AN

HISTORICAL SKETCH

OF THE

PRINCES OF INDIA

AN

HISTORICAL SKETCH

OF THE

PRINCES OF INDIA,

STIPENDIARY, SUBSIDIARY, PROTECTED,
TRIBUTARY, AND FEUDATORY;

WITH A

SKETCH OF THE ORIGIN AND PROGRESS OF
BRITISH POWER IN INDIA.

BY JOHN CLUNES

(OFFICER, THE HONOURABLE EAST INDIA COMPANY)

GYAN

Published by

GYAN

Gyan Publishing House
5, Ansari Road
Daryaganj, New Delhi-110002
Phone: 011-47034999, 9811692060
E-mail: books@gyanbooks.com

Distribution Network
gyanbooks.com
India, USA, Canada, UK, Australia

ISBN: 978-81-212-6460-0 (PB)
First Published, 1833

2nd Impression 2024

Printed at: Gyan Press, Delhi.

AN HISTORICAL SKETCH OF THE PRINCES OF INDIA
Author: JOHN CLUNES

HISTORICAL SKETCH

OF THE

PRINCES OF INDIA.

AN

HISTORICAL SKETCH

OF THE

PRINCES OF INDIA,

STIPENDIARY, SUBSIDIARY, PROTECTED, TRIBUTARY, AND FEUDATORY;

WITH A

SKETCH OF THE ORIGIN AND PROGRESS OF BRITISH POWER IN INDIA.

BY AN OFFICER IN THE SERVICE OF THE HONOURABLE EAST INDIA COMPANY.

EDINBURGH:
PRINTED BY ANDREW SHORTREDE,
AND PUBLISHED BY SMITH, ELDER & CO. LONDON.
MDCCCXXXIII.

CONTENTS.

PREFACE.

At a time when India is about to come under the consideration of Parliament, and when the subject cannot fail to be one of great interest to the whole nation, an "Historical Sketch of the Native Princes," shewing at the same time the origin and progress of their connection respectively with Great Britain, and the present state of their political relations, may not be without interest. Such a work may be at least acceptable to those whose avocations do not permit them to wade through voluminous works, from which much of the substance of these pages have been drawn. Besides the MSS. collected by the compiler while in India, some of which were translated by, or for, him, from the original Mahratta and Persian, he has abstracted largely from the following works:—

The Fifth Report of the Select Committee, &c. 1812.
Papers respecting the Pindarry and Mahratta War.
Treaties with Native Princes, published in 1812 and 1824.
Minutes of Evidence on India Affairs, from 1828 to 1831.
The Asiatic Annual Register.

The Asiatic Journal.
History of British India, by James Mill, Esq.
History of the Mahrattas, by James Grant Duff, Esq.
History of Rajasthan, by Colonel Tod.
History of Boondelcund, by Captain Pogson, Bengal Army.
Hamilton's Hindoostan.
History of Malwa, by Major-General Sir J. Malcolm, G.C.B. and K.L.S.
History of Mysore, by Colonel M. Wilks.
Life of Major-General Sir Thomas Munro, Bart. and K.G.B.
And a variety of other publications.

Every thing in the history of a native Prince, and customs or privileges peculiar to different families, has been sketched. The author lays claim to no merit beyond that of having produced a faithful compilation; and he will be sufficiently rewarded if it prove useful at this juncture. He is sensible of his defects in style; but he trusts to the indulgence of the public to overlook these in the work of one who left England at a very early age, and whose life has been passed in pursuits not well fitted to accomplish him in the niceties of composition.

The author has much gratification in acknowledging the assistance he has received from the Honourable Mountstuart Elphinstone, a gentleman whose name can never be mentioned but with respect; and from Mr James Grant Duff, author of the "History of the Mahrattas." Both these gentlemen had the kindness to look over great part of the work, and their emendations could not be otherwise than adopted. Mr Mill, the well known historian of India, encouraged the design entertained by the author in this publication, but it was afterwards abandoned, and has been resumed only within these few weeks in Edinburgh.

It will be observed, that there is an Introduction to every division of this work:—instancing the Stipendiary Princes, it shews the relation in which they stand generally to the British Government, while at the end of that division is shewn in a table the stipends which they receive, and the revenues which they have relinquished. The same observation applies to the Subsidiary, Protected, Feudatory, and Tributary Princes.

It should be noticed, also, that in accordance with the author's plan of compressing as much as possible, he has thrown into the form of notes, the early, and to the general reader, least interesting part of the history of some of the Princes, and commenced from the time of their first intercourse with the British Government.

The Index is so arranged, that while it directs to the page, it also directs to the province in which the dominions of the Prince are situated.

INDEX TO THE PRINCES;

SHEWING ALSO

THE PROVINCES IN WHICH THEIR TERRITORIES ARE SITUATED, OR THEIR USUAL PLACES OF RESIDENCE.

MAHOMEDANS.

MAHRATTAS.

RAJPOOTS.

PROTECTED SEIKS.

HISTORICAL SKETCH

OF

THE ORIGIN, PROGRESS, AND RESULT, OF THE BRITISH POWER IN THE EAST.

SECT. I.—*Introductory.*

THE British power in the East exhibits at this day a mighty structure, raised on the ruins of the Moghul Empire, which the most gigantic conceptions of the founders never could have imagined. A survey of the principal causes or events which have occasioned the introduction of foreign rule into these territories, is well entitled to the attention of Englishmen. The victories which have led to the establishment of British dominion, and the wisdom of the political conduct which has retained it, have already employed the pen of able historians. But while the achievements of his ancestors may form a proud theme for the Englishman, the errors of ruling authorities, with the remedies successively applied by the legislature, afford an instructive and useful lesson; though in judging of the acts of a former period, it is not always safe to apply the ideas and views of our own. A sketch in chronological order, in as perspicuous a manner as the subject will admit, of the progress of reform in India, from the dawn to the ascendancy of British power, is all that is here intended.

The Emperor Aurungzeb, the last of the dynasty of Timoor, in whom a vi[illegible]orous and wise administration of legislative power existed, [illegible]t a defective will, which originated unnatural contests among [illegible] surviving children, the eldest of whom, Sultan Mauzim, styled Shah Alum, having seen his brothers fall in successive battles opposed to him, was, after a reign of five years, taken off, it is supposed, by poison. The eldest and most profligate of his sons, Jehander Shah, was raised to the throne, his succession being contested by three brothers, who, like their uncles, closed their career in rebellion. After a disgraceful reign of about one year, he was overcome in battle, and strangled by command of his opponent and successor.

A rapid succession of wicked, weak, or infant princes, the tools, and, in succession, the victims of conspiracies, left the affairs of the empire to be conducted by those who had power to usurp and energy to hold the reins of government, which contained in itself intrinsic seeds of dissolution. This event was accelerated by a power recently sprung up, amidst the confusion of the period, into a nation of conquerors: these were the Mahrattas. This people, who had achieved their independence, though opposed by the power of Aurungzeb during twenty years, appeared on the arena of war, in Upper Hindostan, to profit by the anarchy created by the contests among his descendants. Their chief leaders, the Peshwa and Suenaputee, the former of whom was the great Bajeerow, served with the imperial forces in Hindostan as auxiliaries; and, in 1720, obtained for their services, from the party whose power they upheld, those grants for tribute, which, effectually to realize for national benefit, transformed a nation of husbandmen into warriors, and peaceful Bramins into military leaders and statesmen. Bajeerow, equally eminent for political abilities as military skill, had observed, that feuds and personal animosities among the nobles of the imperial court had broken the strength of the house of Timoor; and he returned to the Deccan to arouse the enthusiasm of his countrymen, and to inspire them with the desire of conquest. The flag of the Mahrattas soon after appeared in every part of the country, and for a time they became the paramount power in India; until the British merchants, urged by the principle of self-preservation, were, by the tide of events, transformed from traders into soldiers. From defending their factories, they carried their arms beyond them, till, progressively, the result of their victories first divided with, and afterwards wrested from, the Mahrattas, the supreme power, by which the greater and most fertile portion of India has become a dependency of the British crown,—a dependency yielding a revenue of twenty-one millions sterling, and in which the number of subjects owing fealty to the crown of England is four times the amount inhabiting Great Britain and Ireland, spread over a continent as large as Europe, and comprehending a variety of warlike and peaceful nations, differing from each other in religion, laws, and usages, and having nothing in common with their present rulers.

SECT. II.—*From the commencement of the British intercourse with India, to the first Exclusive Charter.*

Three hundred years ago, individual Englishmen, stimulated by the success of the Dutch and Portuguese, first adventured to India, with views not wholly confined to commerce. Their enterprises were few and far between, from which it would appear that they were unpromising. After a lapse of eighty years, the manifestly better success of their European rivals inflamed the cupidity or ambition of the English nation, and, in 1599, led to the formation, in London, of the first East India Company, to which a Charter of privileges was granted by Parliament in the following year. Ten years after, they were constituted by royal ordinance a permanent body corporate, to continue embodied so long as their exclusive privileges were not considered injurious to the nation.

It is curious to observe the progress of the English in India from this time,—their submissive missions to the Emperor to obtain permission to establish factories at various places on the coast, their conciliatory demeanour towards neighbouring states, and their wars with the rival European traders, the Dutch and Portuguese. But the details, which are sufficiently interesting, belong to the historian.

Their first establishments were effected in 1611, at Surat, Ahmedabad, Cambay, and Gogo; in 1652, at some place, now unknown, in Bengal; and, two years after, at Madras. In 1664, the Island of Bombay was ceded by Portugal to England, in part of the dowry of the Infanta Catherine, married to Charles II.

In 1661, the Company obtained a renewal of their charter of privileges for the fifth time, which then first conveyed to them authority to make war or peace with the native princes.

In 1684, the Directors instructed their local governors to reduce the allowances of the military, which induced the officer commanding at Bombay to confine the deputy of the Governor of Surat, and to declare that they held the island for the King. The garrison retained it for a year, when, in the meantime, a commission being obtained from his Majesty by the Governor of the factory of Surat, and amnesty being promised, the island was surrendered to the Company's authority; and in 1687 it became the capital of all the British possessions in India.

In 1687, differences took place in Bengal between the Company's servants and the natives, and a large armament was sent out, to obtain redress by force of arms. The officer commanding was instructed to seize and fortify Chittagong; to make reprisals on the Soobehdar, or compel him to make reparation. The object of the expedition was not obtained, though matters were accommodated with the Soobehdar. Nevertheless, another attempt was made to take Chittagong, which failed, and the English, in consequence, felt themselves necessitated to abandon Bengal.

Aurungzeb, in 1789, exasperated at the conduct of the Company's servants in Bengal, and at the piracies committed by English vessels, exerted his power to drive them out of India. Their factories at Surat, Masulipatam, and Vizagapatam, were seized; their governor at the former place was imprisoned, and made responsible for one of the largest of the Moghul ships, which had been captured while proceeding from Surat to the Red Sea with pilgrims; and at Vizagapatam, the Company's servants having defended themselves, were all put to death. The Seedee of Jinjeera, (governor of a colony of Abyssinians, planted near Bombay, and hereditary admiral of the imperial fleet,) was instructed to drive them from Bombay, which sustained a siege for many months, until

Aurungzeb being appeased by the humblest submission, supported by the usual bribes at court, allowed them to resume their trade.

In 1698, a charter of privileges was conferred upon a new Company, which took the title of "The English Company trading to the East Indies." The exertions of both old and new were excited by an injurious spirit of rivalry, until the obvious effect of it, a ruinous competition, induced the new Company to propose their union. In 1702, this was accordingly effected, when they assumed the title of "The United Company of Merchants, trading to the East Indies;" but it was not until six years after, that their several properties were blended into one stock. From this commences the first great era in the Company's history.

The business of the Company was now managed by the Proprietors, assembled in General Courts, meeting quarterly, in whom was vested the legislative power; and by Directors, twenty-four in number, who were chosen annually from among themselves, for the performance of the executive. The business was separated into departments, each of which was placed under the superintendence of a committee of the directors, the chairman and deputy officiating in each. The designation of each department conveys the nature of its duties, viz. the treasury, accounts, correspondence, shipping, private trade, warehouses, lawsuits, and since that period, seven other committees have been added. The most important of these committees is that of correspondence, to which the rest may be considered subordinate.

Their affairs in India were, at this time, conducted under three establishments, viz. Bombay, Madras, and Calcutta, the last of which had been, so late as the year before this, a commercial agency dependent upon Madras. The president, or governor, at each was assisted by a council, the former having a casting vote, and the will of the majority was the rule of action. Each establishment was independent within its own limits, but all were responsible to the authorities in England.

Sect. III.—*From the first Territorial Grants, to the acquisition of Bengal, the Northern Circars, &c.*

In 1700, the Company had obtained from the Soobehdar of Bengal, a son of the Emperor, a grant of a small Zumeendaree on the Hooghly, comprising the small towns of Calcutta, Gowindpoor, and Chotanuttee, with permission to strengthen Fort William; and their agents removed to the latter place from Moorshedabad, in 1706. Moorshed Cooley Khan, who had succeeded to the Soobah in 1708, proved adverse to their interests, which induced the Company to send an embassy from Calcutta to the Emperor Ferokhsèr, in 1713, to obtain certain privileges. The exertions of Moorshed Cooley Khañ being opposed to the objects of the mission, they were only obtained by the patriotism of an individual. Ferokhsèr, just then married to a loved and blooming bride, was suddenly afflicted by a white swelling in the back, to cure which baffled the medical skill of Delhi, when Mr Hamilton, attached to that part of the mission from the British merchants at Surat, performed an operation which gave him relief. The royal patient desired him to propose his reward, and he named the objects of the mission. To this man's skill or politic success the East India Company owe the first royal grant, confirming to them the territory which Ferokhsèr's father had conferred on them when Soobehdar of Bengal, together with all the privileges sought for the encouragement of their trade throughout India. But Hamilton's remains rest without a stone in the burial ground at Calcutta, his name and services alike forgotten.

The war which had broken out between France and England in 1745, produced corresponding hostilities in their settlements in India during the following year, and a war commenced, which, after forty-six years' fighting, with occasional intermissions of peace, terminated in the expulsion of the one nation from India, and fixing the other there, a power of the first magnitude. But the French East India Company owed its annihilation, as a power in India, as much to the mismanagement of a controlling ministry as to the result of war.

In 1746, Madras, then the strongest fort held by Europeans in India, capitulated on terms of ransom to the French fleet under La Bourdonnais, after a bombardment of three days, by which a few houses were destroyed, and a few lives lost, forming a remarkable contrast to the siege of the same fortress by the same nation twelve years after, and illustrative of the state of preparation for war of these nations at both periods. On this second occasion, the siege, after being vigorously prosecuted for two months, with a great loss of men on both sides, was abandoned. But every house in the place was laid open to the heavens, the effect of 8000 shells thrown in by the French.

Dupleix now prepared to reduce Fort St David, the only settlement remaining to the Company on the coast of Coromandel; but an English fleet hove in sight, and the French abandoned the position they had taken up near the place. The English, in return, besieged Pondicherry in 1748; but unskilful engineers being opposed to brave defenders, the siege was raised after the trenches had been open thirty-one days. The treaty of Aix-la-Chapelle followed in 1749, and Madras was restored to the English.

About this time both the French and the English began to mix in the politics and intrigues of the native courts. By the reinforcements sent from Europe during the war, they had more troops than was required for the defence of their settlements, and though their respective nations were at peace at home, they were soon opposed to each other in the character of allies to contending native princes, in whose armies they always bore the brunt of the battle. Commissioners were, in consequence, sent from London and Paris to adjust a peace; and Dupleix, whose whole mind was devoted to the aggrandizement of his nation in India, being superseded, returned in 1755 to Europe. Two years prior to this, the French were possessed of more territory than any other European power, great part of which was resigned to purchase peace.

In 1756, the war in the Carnatic was renewed, in which the French and English acted more as principals. It was prosecuted with vigour and activity on both sides until 1763, when it ended with advantage to the English, and prepared the way for the dissolution of the French East India Company, which followed shortly after.

In 1757, the victory obtained at Plassey made the English paramount in the Bengal provinces, and led eventually to their acquisition of them.

Dupleix first discovered the decisive superiority in war of European nations over Asiatic in 1747, at Madras; but Clive put the question beyond a doubt, at Plassey, ten years after. The latter knew well, therefore, when he resumed, in May, 1765, his former situation of Governor and Commander-in-chief of India, the position of the British among the surrounding powers, and the rapid march of aggrandizement since this period may be ascribed to the decisive measures then taken by him. On his arrival in India, he found that the events of war had placed the Emperor of Delhi under protection of, or in dependent alliance with, the Company. He took this opportunity of obtaining from him a grant of the Dewanee of Bengal, Bahar, and Orissa, which superseded the authority of a feeble reigning viceroy. He obtained also, at the same time, 16th August, 1765, a grant of the Northern Circars, which, as the Nizam had previously refused to rent them to the Company on terms considered favourable, an army proceeded to enforce the grant. The Nizam was exasperated; but afterwards appeared pacified by the offer of an alliance for the subjugation of Hyder Ali, and of a body of troops, to be paid out of the rent which the Company consented to pay for the Circars. The Nizam, however, formed a new coalition with Hyder against the English in 1767, and again, with his natural versatility, joined the English against Hyder in 1768.

Presents from native princes, the objectionable foundation of so many private fortunes realized in India before this time, the Company's covenanted servants were now prohibited from receiving on their own account. Since May, 1764, covenants have been executed by them to this end. During the seven years previous to this time, thirty-four servants of the Company had shared among them upwards of a million sterling.

SECT. IV.—*From the first change in the Constitution of the Company until the creation of the India Board.*

The financial difficulties of the Company, in 1769-70, were now destined to bring about an important change in their constitution. Whether by the mismanagement of their servants, or that their possessions did not really yield the revenue which they had been led to expect, the Directors resolved to send out three supervisors to regulate the Company's future interests. They were vested with extraordinary powers, and the ministry for a time opposed their appointment. They sailed nevertheless; but the ship in which they embarked was never after heard of.

But notwithstanding the report of the inadequacy of the revenue to meet the pecuniary difficulties, and the necessity of incurring debt, the Proprietors and Directors concurred in augmenting the dividend to 12½ per cent, for the years 1771 and 1772. Their debt was found to be £1,293,000, and they were under the necessity of petitioning the Crown for a loan of £1,500,000, and hence originated those discussions between the Company and the ministry, which determined the right of the Crown to all territory acquired by military operations, or by treaty with foreign powers. An entire change in the constitution of the Company was now effected by the minister, and the royal assent to two acts for this amendment was obtained on the 1st July, 1773.

The qualification to vote in the Court of Proprietors, for the appointment of a Director, was raised from £500 to £1000; every proprietor possessing £3000, to have two votes; possessing £6000, three; possessing £10,000, four: the holders of £500 stock were still to retain their seat in the Court of Proprietors, with liberty to debate. Only six of the Directors were to go out of office annually. It was declared that the government of Bengal, Bahar, and Orissa, should be vested in a Governor-general, with a salary of £25,000 per annum, and four Members of Council, with £8,000 each. All the other presidencies were henceforth to be subordinate to that of Bengal; a supreme court of judicature was established at Calcutta, consisting of a Chief Justice, with £8000 a-year, and three other Judges, with each £6000 a-year, appointed by the crown. The first Governor-general and Members of Council were nominated by Parliament, and to hold their office for five years; after which, the nomination was to be exercised by the Directors, though the approbation of the Crown should always be necessary; the whole of the Company's political correspondence to be laid before the ministry; the Governor-general, the Members of Council, and Judges, were excluded from all commercial pursuits; and no person in the service of the King or of the Company was allowed to receive presents.

The operation of the two acts embodying these conditions was to have effect in what concerned the home business, from the 1st of October, 1773; and in reference to the foreign, from the 1st of August, 1774.

Mr Hastings succeeded to the government of India in April, 1772, and proceeded immediately, agreeably to previous instructions, to take his seat as Dewan of the Bengal Provinces, and to assume the management of the revenues. The supervisors, who had been appointed, in 1769, to superintend the collection of the revenues and administration of justice by the native officials, were converted into collectors; the revenues were farmed for five years, and the Governor-general and four members constituted themselves a Revenue Board of Circuit.

Resident envoys were first appointed to native courts, Mr Mostyn to Poona, in 1772, and Mr Middleton to Oude, in 1773.

The Governor-general and Council assumed the powers of government, under the new constitution, towards the end of October, 1774. Their first consultations were marked by that hostile feeling which divided the supreme council, and afterwards occupied so much of the time of the British Parliament.

The new Supreme Government was vested with a controlling power over the three Presidencies, and very early demanded from Bombay and Madras an account of its political, financial, and commercial situation. The government of Bombay, before the controlling administration was formed, had entered into a treaty with Rugoba, the expelled Peshwa, for his restoration, which eventually led, in 1775, to the first Mahratta war. The supreme government, however, declared the treaty invalid, and directed the recall of the troops which had advanced into the Deccan in support of Rugoba, while they sent an envoy of their own to treat with his enemies, the ministerial party. The Bombay presidency, lowered in their political importance in the eyes of the native princes, and compelled to a breach of treaty, sent a member of their council to Calcutta, who advocated their cause, but without success. A treaty was concluded with the ministerial party, which the latter never meant to abide by, and broke when the performance of their part of it was required. The Supreme Government then proceeded to treat with the other party, when the ministers changed their tone, and agreed to a treaty, though much less advantageous in its terms than that formerly concluded with Rugoba.

These were part of the inconsistent or impolitic measures which emanated from the divided councils of the Supreme Government, three of the members of which, being violently opposed to the Governor-general and the remaining member, had virtually assumed the powers of government.

The Company applied, in 1769, for a part of his Majesty's navy to protect their commerce on the Indian seas, when the minister required, in return, that the chief naval officer should be empowered to negotiate, and conclude arrangements with the native princes; and to exercise, in fact, the principal authority in the political concerns of the country. To this measure there was naturally opposition; and the minister appears to have ceased to contend for it. Nevertheless, on the 26th July, 1770, a commander of the navy in India arrived at Madras, and exhibited his commission under the great seal, as his Majesty's minister plenipotentiary, with plenary powers, which superseded the Governor as the representative of the British monarch. No intimation had been given to the Company, and their servants in India were unprepared to acknowledge this superior commission; he was, therefore, received with jealousy, and their communications were conducted with every feeling of hostility. Admitting the plenipotentiary to have been possessed of both talent and temper, his want of local knowledge, or knowledge of native character, exhibited him a fit subject to be the dupe of native cunning. He seconded the idle views of Mahomed Ali, both in urging the Madras government to unite with the Mahrattas against Hyder Ali, in the face of the late treaty, by one article of which the English and Hyder had mutually agreed to assist each other; also to commence hostilities, in 1771, against the Raja of Tanjore, to enforce arrears of tribute due to Mahomed Ali, and, finally, in 1773, to subjugate the former prince to the latter. The interference of the plenipotentiary was fortunately not repeated or exercised at any other presidency; but on this occasion it was abundantly pernicious.

Whether the Company's servants or the King's plenipotentiary were to blame in regard to the transactions at Tanjore, it is difficult to say; but Lord Pigot, who had been governor of Madras before, was reappointed in December, 1775, and directed to restore the Raja.

Lord Pigot's administration was marked by extraordinary events. Violent discussions at the council-board took place; and the majority being against the President, they constituted themselves the government, and proceeded to the extreme measure of directing the Commander-in-chief to arrest his person. Both parties had their advocates in Parliament; the result, however, was an order to restore Lord Pigot to office, but he had died in confinement in the meantime; to recall the refractory members of council to England; and to try the military officers concerned by court-martial.

His successor was Sir Thomas Rumbold, who entered upon office in February, 1778, and, in 1781, was dismissed the Company's service, together with two members of the council, the latter of whom had been found guilty of bribery and corruption; the remaining members were also deprived of their seats. Articles of charge were exhibited in the following year against the three former in Parliament, and Sir Thomas was heard in his defence, but he was released without any sentence being passed upon him.

In 1780, while engaged in war with the Mahrattas in the Deccan and Hindoostan, the Company's resources failed at all the presidencies, and they were forced by circumstances into a new war with Hyder Ali, which was prosecuted with alternate success for four years.

But a contest of greater moment was in the meantime going on between the Government and Supreme Court of Judicature of Calcutta, in the efforts of the latter to extend its jurisdiction. To this court the Parliament had intrusted powers, the exercise of which spread terror through the provinces, and endangered the stability of our power in the East.

The Supreme Court, according to the act passed in 1773, consisted of a chief justice and three puisne judges. The power of this court emanated not from the Company, but from the King, who likewise nominated the judges; and it was intrusted with the administration of all branches of English law in India. Its power, in civil cases, extended over all claims against the Company or against any British subject, and over all such claims against natives, as they, at the time of entering into any contract, had agreed to submit to it. In criminal affairs, its powers extended over all British subjects, and over all persons directly or indirectly in the service of the Company, or of any British subject.

During the discussions, in 1780, relative to a renewal of the charter, accounts reached England of these violent contests between the Government and Supreme Court, which, together with the war with Hyder Ali, produced fears for the Company's stability. The charter, however, was renewed from the 1st March, 1781, and an act was passed in Parliament on the 19th June, 1782, to regulate anew the Supreme Court of Judicature, and deprive it of the powers, the exercise of which had been found so destructive. The act particularly exempted from its jurisdiction, the Governor and Council, revenue officers in the performance of their duty, and all matters of revenue.

I now tresspass upon chronological order, to introduce an extract from a minute made by Sir Thomas Munro, in 1822, when the unfortunate proceedings in the Supreme Court, relative to a Jagheer, lowered the government in the eyes of the natives. The necessity of defining more clearly the jurisdiction of the Supreme Court, and preventing it from interfering with the political measures of government, has been instanced at a still later date in Bombay.

"The powers of the Supreme Court, and of the Government, should never be suffered to come into collision; and both the Court and the Government will thus be enabled the more efficiently to discharge their respective duties, and to command the respect of the natives. But, in order to attain these objects, it will be necessary,—

"1st, To exclude from the jurisdiction of the Supreme Court all civil suits between native and native, except where both parties agree to submit to their decision.

"2d, To exclude from the jurisdiction of the Court all lands situated beyond the limits of the Court.

"3d, To exclude from the jurisdiction of the Court all acts done by the Government as a government, and making such acts cognizable only by the superior authorities in England."

Mr Pitt's India Bill was passed into a law on the 13th August, 1784. The principal innovations introduced by it consisted in the creation of the Board of Control, to whom were transferred the power and authority formerly held by the Court of Directors, touching the military, political, financial, and judicial concerns of India. The board was composed of six members of the privy council, chosen by the King, who were appointed to do duty without salary, which was, however, given to the president and two senior members on the renewal of the charter, in 1793. Another of the innovations introduced by it was the Committee of Secrecy, consisting of three of the Court of Directors, chosen by themselves. This committee is placed in direct communication with the Board of Control, and is charged with the management of all political, financial, and military details connected with the government of India, and in its functions is independent of the rest of the Directors. The power of the Court of Proprietors was by this act also diminished.

SECT. V.—*From the impeachment of Warren Hastings to the close of the Mahratta War of* 1817–18.

On the 18th February, 1786, Mr Burke, one of the select committee of the House of Commons, agitated the prosecution of Mr Warren Hastings, the late Governor-general, and his trial by impeachment commenced on the 13th February, 1788, which ended in his acquittal by the Lords in 1795.

On the 12th December, 1787, Sir Gilbert Elliot, in the House of Commons, exhibited articles charging Sir Elijah Impey* with high crimes and misdemeanours, but his impeachment did not take place.

The year 1788 was marked by a struggle between the Board of Control and Court of Directors as to which body was the organ of government for India, which led to their respective functions being better defined.

A very important change now took place in India. The military protection of the Bengal provinces was first provided for by treaty with the Viceroy, in 1758; their financial management was taken out of his hands by the Governor-general, in 1772; and the last remaining prerogative of sovereignty held by him, viz. the administration of justice, which had been exercised by the Nuwab only to oppress, was resigned by him into the hands of Lord Cornwallis in 1787, which enabled him to commence those substantial reforms in the administration of civil and criminal law, for which British India is so much indebted to the first administration of this nobleman, though all his benevolent plans did not meet the success they merited.

In remunerating judges, he substituted salary for the existing system of fees, and rendered the attainment of justice comparatively cheap. But while it is forgotten how much he contributed to the correct administration of justice, the technical forms which load judicial proceedings, the miserable manufacture of some English lawyer, are now the daily

* This is the Chief Justice of Calcutta before whom the Raja Nundcoomar was tried and convicted on the English law for forgery, for which he was executed, —a sentence about as consistent with justice, as has been justly observed, as to hang a Mahomedan or Hindoo for bigamy.

reprobation of both judge and client, since it not only always renders justice tardy, but sometimes defeats it entirely.

His lordship endeavoured to create a landed gentry, and introduced a system of revenue by means of them; but both projects failed. Reforms were also introduced into the rules established for securing a revenue from the monopolies of Salt and Opium, which are the second and third branches of the Company's territorial revenue. To perfect the revenue system, all former regulations were revised, and the code thus framed and printed, in 1793, became the statute book of the British government in India.

During this administration, the power of Tippoo was curtailed, and all prospect of the French becoming a nation in India was finally subverted by the capture of all their possessions there in 1793.

In 1795, all the Dutch settlements east of the Cape of Good Hope inclusive, fell into the hands of the English, viz. Cochin, with those on Ceylon, Malacca, Banda, and Amboyna.

On the 17th May, 1798, the Marquis Wellesley succeeded to the government of India. The first important part of his administration effected the removal of the French army and influence from the Hydrabad dominions. This was followed, in 1799, by the capture of Seringapatam, when the territories of Mysore were divided by the Peshwa, the Nizam, and the Company.

Between the years 1800 and 1802, the dominions and influence of the Company were farther considerably enlarged. Half of the territories of the Vizier, and those of the Nuwabs of the Carnatic, Furruckabad, and Surat, also of the Raja of Tanjore, were annexed to the British possessions, while these chiefs, whose wretched system of misrule had occasioned their deposition, had liberal stipends assigned them for support.

The Mahratta war, which had commenced in 1803, had not terminated in August, 1805, when the venerable Marquis Cornwallis returned to India as Governor-general, with instructions to bring about a peace. He found that the hostile chiefs had, by a series of successful operations against them, been driven to extremity; but he was so anxious to terminate the war, that he granted peace to Holkar and Sindhia on most favourable terms. His lordship disapproved of subsidiary or defensive alliances; but it is questionable how far it was either politic or just to abandon the connection which his predecessor had formed with the petty states on the Jumna, and who had during the war pledged to them the protection of the British government. He directed that the territory conquered from Sindhia, south of the Jumna, should be divided between them as a remuneration, and declared the British government exempted from all obligation to protect them against any of the greater powers, recommending them to unite in their own defence. With the exception of Bhurtpoor and Machery, whose forts were strong, and with whom the treaties remained in force, the rest were all rendered tributary to their more powerful neighbours.

While the Marquis Wellesley believed that the tranquillity of British India was to be ensured only by establishing British ascendency in the councils of native princes, the Marquis Cornwallis conceived it to be attained only by abstaining from all interference with their internal administration, or mixing in their politics, considering it preferable, and more consonant to national dignity, to leave them to settle their own disputes.

The pacific or non-interference system of policy adopted at this time, and an unwillingness to depart from it, permitted the growth unchecked of the Patan and Pindhary powers, both systematic plunderers. At length, the latter having carried their devastations and atrocities into the British territories, and it being discovered that they were abetted by some of the great Mahratta powers, a hostile attitude became, in 1817, one of strict self-defence. The military operations, and political alliances which followed in consequence, have brought all states of the secondary class within the pale of British protection, and gives a prospect of long undisturbed tranquillity to India.

In closing this brief sketch of those events or transactions, which have had a moral or political effect in erecting the gigantic empire which England holds in India, it may be remarked, that of the states, whose histories form the subject of the following pages, few are of ancient date. All the Mahomedan have been founded in rebellion, crime, and usurpation. None of them can claim the antiquity of one century, and some of them were swallowed up in the British empire, to which their princes became pensioners ere they had existed many years. The Mahratta principalities have been formed out of fragments of their own empire at a much later period, while the only states which can boast antiquity are the Rajpoots, a race which can truly boast a soldier's soul, and a native valour, but whose strength has been heretofore always expended in feuds among themselves.

CONSTITUTION OF THE NATIVE ARMY—EXTERNAL AND INTERNAL POLICY—CIVIL AND CRIMINAL COURTS—AND REVENUE MANAGEMENT.

SECT. I.—*Introductory—Commerce.*

HAVING, in the preceding division, sketched the origin and progress of the English East India Company, to the sovereignty of an extensive dominion, the subjects of this division, did my ability for the task correspond with my will, would be, to afford a few suggestions for improving the condition of the natives of India. This subject, let us hope, will obtain the attention of the Legislature, in the ensuing session of Parliament. The chief considerations towards effecting this desirable object, are two: *First*, To employ the natives in responsible situations; and, *secondly*, To make such commercial laws as shall afford a market for their produce, and revive manufacturing industry. The former proposition demands a more ample discussion than my limits allow, nor are the natives yet educated to receive the boon; but the latter is obviously beneficial to both countries, and so necessary to be done speedily, that a few observations on the subject may be indulged in.

Nothing can be more shortsighted in a government, than to permit laws or restrictions to exist, which, in their operation, effectually destroy the commerce of a country of which it draws the revenue. Commerce—the grand principle of union between countries—should always be so regulated, as to continue a mutual source of prosperity. In India, however, the manufacturing population have long been depressed; the chief mart left to them being, in a great degree, shut against the produce of their industry by commercial laws, intended to benefit England, but which, in truth, are injurious to her. The improvement of machinery also, which would have borne its advantages to India, had the sources of wealth not been dried up there, has completed the injury; but still there are manufactures in India, which would, (if the duties were taken off,) probably find a ready sale in London, the market to which all Europe should be induced to resort for them. This would be one course, by which part of the wealth of exhausted India might flow back to it in refreshing streams. England would lose nothing by this, the money thus circulated passing through the artisan to the cultivator, would find its way into the collector's treasury, or would be expended on the cheap produce of British machinery. Let us give the natives the means, as far as enactments will allow them, of raising themselves to opulence by their own exertions and industry, nor will the mother country otherwise than benefit by being kind to the orphan child of her adoption.

SECT. II.—*Native Army, and Subsidiary Alliances.*

Nothing shews more powerfully the effect of European talent in India, than the wonderful combination and constitution of the Native Army, by which the British have acquired such extensive power, and by means of which that power continues to be upheld. It would, some centuries ago, have been a very extravagant conceit in any one to have imagined, that Christians from islands in the Atlantic, in search of traffic in Hindoostan, should train the natives to be soldiers; and that, in leading them against their own countrymen, they should find in them that devotion and perseverance which is usually rewarded by victory, and that faithful attachment which alone can secure its fruits. The wonder is increased, when we consider that these men, wholly unacquainted with the English language, beyond the range of terms used at drill and parade, should fully understand and skilfully perform all the evolutions and exercises of the British line, in which they take their place, and on which they have never been known to bring disgrace.

In India, the military class held the profession of arms exclusively by inheritance, ranking next to the Bramins, or priesthood, in the community; all other classes being inferior, treated them with profound deference. These inferior classes were, therefore, elevated, when enrolled as soldiers in the armies of European nations. In return they were faithful; and by the powerful influence of discipline, the proud hereditary soldiery, who had heretofore looked on them as beings of a lower grade in creation, have been driven from the station they held, into obscurity.

It may be giving too great antiquity to the Native Army, to date its origin from a body of three hundred men, raised to aid in the defence of Fort William, about one hundred and twenty years ago; the nucleus will more probably be found at a subsequent period at Bombay. From the latter place, a reinforcement of troops was sent by sea, to Fort St David's, in 1747, when one hundred disciplined sepoys formed part of it. Whatever may have been the period when natives were disciplined for the British regular army, it does not seem to be questioned, that the formation of sepoy battalions, as well as subsidiary alliances, originated with the celebrated Dupleix—the one arising out of the other. Subsidiary treaties were first entered into by the British, under the government of Warren Hastings, but systematically extended by the Marquis Wellesley, with the view of controlling all India, ensuring some protection to the subjects of the Native States, and preventing the resources of the countries from being employed against the British government. The wisdom of this policy has been less questioned than its justice; but if it had been more strictly pursued, it would probably have prevented the necessity of so rapid an extension of territory, on the part of the East India Company.

When a native Prince receives a subsidiary force, districts are ceded, yielding a revenue equivalent to its maintenance; without such security, neither their payment nor employment would be certain for any length of time. The amount ceded by each state is shewn in its proper place.

Each Presidency has its own army. The forces are as follows:

	Bengal.	*Madras.*	*Bombay.*	*Total.*
	EUROPEAN.			
Infantry,	2 Battalions.	2 Battalions.	2 Battalions.	6 Battalions.
Horse Artillery,	3 Brigades.	2 Brigades.	2 Brigades.	7 Brigades.
Foot Artillery,	5 Battalions.	4 Battalions.	3 Battalions.	12 Battalions.
	NATIVE.			
Cavalry,	10 Regiments.	8 Regiments.	3 Regiments.	21 Regiments.
Infantry,	74 Regiments.	52 Regiments.	26 Regiments.	152 Regiments.
Artillery,	2 Battalions.	—	—	2 Battalions.

Besides European and Native veteran battalions, provincial corps, and irregular horse. If the power to raise armies, to provide the ways and means for their maintenance, and frame laws for its governance, be an indication of sovereign power, the East India Company maintains the largest standing regular army in the world.

The composition of the Native Army, being a variety of tribes and nations differing in religion, is admirably calculated to ensure its fidelity, from the difficulty of organizing conspiracy. The men, however, like their officers; and their allegiance and attachment may be depended on, so long as they are paid regularly—self-interest, in the absence of patriotism, constituting the obligation to obedience. Every allowance, moreover, must be made, in the strict enforcement of discipline, that the prejudices and established habits of the men be not outraged.*

The cavalry of all the Presidencies is principally composed of Mahomedans and Rajpoots, but the former predominate. The Bengal infantry is similarly constituted; but in it the Rajpoot, and Hindoo of the provinces, are most numerous. The Madras and Bombay infantry is composed of all the people of all the nations which belong to, or are domiciled in Hindoostan,—Mahomedans, Rajpoots, Mahrattas, Jews, Christians, and Hindoos of the low classes; and even Deccany Bramins, are sometimes to be found in the ranks. The Bengal troops, both cavalry and infantry, are larger, and altogether finer men; but are neither so well drilled, nor so soldier-like, as their brethren in the other Presidencies.

SECT. III.—*External and Internal Policy.*

The course of policy pursued in India by the East India Company as rulers, has depended as much upon the personal character of the head of the local administration, and the experience and knowledge possessed by him, as upon the circumstances of the times; for the only policy which a legislative body, deliberating at such a distance as England, can authorize, arises out of the official reports made by the officers charged with the administration in India. That

* The writer was with a division of the army in the field, about twenty years ago, when a strict martinet, with the advance picket, by an injudicious severity on one occasion, outraged the feelings of the men, and next morning, though they stood to their arms as usual, they refused to obey his orders. However injudicious the officer was, in this particular instance, in applying the rules for European troops indiscriminately to natives, his conduct involved the necessity of decisive measures, to check insubordination. The division, about 6000 men, Europeans and natives, were instantly under arms, and formed in hollow square, in which, after, a summary drumhead trial, every tenth man of the picket was tied up, and received at the same instant, 200 lashes, and the native officers were reduced. But had it not been for this judicious and prompt measure, the dissatisfaction would have been more general, the prisoners would have been considered martyrs, and possibly an attempt might have been made to prevent the punishment.

system, perfected by the Marquis of Hastings, and his coadjutor and successor Mr Adam, affords the best grounded hope of permanency to the British empire in the East. In contrast with other countries, perhaps no system of government in existence has attained so high a degree of perfection as that now administered in British India; and if there are minor points on which the expediency of change has been suggested, we must recollect that no human institution has ever been found perfect.

Their policy must be treated of under two distinct heads: Externally, as regards their relations, or connections, with independent and protected states; and internally, as regards their system of management in their own possessions.

Interference with the political concerns of independent states, or those with which no treaties of alliance exist, the British government has naturally avoided, so long as such states abstain from aggressions on it or its allies. The independent states with which treaties exist, are Lahore, Caubul, Sinde, Nepaul, and Sindhia. A British envoy is stationed at the courts of the two latter.

The political measures and external relations of protected states, are subject to British control. The power of restraint over actions having a tendency to bring the exercise of the duty of protection into operation, required that they should submit their disputes to the arbitration and decision of the protecting power. Contests among themselves, or interference in the concerns of other chiefs and states, are thus prevented. In the federal arrangements of 1818, protection on the one side, and acknowledgment of supremacy on the other, was therefore the basis, and formed the preliminary articles, of all the treaties.

The substantive states, in return for the security afforded them, have each assigned a portion of their territory, proportioned to the magnitude of the state, the revenue of which is applied to the maintenance of a body of troops; while petty chiefs, or principalities, either contribute towards their military protection in the shape of a tribute, or, if too poor, they are merely required, in cases of exigence, to hold their troops ready to co-operate with the British. With the internal concerns of these states the British do not interfere, except in the case of a disputed succession, when they are bound to support the rightful heir, and prevent civil war.

The humane and liberal policy of the Legislature and Court of Directors towards those who have become their subjects, has been guided by an attention to established usages, religious prejudices, and respect for caste and station, as far as may be consistent with the desire, eventually, to introduce an improved system of government. Justice and liberality to a people differing so widely in religion, habits, and general knowledge, from their new rulers, required the preservation to the Hindoo of his ancient institutions with as little change as possible, as well as an unrestricted exercise or toleration in his religious rites, abhorrent though some of the latter are to the feelings of civilized life. The native is still subject to the law he has hitherto been accustomed to, but divested of all incongruities at variance with Christian notions. Upon this law, and the practice of European judicature together, are founded the principles of the regulations by which the British territories are governed. They are essentially the same throughout India; but each presidency has its own code, the rules of which are framed so as to be best adapted to the promotion of improvement in its own limits.

To persons of rank every allowable deference is shewn; and, in 1818, when the British possessions were so greatly extended, the rights and privileges which they enjoyed under the Moghul or Mahratta governments were continued and secured. The first class of chiefs are wholly exempted from the process of courts, and from all criminal jurisdiction, except in cases of political importance; the second and third classes are treated with forbearance, and the same rules of decorum observed towards them which are practised among themselves, and their personal appearance is never required in civil cases. But though the government has exempted these chiefs from the operation of the judicial establishments, it nevertheless reserves to itself the power, when reasons of state or the peace of the country render it necessary, to place them under personal restraint, and temporarily to attach their lands, without any judicial process.

Sect. IV.—*Company's Civil Courts.*

In 1787, when the committee of revenue was reformed, and designated a Board of Revenue, a European civil servant was appointed superintendent over each district, with the united powers of revenue collector, judge, and magistrate. There was economy in this arrangement, but it would be difficult to persuade the cultivator, who had to represent a grievance of over assessment, or other supposed oppression, that he would be certain of redress by complaining to the judge against the collector, *i. e.* against himself. It is true, an appeal from the decision lay to the Board of Revenue first, and afterwards to the Governor in Council; but Lord Cornwallis, in 1793, rightly deeming it incompatible that officers of the revenue should decide on suits originating in their own department, relieved the Board of Revenue from the exercise of judicial functions. Zillah and City Courts of Adawlut were, from this time, established for the decision of civil suits, under the superintendence of a European covenanted servant of higher official rank than the collector, in whose person were united the powers of judge and magistrate, and to whom was intrusted the superintendence of the police within his division.

To the Zillah and City courts of justice so constituted, a Register with assistants was appointed from the junior European civil servants, with Mahomedan and Hindoo officers to expound the Koran and Shasters, as well as authorized native pleaders to conduct the proceedings of suitors under the established regulations. These pleaders are engaged by a retaining fee, and ultimately rewarded by a per centage on the sum sued for.

The trial of petty suits is left to the Register, but his decree is not final, an appeal lying to the judge, who is moreover empowered to try it again himself if he sees fit.

For the convenience of parties residing at a distance, and for the more speedy administration of civil justice, native commissioners are authorized to hear and decide on suits of personal property under a certain amount; but from their decision an appeal lies to the Zillah and City court. These native commissioners act under instructions, devised to ensure a faithful discharge of the trust reposed in them; they have no salary, but, as a compensation, receive a small per centage on the amount of all causes settled by them. The law in the provincial civil courts is both Mahomedan and Hindoo, that of the defendant being followed. The judicial code, modified by regulations from time to time, is general throughout India, with some exceptions. For instance, in Malabar and Canara the local law, differing wholly from the ancient Hindoo law, is followed in civil cases.

The popular mode of determining civil suits throughout the countries south of the Nerbudda, is that by Punchayet or arbitration, the practice of which is as follows:—Both parties having bound themselves by a deed of submission to abide by the award, each then nominates an equal number of referees, usually two each, to compose the Punch, or court, which, being met, agree upon an umpire, or Ameen, who has the casting vote: the latter is, however, sometimes appointed by the judge from among the Ameens or referees who belong to the court. But the members are usually so determined in favour of the party who nominates them, that the justice obtained proves after all the decision of an individual, viz. that of the Ameen, who has, however, the advantage of hearing all the arguments before he passes judgment. It is an expeditious and satisfactory mode of distributing justice, preventing those perpetual appeals to which the present system is liable. The Punchayet, however, is, though the popular mode, not in practice in the British courts. Superior to the Zillah and City Courts are the Provincial Courts of Appeal, who are empowered to take farther evidence, or refer the suit back to the court in which it originated, as may be deemed most conducive to justice.

From the Provincial Court a farther appeal may be made to the Sudr Dewanny Adawlut, the chief judge in which, at Bombay, is a member of the government. The last petition of appeal is to the King in Council, which must be presented within a given time after the judgment, the execution of which is suspended during the appeal, and security is taken from both parties, as well for the safety of the property in dispute and for payment of costs, as for the performance of such order and judgment as his Majesty shall think fit to give thereupon.

Proceedings in the Honourable Company's courts of law were, at one period, conducted without expense to the suitors, save and except the fees to the pleaders whom they might employ; but in a community peculiarly disposed to litigation, this was found to produce such an inundation of suits as to threaten a stop to the course of justice altogether. To render law, therefore, more expensive, without discouraging a recourse to it where the cause of action might be well founded, an institution fee is exacted, and the petition is required to be drawn on stamped paper, bearing a duty in proportion to the amount sued for. The imposition of this expense, by rendering the proceedings costly to the party, tend to repress litigation.

To afford to pleaders and all other persons the means of gaining a knowledge of the regulations introduced by the British government, printed copies and translations of them are kept for public inspection upon a table expressly allotted for that purpose in every court room, where any person may refer to them, and take copies.

SECT. V.—*The Criminal Courts.*

On the introduction of the new system of internal government, in 1793, the functions of magistrate, as well as of judge,* were transferred from the collectors to the Zillah and City

* The Nuwab of Bengal still held the office of Supreme Criminal Judge, his last remaining prerogative, the duties of which were left to an officer styled the Naib Nazim. The District Courts were filled by officers who purchased their appointments, and reimbursed themselves by fees and a tax of twenty-five per cent upon the litigated property. This miserable mode of distributing justice was put a stop to in the Bengal provinces, by Lord Cornwallis prevailing on the Nuwab to appoint the Governor-general and Council his delegate as Supreme Criminal Judge.

judges. It is declared to be the duty of the magistrate "to apprehend murderers, robbers, thieves, housebreakers, and all persons charged before him with crimes and misdemeanours." In certain cases, he is authorized to pass sentence himself, though subject to the control of the Courts of Circuit and Nizamut Adawlut. When the magistrate has satisfied himself as to the nature of the case before him, he either releases the prisoner, admits him to bail, administers the punishment within the limits of the power delegated to him, or commits him for trial before the Court of Circuit.

The British government has followed the practice of their predecessors in making the Mahomedan law the rule for the administration of criminal justice in Bengal, reserving to itself the right of introducing such alterations and modifications as reason and humanity may suggest, all necessary amendments being legally sanctioned by 13 Geo. III. ch. 63. The Koran, the understood standard of Mahomedan law, containing few passages applicable to the ordinary occurrences of life, the deficiency is supplied by numerous commentators, both Sheea and Soonee, not only on the text, but on the traditional accounts, precepts, actions, and decisions of their prophet; and on the formation of the new code of regulations, in 1793, a wider range was taken in modifying and supplying the defects of the Mahomedan and Hindoo written law, for the government of decisions to be passed in the provincial criminal courts.

As soon as practicable, after the conclusion of each trial, a copy of the record is transmitted to the Nizamut Adawlut, or superior criminal court, whose sentences are final, in cases involving the highest pains, as well as in all cases of corporal punishment, fine, and imprisonment. A power of remission, or mitigation of punishment, is, however, reserved to the Governor in Council, this being necessary, from the native law being barbarous and imperfect in itself, and quite at variance with the notions of Christians. The Company's Regulations are general throughout British India, with special indulgences in particular places, on account of religious prejudices, or other causes.

SECT. VI.—*Revenue Management.*

The public resources in India, are drawn chiefly from the land-rent;* the share contributed by commerce, in the shape of customs,† taxes, &c. towards the support of government, forming only a small portion of its revenue; and the produce of the monopolies of salt and opium,‡ is the profit on a mercantile speculation, rather than a branch of legitimate state revenue. The administration of the land revenue may be divided into three systems, which are here briefly sketched, agreeably to the opinions of the advocates of each system, rather than my own:

The first is the Zumeendaree system, by which an individual farms a number of villages, formed into one or more districts, for which a fixed sum of rent is payable during a period of years. The Zumeendars, or farmers, in former times, received a percentage on their collections, and generally held some land on their own account. These men, taking advantage of the weakness of their government, established their independence, and on the accession of the British government, were confirmed in their possessions, on condition of continuing to pay the revenue assessed on their districts. Sometimes persons, strangers to the district, but possessed of wealth and enterprise, make this kind of farming a profession. The system is a pernicious one; the cultivator being left in the hands of the Zumeendar, who doubtless takes from him as great a proportion of the produce as he is able. Moreover, in the one, it fosters fraud to conceal his produce, and oppression in the other, who, to be just to his landlord, or to himself, must be unrelenting to the tenant. But it relieves the officers of government from all details, and saves the expense of a host of fiscal officers: it affords, at the same time, the best chance of bringing to account all suppressed revenue or produce.

Revenues of the whole of British India for 1827–28.

* The land-rent of the British possessions in India, is, L. 16,766,000, or per cent, 64.34

† Customs, Stamps, Post Office, &c. . . 1,195,000, or per cent, 7.16

‡ Salt and Opium Monopolies, realize . . . . 4,779,000, or per cent, 25.5

The second is the Mouzawar, or village settlement, by which the rent is agreed upon by all the Meerasadars, or hereditary cultivators jointly, for a determinate sum, to continue for a period of years. The villagers arrange among themselves their respective shares of the general engagement, and equally participate in the profit and loss. Sometimes an individual undertakes for the whole rent, who again sub-lets each field; and by this mode of settlement, the annual rent is not liable to any deterioration, by the corruption or incapacity of the native fiscal officers. The inferior tenancy will sometimes be over assessed by their superiors, but the system supports that unity of interests which usually exists among Meerasadars of the same village, and it is more desirable to preserve than to destroy it.

The third is the Ryotwar, or individual settlement, by which the Ryot, or cultivator, pays rent for those fields only which he himself cultivates, and should they prove unproductive, he is entitled to an abatement. By this mode, the industrious are not made to support the indolent portion of the community, as in the village settlement. A permanent Ryotwar rent is a fixed sum paid in all seasons, for all the land that the cultivator occupies. Such a settlement, on a moderate scale of assessment, must be advantageous to both landlord and tenant; but it is to be feared, that from the improvidence of the cultivating class, government would be called upon to extend its fostering aid every year in which the periodical rains failed; but against this consideration, there is to be weighed the remissions which government is now obliged to make on such occasions, and the multitude of revenue servants who might be dispensed with by the change.

The system in operation in the old provinces under Bengal, is the Zumeendaree, while in the ceded and conquered provinces of that Presidency, the lands are in the immediate management of Government, and subject to fresh assessment, as new capabilities in the lands are developed. The former is obviously the least expensive process of management, as the Zumeendar doubtless does not settle with his agents on the same liberal scale by which they are paid under the Ryotwar system.

In realizing the territorial revenues, experiments have been tried under all the systems, Zumeendar, Mouzawar, and Ryotwar; and of annual settlements, or triennial, quinquennial, and decennial leases. The success with which these experiments have been attended, or the modes of revenue management which existed in different provinces before they were assumed by the British government, cannot be treated of in so brief a narrative as the present.*

In the territories under Bombay and Madras, the Ryotwar chiefly prevails; but when the average rent of every village and field can be determined, from the practice of a number of years, so as to protect the cultivator in his ascertained rights, it is to be hoped that the introduction of long leases, or a perfected Zumeendaree settlement, will save the enormous expense of collection, and that its amount, being the difference between the present and a moderate assessment, will be conceded to the cultivator.

In the territories which have fallen under British rule the aristocracy have greatly disappeared: there are, however, a

* *Q.* "Comparing the extraordinary increase which has taken place in the revenues of all the countries permanently settled, with the decline which, with a solitary exception, has taken place in all those parts in which temporary and periodical settlements, and above all, Ryotwar settlements, prevail; does this fact not throw some doubt over the supposed advantages of temporary settlements? *A.* What is assumed in the preamble of the question, I do not altogether admit, because I should say, that a continued increase is only exemplified in Bengal and Benares. I do not admit that there is this increase in the permanently settled districts at Madras. In Bengal, the increase has arisen mainly from salt and opium; and when it is considered that Bengal is not only the most fertile portion of India, by many degrees, but one of the most fertile places on the face of the earth, under circumstances peculiarly favourable, from the regularity of the irrigation; when it is farther considered, that the land-revenue, speaking in round numbers, is, in the lower and permanently settled provinces, three millions, and that in the upper provinces, it is also three millions; considering, in the next place, that Bengal enjoys the great advantages of a navigable river running through the heart of it; considering, above all, that the population of Bengal is double the amount of that of the upper provinces, the small amount of comparative financial prosperity it exhibits, appears to me one of the strongest proofs which can be adduced, that it is under some very pernicious system of management."—*Extract from the Evidence of James Mill, Esq. before the Committee of the Commons on India Affairs, August* 23, 1831.

few Chiefs met with as subjects, and, in some instances, an absolute power on their own estates has, in civil cases, been conceded to them. They may be divided into two classes, viz. those who hold land on the condition of military service with a body of troops, agreeably to the magnitude of their Jagheer or assigned lands, and those who pay tribute. In their internal management neither are interfered with, so long as they perform towards Government what is expected from them. Their estates are thriving or otherwise, agreeably to the personal character of the Chief; and it has been remarked of the Jagheerdars of the Southern Mahratta Country, that the industrious portion of the inhabitants of the adjoining lands have contributed to make their estates respectively a garden; and it is obvious, that were more of the country under such proprietors, the revenue would be realized, under the shape of tribute, with greater facility and infinitely less expense. A race would at the same time be interposed between the conquerors and the conquered, who would be bound, if not by gratitude, at least by self-interest, to their feudal superiors. Landholders of this description see an increase of revenue to themselves by an attention to the interest of their cultivators, and a personal inspection of the uncut crops enables them to judge where remissions should be afforded. Their range of supervision would permit this, which it does not to a government collector, and they know that a rigid exaction of their dues occasions emigration and loss of revenue. In a country where the income of the state is principally derived from cultivation, equitable and fixed assessments are primary considerations. The provinces in the Guzerat peninsula are divided among some hundreds of tributary chiefs, whose tribute is fixed, and not liable to be augmented, agreeably to the questionable system elsewhere, of raising the assessment upon either tributary or landholder, upon every occasion of improvement in his revenue, though effected by him at his own risk and expense!

STIPENDIARY PRINCES.

Introduction.

A LARGE portion of the dominions of British India is made up of the former possessions of Princes, who, either themselves or their descendants, now enjoy stipends, paid to them out of the revenues. The first connection with most of these Princes was of a subsidiary nature; some of them formally ceded their territories; others lost them to us by the result of war; while those of others were assumed from the absolute incapacity and misgovernment of their rulers, whom the British Government, with which they stood connected, could no longer consent to support by its countenance against their oppressed subjects. The Princes of the first and last classes are formally installed on the Musnud,* and allowed to exercise sovereignty over the tenants on their household lands, and they are exempted from the jurisdiction of the British Courts of Law. They have their own civil and military functionaries, with all the insignia of a state, and a British envoy is usually is resident at their Court, whose duties chiefly relate to their pecuniary affairs, or supposed encroachments on their ceremonials of sovereignty. Their stipends have been fixed on a most liberal scale, and are sufficient to maintain them in affluence and splendour; a fixed sum, besides one-fifth of the net revenue, being, in most cases,

* *Ceremonial of Installation at Tanjore, 24th March,* 1832:—After the due performance, in the palace, of the sacred *abshégum*, prescribed by the Hindoo law, on the coronation of a prince, in the presence of his assembled relatives, and chief officers of the court, his Highness sent for the signet ring and sword of state, which he delivered into the hands of R. Babajee Ramajee Pundit, thereby appointing him Surkhel of the State, agreeably to an arrangement previously made by his late Highness. The Surkhel and Foujdar, R. Baboo Rao Inglay, then proceeded, with their retinue, to pay their compliments to the resident, who, with the judge, proceeded to the palace, and placed him on the throne of his ancestors. After congratulations, khelauts, nuzzurs, &c. &c. and the proclamation read, in Mahratta, by the Resident and Sheristadar, the ceremony ended.—*Asiatic Journal.*

set aside for this purpose, which, as a general rule, is probably more than any state in India can well afford for the private expenses of its Princes. The other Princes, who have not the same claims to consideration, are also most amply provided for.

HIS MAJESTY THE KING OF DELHI.

MANY writers having recorded the history, achievements, and once unequalled splendour of the house of Timour, whose present representative is a dependant upon the East India Company, this brief memoir is confined simply to the origin and progress of the events which have led to that connection.

The Empire of Hindoostan was anciently divided into Soobehs, or Viceroyalties, the Governors of which were appointed by the Emperor, and held office during his pleasure. On the death of Aurungzeb in 1707, the conflicting pretensions to sovereignty among his sons and grandsons, subjected the country to be periodically overrun by rebellious, or foreign armies, which together weakened the imperial power, and destroyed all control over powerful Viceroys in distant provinces, who became independent, and sought, as opportunities offered, to extend their dominions at the expense of their neighbours. Europeans, who had settled on the coasts of India as merchants, took part, as auxiliaries, in these intestine wars, and treated with their employers as sovereign hereditary princes; though grants of land, awarded them for services by these potentates, required confirmation from the Emperor.

A joint embassy from the three Presidencies was deputed from Calcutta in 1713 to the Imperial Court, but it was not until early in 1716 that they succeeded in obtaining the objects of the mission. These were, that English goods should be exempted from customs; that three villages contiguous to Madras, formerly granted but since resumed, should be restored to the Company; that the island of Diu should be conferred on them; and, that they should be allowed to purchase the occupancy of thirty-seven villages contiguous to Calcutta. These were the first imperial grants of any importance conferred on the British East India Company. The next territorial assignment obtained from Delhi, was in

1759, during the reign of Shah Jehan II, for the support of the imperial fleet, of which the Company's agent at Surat was appointed Admiral.

But the first grants which elevated them to rank as one of the powers of India, was from Shah Alum II, who, therefore, claims particular notice in this memoir. He was the ninth Prince exalted to the imperial throne during the eventful fifty-three years which followed the death of Aurungzeb. Shah Alum, when heir-apparent, had been invested as Soobehdar of the Bengal provinces, and proceeded, in 1759, to recover them from Jaffier Ali Khan, who was supported by the English. But the Nuwabs of Oude and Allahabad, the chief supporters of the expedition, quarrelled, and the latter was put to death by the former. A seasonable offer of a sum of money to the Moghul Prince induced him, on this emergency, to give up the enterprise. In the following year, however, on succeeding to the empire, he again invaded Bengal at the head of 60,000 men, principally the troops of Oude and the Rohillas, together with a party of French under M. Law. But a succession of defeats induced the Emperor to accept terms of peace, which were offered to him by the English commander; and in return, the Soobehdar of Bengal received at his hand the royal investiture. In 1764, the Emperor again appeared in the Bengal provinces with the army of the Vizier, in support of the deposed Naib Meer Cassim Ali. The Vizier Shuja-ood-Dowla, at this time, however, held paramount influence in the state, and the Emperor felt himself but a pageant, when the decisive battle of Buxar, in October of that year, afforded the latter an opportunity of separating from the former. He joined the victorious army, and accompanied it to Benares, where he manifested his good will towards the Company, by making over to them the Zumeendaree of Benares and Ghazipoor, on condition of their subduing, and establishing him in possession of, the rest of the dominions held by the Vizier.* To his Majesty's

* In Grant's History of the East India Company, 1813, page 255, the deviation from this part of the treaty is conclusively explained and justified. This book had not fallen into my hands until these sheets were in the press.

disappointment, however, the war terminated in a treaty of peace, dated 16th August, 1765; by which the Vizier was confirmed in his possessions, with the exception of the districts of Corah and Allahabad, which were formed into a royal demesne for the Emperor: Benares and Ghazipoor were at the same time restored by the Company to the Vizier. Shah Alum, dissatisfied with this arrangement, made secret overtures, in 1766, to the Mahrattas, to be taken under their protection; and, in May, 1771, when they appeared in sufficient force in Upper Hindoostan, he quitted Allahabad, with the consent of the British Government, and proceeded with his new allies to Delhi, where he was reinstated on the throne of his ancestors.

It is here necessary to revert to the 12th August, 1765, four days anterior to the treaty of peace with the Vizier. The Emperor, grateful for the services of the English East India Company in releasing him from the thraldom of the Vizier, and calculating upon future benefit from the alliance, conferred upon them, in perpetuity, the Dewanee* of the provinces of Bengal, Bahar, and Orissa, reserving to himself out of the revenues, an annual tribute of twenty-six lacs of rupees, and stipulating for an adequate provision for the Nuwab of Bengal, whose authority was thus superseded; the rest of the revenue was to be retained by the Company for the protection of the provinces. On the same day he executed a firman, confirming, in perpetuity, to the Company, the districts of Burdwan, Chittagong, and Midnapoor, the revenues of which had been assigned by the Nuwab of Bengal, in 1760, for the maintenance of the subsidiary force. By the same deed, the twenty-four Pergunnahs of Calcutta, &c. are also confirmed. A like grant, of the same date, conferred upon the English Company the farm of the Northern Circars, formerly granted to the French East India Company, by Sulabut Jung, the Soobeh of the Deccan. The grants of

* This office comprises, the collection of the revenue and administration of civil justice. The Dewans were merely stewards, and it was their duty, after paying the expenses of the province, to remit the balance to the royal treasury.

he Soobehdar of the Carnatic to the Company, were also confirmed by a firman of the same date. It is in virtue of these deeds that the Company hold these territories by legal right. The annual tribute of Bengal, &c. twenty-six lacs of rupees, continued to be paid to Shah Alum, until the year 1771, when, having accepted the assistance of the Mahrattas to replace him on the throne of his ancestors, it was withheld, agreeably to instructions provided against this contingency by the Court of Directors, and is still in abeyance. The same grounds justified the resumption afterwards of Corah and Allahabad, which the Emperor had either given over to the Mahrattas, or of which they had been deputed by him (holding, as their Bramins did, all the financial offices of the state) to collect the revenues for his use. These districts were afterwards restored at two years' purchase to the Vizier, to whom they had formerly belonged. The unfortunate Shah Alum, nevertheless, still looked towards the English from time to time, though surrounded by persons inimical to their interests. In 1782, the decease of the nobleman who had, as Ameer-ool-Oomra, guided the administration at Delhi with fidelity and firmness, induced distractions in the Imperial Courts, the nobles breaking into parties, each contending for the chief influence,—or, in fact, custody of the Emperor's person. Finding himself reduced to a cipher in his capital, he, in 1784, deputed his son, the present Emperor, to the camp of the Governor General, then at Benares, to make overtures of alliance to the Company, but which, unhappily for the Prince, it was not considered expedient to accept. From this time he was thrown wholly into the hands of the Mahrattas.

In 1788 the measure of his misfortunes was filled up, by a person who had not merely received an asylum, but who had been raised by him to the highest office of the empire,—that of Ameer-ool-Oomra. This was Gholam Cawdor, son of the late Chief of the Rohillas, who had been before banished by his own father. This wretch having discovered that the Emperor wished to remove him from court, surprised the royal residence, exposed the aged monarch to indignity and torture, and, after maltreating his children before his face, ordered his eyes to be pierced, and filled up the black catalogue of atrocities by dishonouring the ladies of the court, and giving up the palace and city to pillage. The sequel, as regards the chief actor, ought not to be omitted. Flying alone from a fort in which he had taken refuge, his saddle stuffed with precious booty, he was thrown from his horse, and picked up by his pursuers, the Mahrattas, who deprived him of his limbs, and exhibited him at Delhi in a cage, in which he perished; an awful instance of punishment for perfidy and ingratitude.

The wretched Emperor, finding another opportunity, by the Mahratta war of 1803, of renewing his connection with the English, threw himself on their generosity; and the immediate result of the battle of Delhi, on the 11th September of that year, rescued the aged descendant of Timour from the custody of the Mahrattas, and placed him again under British protection. A royal demesne, of which Delhi is the centre, was formed for his maintenance, and that of the other members of the royal household, comprising fifty or a hundred Princes and Princesses. But Shah Alum survived his liberation from the Mahrattas only about three years, when, at the age of eighty-three, he terminated a long career of vicissitude, and a calamitous reign of forty-five years. He was succeeded by his son Akbar, the present king. The real proceeds of the demesne, in 1827-28, exceeded thirty lacs of rupees, of which 13,40,983 rupees were applied to the maintenance of the royal family, including 1,95,604 rupees, payable to the members of it residing at Benares. This is all that remains to the unfortunate descendants of Timour from the wreck of an empire which, at the demise of Aurengzeb, produced a revenue of thirty millions sterling. The imperial dignity was acknowledged by Lord Lake, the British Commander-in-Chief, who presented the usual offering, and was created a Noble of the Empire. His Majesty, however, is no longer allowed to exercise the prerogative of conferring honours, it being incompatible with the situation to which he is reduced. An indication of his nominal supremacy is still conceded to him by the current coin throughout India, even at the British mints, being struck in his name. But exclusion from business of all kinds, and the usual effeminate life of Asiatic pageant royalty, has debased the dignity of the present members of this line, and an increase of wealth would only farther surround them by creatures, whose views, bounded by their own interests, would rather pander to their vices, than correct or check them. His present Majesty is himself a worthy man, and wholly given up to piety.

HIS HIGHNESS THE SOOBEHDAR OF THE CARNATIC.

The first of this family appointed to the Soobeh, was Anwar-ood-Deen Khan, who had been selected in 1743 by Nizam-ool-Moolk, for the office of guardian to the young Nuwab of the Carnatic, and for the administration of the government during his minority. The assassination of the young Prince some time after, by a mutinous soldiery, (not without a suspicion attaching to his guardian,) led to Anwar-ood-Deen's appointment to the Soobeh, which he held until the battle of Amboor, in 1749, in which he was killed, at the extraordinary age of 107 years, and his eldest son was taken a prisoner. His second son, Mahomed Ali, who had been confirmed in the Soobeh, by his acknowledged superior, the Nizam, fled, and sought the aid of the English, whose apathy and an unhappy spirit of division among themselves, prevented them from making any great exertions in his favour, till Lawrence returned from England, and Clive sprung up in India, to revive the military spirit of their countrymen, and conduct them to successful enterprizes. After severe contests with the French and their allies, who supported the cause of the rival candidate, Chunda Sahib, the surrender, in 1752, of the French force as prisoners of war at Tritchinopoly, induced Chunda Sahib to seek safety with the Mahratta general, who, regarding policy rather than hospitality, caused him to be assassinated; and his death leaving Mahomed Ali without a rival, led to his establishment in the Soobehship of the Carnatic. The war in the Carnatic was, however, renewed in 1755, after a peace of scarcely a year's duration, and continued for seven years. The French and English, who had joined the rival candidates as auxiliaries, contended now, in fact, as principals for the political existence in India of their respective nations. The importance of this object called forth all the skill and energy of the commanders, and afforded a powerful stimulus to the devotion, patriotism, and bravery of their troops.

In 1763, the treaty of Paris terminated the war between France and England, and Mahomed Ali being acknowledged by it the lawful Soobehdar of the Carnatic, and an ally of the British crown, he, in gratitude to the Company, conferred upon them, in Jagheer, the territory round Madras, rated at 4,42,881 pagodas, comprising the districts of Poonea, Tripassore, Conjeveram, Chingleput, Carangoly, &c. The confirmation by the Emperor to these grants, was dated 12th August, 1765. By a royal firman of the same date, Mahomed Ali was confirmed as Soobehdar of the Carnatic, and was also released from all dependence upon the Soobehdar of the Deccan, to which the concurrence of the latter was finally obtained by treaty, dated 23d February, 1768, in consideration of a sum of five lacs of rupees.

We have now reached a period, over which the faithful chronicler may not draw a veil. If the bravery and generosity of the Company's troops had established their military reputation, and obtained a high respect for the British character, beyond the bound-hedges of their settlements on the coast, the conduct of certain British subjects, then members of the Government at Madras, who prostituted the influence accidental to their official station, to accomplish their own private views, brought upon the British name a reproach * which is not yet forgotten. At this late period, it is impossible to discover whether the wants of the Nuwab were real or fictitious. He was in possession of a rich country, affording, except in an occasional bad season, a large surplus revenue: it may be

* Ay, but how did you behave in the end to Mahomed Ali? is a question which has been put to the writer more than once, by natives, when in familiar conversation.

doubted, therefore, whether he might not consider that the large amount advanced to him by influential men at Madras, at the iniquitous interest of 30 and 36 per cent, was not one way of securing him in his government. The interest was subsequently reduced to 25 and 20 per cent, and at last, by a general regulation, it fell to 10; but it had not been regularly paid, and interest heaped on heavy interest, formed an enormous accumulation of debt. In January, 1767, three members of the Government at Madras secretly obtained from the Nuwab, for the liquidation of their own and friends' claims, an assignment of territory yielding eight lacs of pagodas, and the Tanjore tribute, of four lacs of rupees more. On this transaction and others, the Court of Directors have observed, and placed upon record, that the Governor and Council of Madras had, in notorious violation of the trust reposed in them, preferred individual interest to that of the Company.

The violation of Hyder Ali's country in 1767, is supposed to have originated in the intrigues of those servants of the Company, who were creditors of the Nuwab. They flattered him that he might be put in possession of Mysore, to the revenues of which they looked for the discharge of their own debts, and probably as a fresh field for extortion. That formidable Chief overran the Carnatic in return, and appeared in a few months at the bound-hedge of Madras. Throughout this extensive tract of country, war and famine raged during eighteen months, producing universal desolation. The population migrated to escape captivity or slaughter, and the vicinity of Madras exhibited hundreds of these emigrants daily dying of exhaustion and want of food. Hyder Ali at last put an end to the war: Having eluded, by a manœuvre, the army opposed to him, he appeared a second time before Madras, where, on the 3d April, 1769, he dictated a peace, embracing an exchange of prisoners, and a mutual restoration of conquests. The periodical rains which had failed the year before, again disappointed the country in this year, and produced a scarcity by which the inhabitants of entire villages perished.

These events would have been sufficient to press upon the resources of Mahomed Ali, who had, moreover, to bear part of the military charges of the Madras Presidency. His public debt to the Company continued to increase; and that the revenues of the Carnatic might not be diverted in favour of private creditors, the claims of the latter were, in 1777, incorporated with the former. These debts, which were, in 1785, the subject of Parliamentary inquiry, then amounted to the enormous sum of £4,440,000 of sterling money of Great Britain, producing annuities, at their several rates of interest, of £623,000, of which £383,000 stood chargeable to the revenue of the Carnatic.* By articles of agreement with Mahomed Ali, in June, 1785, he consented to pay twelve lacs of pagodas per annum towards his public and private debts, and four lacs of pagodas per annum as his share of the Company's Military Peace Establishment. By treaty, executed in February, 1787, the permanent subsidy was increased to nine lacs of pagodas, with a provision, that in the event of war, four-fifths of his whole revenue should be made available to the discharge of its expenses; the annual payment of twelve lacs towards his debts continuing as before.

In 1792, it appearing that the resources of Mahomed Ali were not equal to his engagements, a new treaty became

* A Committee in India was appointed in 1805 to investigate into those private debts of the Nuwab, which had not been registered, and as such, had not been adopted by the Company. The amount of claims, up to June, 1831, exceeded thirty millions sterling, on which the adjudications *against* claimants exceeded twenty-seven millions: the adjudications *in favour* of parties having amounted only to £2,600,000. In the words of one of the reports,—"the investigation has defeated some of the most iniquitous combinations of fraud which were ever submitted to a legal tribunal." The expense, however, incurred by the East India Company, in this investigation, cannot have been much less than half a million of sterling money of Great Britain. Three Commissioners in India, whose united services exceed eighty years, cannot draw less, with their secretary (judging by the salaries usually given to old civil servants,) than £10,000 per annum; and with the establishment, &c. may not be under £15,000 per annum: they have now met upwards of twenty-six years. Besides the Committee in India, there is the London Carnatic Committee in Manchester Buildings, the cost of which exceeds, probably, £3000 per annum.

necessary. His share of the Military Peace Establishment remained at nine lacs, in part payment of which the Company took the risk and trouble of collecting the tribute of the forty-four Poligars, or feudal Chiefs of the Carnatic, whose united tributes amounted to 2,64,704 pagodas. The annual sum fixed for the liquidation of his debts, was 6,21,105 pagodas, making, with the subsidy, a sum of 12,56,400 pagodas, payable in twelve monthly instalments into the Treasury. His forts were to be garrisoned by Company's troops, and it was agreed, that in the event of war, or failure on the part of the Nuwab to make good his engagements, the Company should temporarily assume the management of the revenues of the Carnatic; on the occurrence of which contingency, the Jagheerdars of the Nuwab's family should be secured in their Jagheers, rated at 2,13,911 pagodas, and one-fifth of the net revenues should be paid over to the Nuwab. Mahomed Ali died in October, 1795; the firm ally of the English for forty years. The connection gave to him a throne, and to the Company possessions half as large as Ireland. He was succeeded by his son, Oomdut-ool-Oomra, who died in 1801.

A long course of mal-administration, conjoined with a discovery, made on the capture of Seringapatam in 1799, of a correspondence between Mahomed Ali, in his latter days, Oomdut-ool-Oomra, and Tippoo Sultaun, for the re-establishment of the banners of the Prophet in the Carnatic, and expulsion of the English, determined the Company, agreeably to certain articles of the treaty of 1792, to assume the government of the Carnatic. On the installation, therefore, of the Nuwab, Azeem-ood-Dowla, on the Musnud of the Carnatic, a treaty was executed, by which all his possessions, with the exception of his household lands, were transferred to the Company, which took on itself the whole of the debts of the late Nuwabs. A fifth part of the net revenue, which was never to be less than 12,000 pagodas a month, was assigned to the Nuwab and his heirs, for maintenance. Provision was also made for the families of the late Nuwabs, Mahomed Ali and Oomdut-ool-Oomra; and the Jagheer lands, agreeably to the treaty of 1792, yielding a revenue of 2,13,421 pagodas, were secured to the principal officers of the late government. By this arrangement, the Company acquired possession of the districts of Nellore, Ongole, Arcot, Pulicat, Chinleput, Pondicherry, Tritchinopoly, Tanjore, Tinevelly, Dindigul, Ramnad, Madura, &c. which are divided into eight collectorships. Azeem-ood-Dowla died in 1819, and was succeeded by his son, Azeem Jah. The family reside in the Chepauk gardens, which being situated within the jurisdiction of the Supreme Court at Madras, has given rise to complaints of proceedings at law as being inconsistent with the Nuwab's rights of sovereignty.

THE NUWAB, SOOBEHDAR OF BENGAL, &c.

The first of the family who held the vice-regal throne of Bengal, was Meer Jaffier Ali Khan, an officer who had served with distinction under three former Viceroys of these provinces, and who commanded the principal part of the army under Suraja-Dowla, whose memory is rendered so infamous by his destruction of the English prisoners in the Black Hole at Calcutta. The determined hostility of Suraja-Dowla towards the English, and violence towards his nobles, originated a conspiracy among them, which led to a treaty between Jaffier Ali Khan and the English, by which the latter undertook to raise him to the Soobehship of Bengal, Bahar, and Orissa. This was effected by the overthrow at Plassey, on 20th June, 1757, of the reigning Soobehdar, Suraja-Dowla. By the treaty which took place at this time the limits of the factories were extended by a grant of adjoining lands; and the Zumeendaree, or lease, of the twenty-four Pergunnahs lying between Calcutta and Calpee, was conferred upon the Company at an annual rent of 2,23,000 rupees. By the same treaty, the commercial privileges of the Company were extended, the French expelled from Bengal, and those who had suffered by the capture of Calcutta were amply remunerated.

Some years afterwards, it was discovered that intrigues had

been set on foot, having for their objects the expulsion of the English from Bengal, in which it appeared to a committee of investigation that Jaffier Ali bore a part. A hostile feeling had been evinced by an obstruction of the Company's commercial agents in the performance of their duty, and there being a great deficiency of revenue, notwithstanding the most oppressive exactions, a sense of justice towards the oppressed people of Bengal, over whom it was now discovered that a person had been raised inadequate to the task of governing, induced the Company's servants to exercise the right of interference which they had acquired, and resolve upon the deposition of Jaffier. His son-in-law, Cassim Ali Khan, was therefore invested, as Naib, or deputy, with the administration of affairs, and declared his eventual successor.

The force maintained at this time for the defence of the Bengal provinces, was 500 European cavalry, 2000 European infantry, and 8000 sepoys. Experience had shewn the necessity of securing a fixed resource for defraying its charges, not dependent upon the caprice, or mismanaged revenues, of a native prince. This security was obtained by a treaty with Cassim Ali Khan, dated 27th September, 1760, in which he assigned to the Company, for the expenses of the army, the districts of Burdwan, Midnapoor, and Chittagong. Cassim Ali disappointed the expectations formed of him. He abolished those particular immunities granted by his predecessors to European traders, which gave them so great an advantage over native inland merchants. But being compelled to rescind his orders on this head, he exempted the latter also from the payment of customs, which measure, undoubtedly just in itself, seems nevertheless, from the pernicious practice of permitting civil servants to traffic, to have engendered against him much displeasure. He also raised an army disciplined by Europeans, and, it is believed, contemplated the expulsion of his patrons from Bengal. An English envoy, and most of his party, though furnished with Cassim Ali's passports, were waylaid and shot, and 200 English prisoners were assassinated at Patna at his instigation, by his favourite General, Sumroo, a renegade German. The operations against him were vigorous and rapid. Cassim Ali's army sustained a signal defeat at Gheriah, and Moongheer, which he had made his capital, was taken after a regular siege. Patna was carried by storm on the 6th November, 1763; but Cassim Ali escaped to Oude, where he afterwards persuaded the Vizier to espouse his cause. It was the overbearing conduct of the Company's servants which made Cassim Ali an enemy, but his atrocious crimes justified their dethroning him.

In the meantime, Jaffier, who, it was discovered, had been unjustly degraded, was reinstated in July, 1763; but, worn out with age and infirmity, he died in the following year. With regard to the accusations which had chiefly led to his deposition, the committee who planned it had been grossly deceived. For the more effectual defence of the provinces, he raised, on his restoration, an auxiliary force, in addition to the subsidiary, of 12,000 cavalry and 12,000 infantry.

Jaffier was succeeded by his son, Nujeem-ood-Dowla, a boy of eighteen years of age, with whom a treaty was concluded in February, 1765, by which the Company engaged to secure him in the Soobehdary, and support him against all enemies; on his part, he promised to continue an advance of five lacs of rupees per month, agreed to by his father, towards the extra expenses of the war with the Vizier. The Emperor of Delhi having, subsequently, been graciously pleased to grant to the Company the Dewanee of these provinces, with the revenues thereof, on certain conditions, one of which was to provide for the personal expenses and dignity of the Soobehdar, this grant entirely superseded his authority, and vested the sovereignty in the Company; but his concurrence in it was not obtained until six weeks after, on the 30th September, 1765, when he consented to accept for personal expenses, the sum of 17,78,854 rupees, and for Aswarry (troops, &c. for parade) the sum of 36,07,277 rupees, agreeably to schedules given in by him. Nujeem-ood-Dowla died in the following year, and was succeeded by his brother, Suef-ood-Dowla. On his accession, a treaty was concluded, dated 19th May, 1766, when the amount for Aswarry was reduced to 24,07,277 rupees. Suef-ood-Dowla died in 1770, and his brother, Moobaruk-ood-Dowla, was invested as his successor. The principal conditions of this accession treaty, on the part of the Nuwab, were, that the tribute of Bengal should continue to be paid in instalments of 2,16,666 rupees per month to the Emperor, and specifies annually for himself 15,81,991 rupees for personal expenses, together with 16,00,000 rupees for Aswarry. The whole stipend of this family was, two years after, reduced to 16,00,000 rupees (or £180,000) per annum, which is the sum now paid to the representative of the family. Moobaruk-ood-Dowla died in 1796, and was succeeded by his son, Nazim-ool-Moolk, who died in 1810, and was succeeded by his son, Syed Zein-ood-Deen Ali Khan, then seventeen years of age. The family reside at Moorshedabad, the ancient capital of Bengal.

THE RAJA OF BENARES.

Munsuram, the founder of the Zumeendaree of Benares, possessed originally no more than half the village of Gungapoor, but through the favour of the Soobehdar of the province, and by modes of ambition usual in Hindoostan, becoming security for the rents of landholders, outbidding some, and expelling others for non-performance of engagements, he had acquired in nineteen years, until his death in 1740, districts yielding a gross revenue of 24,50,000 rupees. Bulwunt Sing, son of Munsuram, obtained the usual Musnuds for his father's possessions, and in the thirty years of his management, acquired from the Viziers Sufdur, Jung and Shuja-ood-Dowla, and also from the Emperor, additional possessions, rated at 35,00,000 rupees. He made private overtures to the English when they were at war, in 1764, with his feudal superior, the Vizier, who treated with him, from not knowing better at that time, as a sovereign Prince.

The King of Delhi, who had placed himself under protection of the English after the battle of Buxar, transferred the sovereignty of his possessions to the Company, on condition of their reducing the Vizier to obedience. But on the conclusion of the treaty of 16th August, 1765, these districts were restored to the Vizier, as a free gift by the Company, he engaging to exact only the same tribute as heretofore, viz. 20,00,008 rupees per annum. On the decease of Bulwunt Sing, in 1770, his son, Cheyt Sing, was confirmed in the succession by the Vizier, on an increased rent of two lacs and a half. In May, 1775, a subsidiary treaty was executed between the Vizier and the Company, when the sovereignty and possessions of the districts rented by Cheyt Sing were made over in perpetuity to the British Government. In the following year, by a deed, dated 15th April, 1776, the Zumeendaree was confirmed in the family of Cheyt Sing for ever, at a fixed annual rent, or tribute, of 22,21,745 rupees. This deed, being afterwards discovered to be contrary to the usages of India, was annulled; and an attempt being made to reduce the Raja to his original condition of a farming landholder, he, in 1781, rose in insurrection against the measures of the Governor-General. After an unequal conflict, Cheyt Sing took refuge in Sindhia's camp, where he was honourably received, and appointed to a command. He died at Gwalior in 1810, and his family now enjoy pensions at Benares, amounting to 23,000 rupees. On the flight of Cheyt Sing, his sister's son, Mehipnarain, a minor, was, by a deed dated 14th September, 1781, confirmed in the Zumeendaree, his father being appointed to the charge of it, under the title of Naib, or deputy, to his son. The tribute, however, was raised to forty lacs of rupees, being within 9,02,741 rupees of the full amount of his assessment, which sum was left for the personal expenses and Aswarry of the Raja, including stipends and lands to his relations and dependents. At length, in 1787, negotiations were commenced, to prevail on the Raja to relinquish the administration of his Zumeendaree concerns into the hands of the British Government, which he had heretofore been allowed to exercise with a degree of regal authority. These ended, in 1794, in an agreement, by which the Raja retains his authority over certain patrimonial lands of inconsiderable extent, and the rest of the province of Benares is now administered by the Company's officers, a certain share of the surplus revenue, or excess above the fixed tribute of forty lacs, being assigned for the personal expenses of the Raja, which, in 1827-28, amounted to about 1,20,000 rupees.

HIS HIGHNESS THE RAJA OF TANJORE.

TANJORE formed part of the conquests achieved by Shahjee, the general of the Mahrattas in the service of the King of Beejapoor, and father of Sivajee, the renowned assertor of Hindoo independence. On Shahjee's death, in 1664, his second son, Venkajee, was confirmed successor in his Jagheers, and held them undisturbed until 1678, when Sivajee, having settled his conquests in other quarters, visited this part of the peninsula, and, after a slight unequal contest between the brothers, Venkajee was confirmed in the possession of Tanjore, on condition of paying half the revenue to Sivajee. These are the ancestors of the present family. The kingdom of Bejapoor, of which Tanjore formed a part, ceased to exist in 1683.

The first time that the British came in contact with this state was in 1749, when they sent a body of troops from Fort St David, to restore to the Musnud Syajee, the grandson of Venkajee, and only legitimate son of his father, Tookajee, who was the youngest son of Venkajee, but the only one of them leaving heirs. The object of the expedition failed, but the price of the assistance, the Fort of Devi-cotta, was obtained from the reigning Raja. The Raja of Tanjore was tributary to the Nuwab of the Carnatic, who found it necessary, in September, 1771, to send an army into his territory, principally composed of Company's troops, by which the Raja, Tooljajee, was compelled to pay the two years' arrears of tribute, at four lacs of rupees per annum, and to assign districts to the Nuwab, yielding sixteen lacs, to pay the expenses of the war, which were estimated at thirty-two lacs.

In August, 1773, another expedition proceeded against him, when he was dethroned* by his feudal superior. The

* Page 12.

measure was not approved of by the Government in England, and the Madras Government was directed to effect the restoration of the Raja, which was formally done in April, 1776. The Raja then applied for a subsidiary force, and offered territory in the district of Munargoody, including the sea-port town of Nagore, yielding four lacs of pagodas, for its maintenance. This does not appear to have been complied with until 1787, when the growing power of the Mysore state, and the obviously ambitious views of its Chief, suggested the expediency of a coalition for the future defence and protection of the Company's territories, as well as those of their allies: it was arranged, therefore, that the Nabob of the Carnatic, and Raja of Tanjore, should bear their share, in proportion to their respective revenues, of the expense of the maintenance of the Madras army, about to be increased. By treaty, dated 10th April, 1787, with Ameer Sing, who had succeeded his father, Tooljajee, during the preceding year, it was agreed, that he should pay four lacs of pagodas annually, into the Company's treasury, towards defraying the Military Peace Establishment; and that four-fifths of the whole fiscal revenues should be applied to the military expenses, on the occurrence, and during the continuance, of war. The tribute to the Nuwab of the Carnatic, which had been allowed to remain in arrear for eleven years, was transferred to the Company, who also became guarantee for certain of his debts to British subjects, amounting to about four lacs of pagodas. Towards the liquidation of these debts, the arrears of tribute, and prospective tribute, a farther yearly sum of three lacs of pagodas, was allotted; leaving thus to the Raja, after deduction of these sums, a balance of three lacs for his current expenses, when the full revenue of his country, estimated at ten lacs of pagodas, should be realized. An Asiatic territorial revenue being dependent upon the periodical rains, is ever fluctuating: a fixed tribute becomes, under such circumstances, in one season light, in another oppressive; but whether a fixed sum, or a per centage of the realized revenue, be the more equitable, is discussed in another place. It soon became obvious, that the Raja's resources were unequal to his engagements, and a new treaty was executed in 1792, by which the subsidy was reduced to 3,50,000 pagodas; and as the condition of the Tanjore country rendered a suspension of the tribute absolutely requisite, the payment on that account, and private debts together, was fixed at 1,10,000 pagodas per annum, for three years, at the expiration of which period, the whole sum to be paid by him annually, including subsidy and private debts, was fixed at 5,74,285 pagodas. A failure on the part of the Raja was to entitle the Company to assume the management of certain districts, estimated to yield this amount. A provision for the support of Surfoojee, the adopted son of Tooljajee, and the maintenance of the widows of the latter, formed another alienation of 14,000 pagodas from the fiscal revenue.

In 1798, the Raja, Ameer Sing, was deposed, and a sum of 25,000 pagodas per annum set aside out of the revenue for his maintenance. Surfoojee, the adopted son of Tooljajee, was raised to the throne, but the British administration, revenue and judicial, was introduced into the country. The Company, in assuming the management of the revenues, set aside out of them a fixed sum, amounting to one lac of pagodas annually, besides one-fifth of the net amount realized, for the maintenance of Surfoojee. The payments to his Highness on this account, amounted, in 1828-29, to 9,31,182 rupees. He has his own Court of Justice, and his only military expenses are for the garrisons of the two Forts of Tanjore, which together consist of about fifteen hundred irregular infantry.

Surfoojee died on the 7th March, 1832, and on the 17th the installation of his son took place, under the titles of Shreemunt, Rajasree, Sivajee, Maharaja, Chuturputee.

BAJEEROW RUGOONATH, THE EX-PESHWA.

The first of this family who attained eminence, Ballajee Wiswanath, officiated as an accountant with the Mahratta army in 1713, from which comparatively humble station he was elevated, in 1717, to the rank of Peshwa, or Chief

Minister: he held the office at his death in 1720, and left it to his son, Bajeerow Bullal. The Mahratta nation owe to the conduct of this line of Peshwas, at once their glory and their downfall; their right to tribute from every nation in India, and the decline, subversion, and eventual incorporation of their country with the Anglo-Indian Empire. The details of military operations, or properly, perhaps, predatory excursions of this people, including every fact connected with their rise, progress, and decline, being already before the public, in Mr Grant Duff's "History of the Mahrattas," a brief notice is only intended here.

The first treaty of Bassein, in July, 1739, (in which Bajeerow, and not his master, was the party treated with,) limits the British possessions at Bombay to that island, and about a mile of the ocean. Bajeerow died in 1740, leaving the Peshwaship to his son, Ballajee Bajeerow, styled Nana Sahib. In 1749, Sahoo, the pageant Raja of the Mahrattas, died, and though a nominal supremacy in the state was continued in his family, it was only an elevation to a throne and a prison; the custody of the Raja's person, and an uncontrolled power, being vested in the Peshwa, who became, *de facto*, Suzerain over all the Chiefs of the Mahratta confederacy. The successful expeditions under Commodore James, and lastly, Watson and Clive, against the piratical power formed on the west coast of India, by the Angria family, led to a treaty in October, 1756, by which Bankoot, and many important commercial advantages, were conceded to the Company.

Nana Sahib died in 1761, it is supposed of grief, occasioned by the result of the disastrous battle of Paniput, and was succeeded by his son, Madhoorao Ballajee, styled the Great, who, by a treaty in September of that year, granted farther advantages to the Bombay Government. After the decease of Madhoorao, his brother, Naraen Rao, a minor, succeeded to the office of Peshwa, under the guardianship of his uncle, Rugoonath Rao, so well known to the English, under the name of Rugoba. Naraen Rao was assassinated by ruffians, employed, it is believed, by Rugoba, who officiated as Peshwa for a few months, until it was discovered that the widow of the murdered youth was pregnant. Here commenced the downfall of the Poona state. A number of Chiefs confederated, formed a Regency, and expelled Rugoba, who took refuge at Surat; but the Bombay Government agreed to support his pretensions to the Peshwaship, or Regency. A treaty with him took place in 1775, embracing territorial cessions, and providing present funds for the maintenance of the troops with which he was assisted. The Bengal Government, who had been applied to by the opposite party, disapproved* of the measures of the Bombay Government; the troops were recalled in consequence, and the treaty annulled. The interference of the Bengal Government ended in the conclusion of a disadvantageous treaty in May, 1776, which, notwithstanding, was violated by the Regency in almost every article. Both Presidencies now concurred in affording assistance to Rugoba, with whom a new treaty was formed in 1778, which led to the invasion of the Mahratta territory for that purpose, and the disgraceful convention of Wurgaom* in the following year. In May, 1782, the necessity of meeting the aggressions of Hyder Ali, constrained the Company to conclude a peace with the Mahratta Regency, by which they relinquished all their material conquests, though they secured an honourable provision for Rugoba.

In 1790, the Peshwa Sewai Madhoorao was one of the parties of the triple alliance formed against Tippoo Sultaun, and shared in the division of half that Prince's territories, which, at the termination of the war in February 1702, he was compelled to cede to the Allies, together with 330,00,000 rupees, or upwards of £3,000,000 sterling. The territory acquired by the Peshwa, amounted to 13,16,666 rupees of revenue, and was situated contiguous to the hereditary possession of the Mahrattas in the Doab.

The victory obtained at Poona, 25th October, 1802, by Jeswunt Rao Holkur over Sindhia and the Peshwa, occasioned the latter to throw himself into the hands of the British

* Page 10.

† Nana Furnawees and Mahadjee Sindhia, the one afterwards so celebrated as a statesman, and the other as a military leader, were both at this time members of the Regency which ruled affairs at Poona.

Government, and led, on the 31st December following, to the second Treaty of Bassein, for the restoration of Bajeerow Rugoonath, the son of Rugoonath Rao, to the Musnud at Poona. From former alliance with this family, it was considered obligatory on the British Government to assist him in recovering and maintaining him in his unquestioned rights. The Company therefore engaged to furnish him with a permanent subsidiary force of six thousand native infantry, with the usual proportion of European artillery, for the support of which, territories, rated at twenty-six lacs of rupees, were ceded in the Deccan and Carnatic. By a supplemental treaty in the following year, a regiment of cavalry was added to the subsidiary force, and the territorial cessions differently arranged. The territory ceded in the Carnatic, of which the revenue was rated at 19,16,000 rupees, was restored for a portion of Bundelcund, rated at 36,16,000 rupees, the difference being to provide for the additional regiment of cavalry, the extra expenses of the war, and reduction of Boondelcund. Over this province, the Peshwa's authority had not been more than nominal, as his manager had never remitted any of the revenue to Poona. The military protection of his hereditary possessions may therefore be said to have been secured to him at small cost. By one of the articles of this treaty, he engaged in time of war to co-operate with a contingent of five thousand cavalry, and three thousand infantry, but which he had never been required to keep up, until, forgetting his obligations to the British Government, he engaged in a variety of intrigues against them, when the latter was compelled to have recourse to arms in May, 1817. The treaty of Poona took place in June following, when the Peshwa was compelled to cede territory for the maintenance of the contingent, which the British undertook to raise and maintain. On the 5th November following, when at peace, he attacked, plundered, and burnt the Poona Residency, which led to the battle of Khirkee, where being repulsed, he shortly after became a fugitive at the head of his army, until overtaken on the 3d June, 1818, when he formally renounced the sovereignty of his dominions, to which the Company had now acquired a right by conquest. He was allowed to fix his residence at any place north of the Nerbudda, and has now a liberal stipend allowed him, of eight lacs of rupees per annum, which, as he has no children, will revert to the donors. He is otherwise known to be possessed of considerable treasure. His permanent residence is Bithoor, a place of pilgrimage, on the Jumna, where he keeps up a good deal of state, and maintains a body guard of four hundred horse.

The deposal of Bajeerow, an inveterate, if not a very powerful enemy, wearing the mask of the closest friendship, contributed essentially to the stability of the British power in India. The Peshwa, though no longer the acknowledged head of the Mahratta confederacy, had still a sort of hereditary influence at the Durbars of most of the substantive states, and it had, during a considerable period, been used by Bajeerow in fostering plots to overturn the British power. The conquest of his territories put the Company in possession of a farther revenue, which, in 1828, exceeded one million sterling, exclusive of Jagheers, but including former cessions. These amounted to 36,16,000 rupees in 1802-3, and in 1817 to a farther sum of 34,00,000 rupees, to maintain the contingent. The improved management of these acquisitions, lapses of Jagheers and pensions, together with an eventual reduction of the troops, for which the cessions of 1817 were obtained, will give to the Company, in the course of time, a large surplus revenue from the conquest.

Vinaeek Rao, Bappa Sahib, is the son of the late Amrut Rao, who had been adopted by the Ex-Peshwa's father, when he despaired of having an heir. Amrut Rao assumed the government of Poona during the absence of Bajeerow, in November 1802. He refused the Peshwaship, but he allowed his son, the present Vinaeek Rao, to be invested with the dignity. On the advance of the British forces into the Deccan, for the purpose of establishing Bajeerow, negotiations were opened with Amrut Rao, who was then plundering the country, at the head of a body of horse, which ended in his joining Sir Arthur Wellesley's division, until the restoration of order in the Deccan, and to his eventual retirement to Benares, in 1804, on a stipend of 7,00,000 rupees per annum, during his own and son's natural lives. Stipends were also assigned to certain of his adherents, amounting to 58,050 rupees, some of which have since lapsed. He usually lives at Turrowah, a residence selected by his father.

CHIMNAJEE APPAH, SAHIB, is the younger brother of the Ex-Peshwa, in whose palace at Poona he always resided. He also had been invested as Peshwa by one of the parties in the state, during the absence of Bajeerow in 1802. He accompanied his brother during his flight in 1817-18, until his affairs became wholly desperate; when, in May, 1818, he quitted him, and surrendered to a British detachment, together with the Chief of Neepaunee, and a strong body of horse. He experienced the most humane and liberal treatment on his submission; and, after the discharge of his debts by the British Government, he was allowed a pension of 3,00,000 rupees per annum. His residence being restricted to any place north of the Nerbudda, he chose Benares.

NUWAB OF BANDA.

THE ancestor of this family, the Peshwa Bajerow Bullal, had, on leaving Boondelcund in 1743, brought with him to the Deccan a Mahomedan beauty, the celebrated Mustanee, and from this connection, wholly repugnant to the obligations of his caste, or order, was born Shumsheer Bahadoor, afterwards the leader of a division of the Mahratta army, at the head of which he fell, at the battle of Paniput.

His son, Ali Bahadoor, was sent with a body of troops from Poona, about 1789, to co-operate with Sindhia in extending the Mahratta possessions in Hindoostan. But a dispute arising between Sindhia and the remarkable Himmut Bahadoor, (the spiritual guide and military leader of the Gosaeens,) the latter took refuge with Ali Bahadoor, who held, for the time, a casual supremacy, from being intrusted by the Peshwa with the national standard in this expedition. This led to the secession of Sindhia, and abandonment of that object.

Himmut Bahadoor, who had already acquired, in the confusion of the times, possessions in Boondelcund, valued at thirteen lacs of rupees annually, apprehending their loss by the restoration of tranquillity, suggested to Ali Bahadoor, and united with him for the reduction of the rest of the province, which they accordingly invaded, in 1790, at the head of forty thousand men. The forces of the various native chiefs were successively defeated; and the whole country, and its places of strength, in which it abounds, were nominally subdued, with the exception of the Fort of Kallinjer, which Ali Bahadoor had been two years besieging when he died, in 1802. His elder son, Shumsheer Bahadoor, was at the time absent at Poona, which brought about the elevation of his half-brother, Zoolfikar Ali, an infant two years of age, to the Musnud, by the instrumentality of his uncle, Ghunnee Bahadoor, and Himmut Bahadoor, the former of whom assumed the regency, with the command of the army, and continued the siege.

Shumsheer Bahadoor, then eighteen years of age, on receiving intelligence of the death of his parent, obtained from Amrut Rao, then acting Peshwa, the investiture of his father's succession, and proceeded to Boondelcund, where his first act, after assuming the administration of affairs, was to seize his uncle, and administer poison to him.

About this time the cession of Boondelcund to the British Government took place, and Shumsheer Bahadoor prepared to resist its occupation. After some slight affairs with the British troops, the defection of his chiefs, and particularly of his wily ally, Himmut Bahadoor, who made his own bargain with the invading army, he made overtures of submission. He came over to the British camp on the 18th January, 1804, and on giving orders for the evacuation of all the forts still occupied by his adherents, an annual pension of four lacs of rupees was settled upon him and his successors for ever. He kept up, for purposes of parade, a guard of about five hundred cavalry, infantry, and artillery, dressed and armed like British troops. He was succeeded by his half brother, Zoolfikar Ali, who usually resides at Banda. He admires and endeavours to assume English manners and customs. His dress is partly

English, and the furniture of his palace is almost wholly so. He has an extensive racing stud, and patronizes liberally the turf at Cawnpoor. He, however, abstains from the forbidden juice, though his brother, who was an honorary member of a dragoon mess, made large libations to the jolly god.

Himmut Bahadoor died in 1804, at seventy years of age; but his Jagheer, by treaty, rated at twenty lacs for the support of ten thousand cavalry, was not resumed until 1806; another Jagheer was then conferred on his son, the Raja Neerundur Geer, at Rasdhun, in the Doab of the Jumna and Ganges, yielding annually 1,35,000 rupees; while his other descendants now receive pensions exceeding 60,000 rupees.

THE DESCENDANTS OF HYDER ALI AND TIPPOO SULTAUN.

The Mahomedan dynasty of Mysore may be dated from 1761, when Hyder Ali assumed the regency, and terminated with his son, Tippoo Sultaun, on his death, and the capture of Seringapatam, in 1799. Hyder Ali, the most formidable opponent the British power ever met in India, commenced life as a private horseman in the corps of his elder brother, at Deonhully, in 1749, and for his gallantry at the siege he was, before its termination, intrusted with the command of fifty horse, two hundred infantry, and three hundred Behder Peons, or Ramoosies, a tribe to whose expertness as thieves and spies, he owed much of his success in after life. Hyder's character was a composition of courage, cunning, and cruelty; and, in the words of an able orientalist, "he was distinguished for all the terrible accomplishments of an Asiatic hero,—equally prodigal of faith and of blood—equally victorious in the use of intrigues and of arms!" He could neither read nor write; but the defect was supplied by an exceedingly tenacious memory, and a sagacity which made it a daring experiment for secretaries to practise deception upon him. He came upon the stage when anarchy reigned throughout India, and the sceptre of Mysore was in feeble hands. His father died in the humble situation of a Naik of Revenue Peons, about 1734, leaving a family destitute and friendless. Hyder was a sovereign in 1761.

In 1751, Mahomed Ali was besieged in Tritchinopoly, by his rival Chunda Sahib, and the French; when the Regent of Mysore, with a body of Mahrattas, and the Raja of Tanjore, were induced to join the cause of the former. Hyder accompanied the Regent with a corps of five hundred Sepoys, armed with muskets, for which he was indebted to the activity of his Ramoosies. This corps, disciplined by European deserters, was shortly after increased to twelve hundred men, and was the most efficient of the Mysore division. On the siege of Tritchinopoly being raised, possession of it was claimed by Nunjraj, the Regent, as the stipulated price of his assistance, by a secret treaty with Mahomed Ali, but of which the latter now evaded the fulfilment. The Mysorean remained before the place, and having failed in his attempts, during the absence of Mahomed Ali and his allies, to gain possession by stratagem, he, supported by the French, invested it. The timely return, however, of Mahomed Ali and Major Lawrence, not only saved the place, but led to a series of brilliant actions, in which English valour and skill were conspicuous. It was thus that Hyder Ali, whose command had increased to fifteen hundred horse, three thousand Sepoys, two thousand Ramoosies, and four guns, learned to appreciate European tactics, and obtained experience which afterwards proved highly beneficial to him. Tritchinopoly was to have been given up to Nunjraj in May, 1754, on certain conditions being performed; but subsequent events determined the English to retain possession of it; and the Regent was compelled to return to Mysore in 1755, to defend his own territories, abandoning a favourite project, which had cost much blood, treasure, and time. In this year Hyder was appointed Foujdar of Dindigul, and was for two years actively employed in reducing the Poligars in that quarter, who resisted the tribute due by them to Mysore. He purchased at this time the sovereignty of Sera from Busalut Jung, though the latter had been long dispossessed of it.

In 1760, having returned to Mysore, Hyder had gradually obtained assignments of more than half the revenues, for support of his troops. This stretch of his influence excited the indignation of Khundeerao, the Dewan, to whose sagacity, decision, and friendship, Hyder principally owed his elevation. The feelings of regard being now supplanted by the impulses of revenge, Khundeerao co-operated with Nunjraj, and attacked Hyder, who, escaping to Bangalore, raised another army, and encountering his opponents, was again defeated. Reduced to extremity, he, by a bold artifice, succeeded in dividing his enemies, marched to Seringapatam, assumed the government, and reduced the Raja to the condition of a pensioner. Of the revenues, three lacs of pagodas were reserved for the expenses of the Raja, and one lac for Nunjraj, while Khundeerao was confined in a cage. Henceforth Hyder became the uncontrolled ruler of Mysore. Actuated by the consciousness that the sword of an usurper is never sheathed with safety, the improvement of the army became his chief care; while, at the same time, every part of the administration was vigilantly attended to and watched by his personal supervision. After the fall of Pondicherry on the 16th January, 1761, hosts of European adventurers sought his patronage, and such as obtained it became essentially serviceable to him. The first six years of his reign were wholly employed in extending his dominions. He subdued the Poligars of Raidroog, Harponelly, Chittledroog, and Ooscotta; the Nuwabs of Savanore, Sera, &c.; the Rajas of Cochin, Palghaut, &c.; and the whole of Canara and Malabar.

Hyder's first intercourse with the English occurred in 1763, when he gave permission to the Bombay Government to enclose and build a factory at Onore, with the exclusive right of purchasing all the pepper produced in the province. He granted other advantages or exemptions to facilitate commercial intercourse, and excluded Europeans of other nations from settling there. On his final conquest of Malabar, in 1766, he confirmed the privileges which the Princes in that province had granted to the Company's commercial agents for the exclusive purchase of pepper, sandal wood, cardemoms, &c.

In 1767, commenced his first war with the English, which terminated in an injudicious and hasty treaty of peace at Madras, on the 3d April, 1769, by the second article of which, Hyder Ali seems to have calculated on the future co-operation of the Company against his enemies the Mahrattas, in their periodical invasions of the Mysore. Finding himself disappointed in this hope, he accused the English of non-observance or infraction of treaties; and hence, probably, arose that inveterate hostility towards them, which terminated in the ruin of his family. It is curious to observe, that in the treaty of the year before, between the Nizam and the Company, Hyder is declared a rebel and usurper.

From the above period, Hyder seems to have been solicitous to form a closer alliance with the English. In August, 1770, he concluded a treaty with the Bombay Government, in which he repeats his permission to build and enclose factories at Onore and Carwar; grants the monopoly of the pepper, sandal wood, &c. produced in his own and the conquered provinces; stipulating that part of the price be paid in guns, military stores, &c. Free permission was also given to purchase and export timber (teak excepted) from Malabar, and the English were to take precedence of all other nations, European or Asiatic, in matters of ceremony.

In 1771, hard pressed by the Mahrattas, his army nearly annihilated, and his resources destroyed, Hyder in vain solicited aid from the English, though offering, as the price of it, both territory and money. After fifteen months of hopeless war, he obtained peace, by paying thirty lacs of rupees, and ceding part of his territory to the Mahrattas.

He renewed his proposals for a closer alliance, by envoys sent to Madras, in December, 1773; but after waiting until May, 1775, in the hope of effecting it, he dismissed Mahomed Ali's envoys from his court, and prepared to form a connection with the French. With the latter he then concerted a future co-operation, and they, in the meantime, supplied him with military stores, through their settlement at Mahé.

Hyder's affairs were now becoming more prosperous; his army was numerous and well appointed; and as soon as the reduction of the French settlements in India was resolved on, he had no difficulty in precipitating himself into war, the plea for which was, that Mahé was situated in the territory of a prince under his protection. In 1779, an alarming confederacy was formed between Hyder, the Peshwa, and Nizam, for the extermination of the English; and it was perhaps owing to the accident of a mandate arriving from the Emperor, which Hyder had applied for some time before, conferring upon him all the possessions held by the Nizam, that the latter was detached from the alliance.

From 1780 to 1784, Hyder (and after his death, Tippoo) carried on a desolating war. The inhabitants of the Carnatic were expatriated, or mutilated if caught, and their habitations reduced to ashes; but the cruelties perpetrated in the Coorg country, were of a still more sanguinary character; and in Soonda, 30,000 Christians, or Nazarenes, were forcibly circumcised.

Hyder died in 1782, and was succeeded by Tippoo, who surpassed his father in cruelty. The British operations of this period are extremely interesting. The mistakes of some officers, and consequent disastrous effects—the genius of others, extricating themselves under more than ordinary difficulties—and the enterprising spirit of all,—form important lessons to the soldier. The war terminated in a treaty of peace, concluded at Mangalore on the 11th March, 1784, the terms of which embraced mutual restoration of conquests, the evacuation of the factories at Onore, Carwar, and Sadashewgurh, by the British troops, and giving them up to Tippoo, who, on his part, restored to the British the factories at Calicut, &c. with certain commercial privileges.

Tippoo continued to be fully employed against the Mahrattas, or in quelling insurrections in Coorg, Malabar, &c. until 1789, when his attack on our ally, the Raja of Travancore, was considered a declaration of war against the Company. A variety of petty insults and aggressions, during the past three years, evincing the disposition of Tippoo, led to a league with the Nizam and Peshwa, which had for its object the crippling the Sultaun's means of disturbing the general tranquillity of India. Accordingly, his dominions were invaded at three different points, by divisions which amounted to (exclusive of the armed rabble that followed the Mahratta and Moghul leaders) a force of eighty-four thousand men, of which eleven thousand were Europeans, and thirty thousand Company's regular troops. The war was under the personal conduct of Lord Cornwallis, and terminated at Seringapatam in a treaty of peace, by which Tippoo was compelled to cede half his territories (producing a revenue of forty lacs of pagodas) to the allies, and to pay in specie three crore and thirty lacs of rupees.*

Notwithstanding these reverses, the Mysore state still maintained a large field army, and endeavoured to form foreign connections. In 1798, Tippoo sent envoys to Paris, and concluded a treaty, offensive and defensive, with the French Republic, against Great Britain, and received a body of French troops into his service. Having refused explanation, and evaded the Governor-general's demand for security, the British forces, joined by those of the Nizam, proceeded to hostilities; which ended in the reduction of Seringapatam—the death of Tippoo, who fell in its defence—the extinction of his power, or dynasty, and the partition of his territories among the allies, reserving a portion to form a demesne for the descendant of the ancient Rajas. Out of the share which fell to the Company, stipends, affording a suitable maintenance, were specified to be paid to the families of Hyder and Tippoo, amounting to 7,20,000 rupees, which by lapses, were reduced in 1827-28, to 6,39,549 rupees.

The Mysore, at the beginning of the eighteenth century, was tributary to the Nuwab of Sera; and after he dwindled into insignificance, it became tributary to the Soobehdar of the Deccan, and the Peshwa: to the former, in three lacs and a half of rupees per annum, determined from the invasion of Nasir Jung, in 1746; and to the Mahrattas, from their invasion in 1723. Tribute, however, was not usually paid in

* A lac (100,000) of rupees, may be assumed at £10,000; and a crore or a hundred lacks, at a million sterling; a lac of star pagodas at £40,000; and of Canterai pagodas, at £33,500. There are, however, a great variety of rupees and pagodas, differing sometimes thirty per cent in value.

India, without being enforced by an army; and the invasion of Salabhut Jung, in 1755, and of nine different irruptions of the Mahrattas into the Mysore, between 1761 and 1791, were to collect arrears of tribute. In like manner, the Rajahs, Poligars, &c. tributary to Mysore, always resisted payment, so that the Mysoreans were perpetually engaged in military operations.

NUWAB OF FURRUCKABAD.

THE Afghan principality of Furruckabad was founded by Mahomed Khan, whose adjunct of Bungush denotes his tribe. He held the high office of Soobehdar of Allahabad, and afterwards of Malwa, during which period he twice invaded Boondelcund, in 1731, when he was repulsed, and again, with better success, in 1732. He had reduced the Raja of Jytpoor, son of the famous Chitursal, to extremity, when the Mahrattas joined the latter, and turned the tide of victory. He died in battle against the Rohillas, and his son, Ahmed Khan Bungush, joined the Vizier Shaboodeen, of notorious memory, in his invasion of Rohilcund in 1756. Five years after, when all Mahomedans made common cause against the Hindoos, Rohilla and Bungush fought under the same standard, and Ahmed Khan was conspicuous at Paniput. He died in 1771, and his son, Moozuffir Jung, was invested as his successor by the Emperor when on his ill-starred journey from Benares to Delhi. The Nuzzarana, or offering on investiture, five lacs of rupees, went to satisfy one of the demands of his Majesty's Mahratta allies.

The Furruckabad territories were wholly surrounded by those of Oude; and it was judged equitable that the Nuwab should contribute towards their general military protection. A subsidiary treaty was, therefore, concluded in 1786 between the Vizier and Nuwab, under the guarantee of the British Government, by which the former engaged to raise one battalion of infantry for his protection, for the maintenance of which the latter was to pay an annual fixed tribute, or subsidy, of four and a half lacs of rupees.

In 1787, the country was sequestrated by the Vizier, when the British Government interfered to ensure a suitable provision for Moozuffir Jung, his brother, and the late Minister. Moozuffir Jung was shortly after murdered by his eldest son, when the second, Imdaud Hoosein Khan, a minor, was appointed to the succession, under the guardianship of his uncle, who was intrusted with the administration of affairs during his minority. The tribute of Furruckabad formed part of the cessions made by the Vizier in 1801, and the territory became isolated by the possessions of the Company, affording, had its independence been permitted, a shelter for criminals, for there the jurisdiction of the British Magistrate could have no place. In the province, moreover, no court, civil or criminal, existed for the dispensing of justice; and the ferocious Patans, whose hands may be said to be against every one, whose employment is war, and danger their pastime, indulged their natural disposition with impunity, often at the expense of the inhabitants of the adjacent countries. It was determined, therefore, to assume the civil as well as the military government of the country, and in June, 1802, when the Nuwab had attained his majority, a treaty was concluded by which this hitherto misgoverned province was ceded to the Company in commutation of the subsidy, or tribute. A monthly provision of 9000 rupees was secured to the Nuwab, and his heirs for ever, besides an allowance annually for the support of the palace. The possession of his household, lands, gardens, and houses, was continued to him, and he was exempted from the Court of Adawlut. Allowances were assigned to his relations, and the old pensions and Jagheers of his family and adherents guaranteed. To four officers of his household, who were displaced by the new order of things, stipends were granted at his request amounting to 16,000 rupees annually. Imdaud Hoosein Khan was succeeded by his son, who died of the small-pox, and the present representative is Jumal Hoosein Khan.

THE NUWAB OF SURAT.

THE British acquired a great increase of political power on the western side of India through the offices of Admiral of the Moghul Fleet, and Governor of Surat Castle, which were conferred by the Emperor, in 1759, upon the Government of Bombay, with an assignment of two lacs of rupees upon the revenues of Surat, for their expenses. The government of the city, however, was retained by the Nuwab. But while the Company was charged with the military defence of the city, universal misrule, in the absence of any thing like a police, existed under the administration of the Nuwab, which imperatively called for reformation. On the accession, therefore, of Nasur-ood-Deen, in March, 1800, the Company took the Nuwab's share of the revenue into their own hands; the undivided civil and military government of the city and its dependencies was also assumed, and the Presidency Code of Civil and Criminal Justice introduced. Nasur-ood-Deen was so illiterate that he could not write his name on the treaty being presented to him for that purpose. On his death, he was succeeded by his son, Meer Ufzool-ood-Deen Khan, Buhadoor, styled also Hushmut Jung, and Qumr-ood-Dowla.

The Nuwab has independent authority over all families residing upon his estate, may arrest and imprison defaulting tenants, and may attach and sell their property; but complaints on the tyrannical exercise of this power are cognizable by the government. He is in his own person perfectly independent, not being subject to the process or jurisdiction of the local courts of law. He has about 1600 beegas of land, about 300 cultivators, 200 armed attendants, and 200 servants and slaves. He receives, by the installation treaty of 1800, 1,00,000 rupees annually from the British Government, and one-fifth of the customs collections, and surplus revenues of Surat, which amount to about 50,000 rupees; while his private estate yields about 24,000 rupees more.

THE BUKSHEE OF SURAT, Mahomed Mooeen-ood-Deen Khan, is the great-grandson of Meer Zeea-ood-Deen, commonly called Shah Meetan, the first of this race who held the office of Bukshee of Surat. The family came originally from Boorhanpoor, and settled at Surat about the beginning of the eighteenth century. The brother of Shah Meetan, called Meer Mooeen-ood Deen Khan Achun, was the first Nuwab of this family, and was recognized as such by the Honourable Company about 1750. The Bukshee has certain rights upon the revenues of Surat, which realized to him, in 1827, 12,680 rupees; and he is otherwise very wealthy. The office of Bukshee ceased in 1806, but courtesy keeps up the name.

In 1748, Meer Mooeen-ood-Deen Khan, commonly called Syed Achun, son-in-law of the late Nuwab, with the aid of the Mahrattas, under the nephew of Dumajee Rao Gaekwar, expelled the Nuwab, Sufdur Khan, then styled Foujdar. This was the time the Mahrattas obtained their first footing in Surat. For the service rendered, they had the Chouth conferred upon them in perpetuity, and these continued to be realized for the joint benefit of the Gaekwar and Peshwa, until the share belonging to the latter was transferred as part of the cessions made by the treaty of Bassein in 1802. The Gaekwar's share was obtained at a subsequent period.

THE CHIEFS OF SAGUR AND CALPEE.

THE Raja of Boondelcund, about 1722, assigned over a third of his dominions to the Mahrattas, to ensure their protection of the rest to his descendants. The ceded territory, rated at 30,76,953 rupees, was formed by the Peshwa about 1743 into two sub-governments, the one included Sâgur, Calpee, Julaoon, Dhamonee, Kunnur, Koonch, &c.; the fiscal revenue of which was rated at 15,40,935 rupees; the other comprised Jhansi, &c. The first Soobehdar appointed over the former districts, was Gowind Bullal, who engaged to maintain a contingent of horse for the service of the state, and to send an annual tribute of one lac of rupees to Poona. Gowind Bullal was killed in action at Julalabad, when escorting treasure to the army at Paniput, in 1760. He left two sons, Baloojee Gowind Rao, and Gungudhur Punt, between whom the Peshwa divided the Jagheers held by their father: the former obtaining Sâgur, &c. the latter Calpee and Julaoon. On the decease of Rugoonath Rao, the son of Baloojee Gowind, without heirs, his Jagheer was claimed by Nana Gowind Rao, the grandson of Gungadhur Punt, in opposition to the widow of the late chief, and Vinaeek Rao, who conducted the administration of the country in her behalf. The chiefs of both Sâgur and Calpee had at first opposed the occupation of the territories in Boondelcund, ceded by the supplemental treaty of Bassein; but they submitted at length to the views of the British Government, and engagements were concluded with them in October, 1806. Their subsequent conduct entitled neither of them to favour; but when they became, through the treaty of Poona, in June, 1817, feudatories of the British, Government resolved, while securing its own rights, to reconcile the conflicting pretensions of both claimants. On the advance of the British army, in 1817, towards the positions of the Pindarries, Vinaeek Rao rejected all offers of negotiation, or any acknowledgment of his relative situation towards his feudal superior, contumaciously refusing either to pay tribute, or to furnish his contingent of horse, agreeably to the obligations of his office as manager of Sâgur. It being moreover discovered that he had countenanced and supported the Pindarries, and permitted recruiting in Sâgur for Appah Saheb of Nagpoor, his fief was regarded as forfeited, and after its military occupation, was transferred to British agents. On his subsequent submission, an annual sum of 2,50,000 rupees was set aside from the revenues, which are rated only at seven lacs, as a provision for the Widow, Vinaeek Rao, and other persons connected with the former government, who had fair claims to consideration. The hereditary right of Nana Gowind Rao on the Jagheer, was commuted for a stipend which should never exceed 1,18,000 rupees, being the amount of the surplus revenues of Sâgur, after deducting the amount set aside for the widow, &c. the tribute and pay of the contingent. This stipend is secured to Nana Gowind Rao during his life, after which it reverts to the British Government.

THE NUWAB OF MASULIPATAM.

THE Foujdarry of the northern provinces of the Deccan, commonly called the Northern Circars, was held by Anwar-ood-Deen Khan, under the Soobehdar of the Deccan, Nizam-ool-moolk, with all the powers of chief magistrate, military commander, and comptroller of finance. On the transfer of that officer, in 1732, to the superior Foujdarry of the Carnatic, Roostum Khan was appointed, by the Soobehdar of the Deccan to supply his place. He found, on assuming the government, that, during the lax rule of his predecessor, who governed chiefly by deputy, that the Zumeendars had availed themselves generally of the convulsions which had ensued on the demise of Aurungzeb, to establish their independence, though, in effecting this, they had only their personal advantage in view. They defrauded the treasury, by withholding the revenues collected by them, while they squeezed to the utmost the husbandman and manufacturer. Roostum Khan pursued these petty tyrants to extirpation; those who escaped the sword were proclaimed traitors, and a reward being offered, a sufficient number of the Zumeendars' and their followers' heads were brought in to erect two of those horrible pyramids called Khulla-Minars. This provincial governor is held up as an example for his vigour and integrity.

His successor was probably Hussein Ali Khan, who appears to have been well known to the English some years before these provinces were conferred upon the Company. The grant was obtained from the Emperor in September, 1765; and four of these provinces were formally ceded by the Nizam in the following year; three of them, viz. Rajamundry, Ellore, and Condapilly, were continued under the management of Hussein Ali, on a lease for three years; and he was allowed to retain all the power and splendour of a viceroy, which he had heretofore maintained. In 1769, on the termination of his lease, these provinces were placed under European management, and a Jagheer, comprising the districts of Tuttepoor, Peroor, &c. valued at 1,44,000 rupees of annual revenue, were then conferred upon Roostum Ali Khan, as compensation, and for the maintenance of his dignity. On his decease, in 1771, the Jagheer was resumed, and 1,00,000 rupees out of the revenue thereof were set aside annually for seven years for the use of the family.

In 1820, an investigation of the claims of this family upon government took place, when a decision was pronounced in favour of Roostum Jah, its present representative, who now enjoys a pension from the British of 50,000 rupees per annum.

ABSTRACT of STIPENDS, including SHARES of REVENUE enjoyed by PRINCES and CHIEFS, with the present Revenue and Charges of the territories over which they formerly ruled, but into which the British administration is now introduced.

	When Pensioned	Stipends in Rupees.	Gross Revenue in 1827-28.	Charges, &c.‡	Net Revenue.
The King of Delhi and family,	1803	13,40,983	included in	the cessions	from Oude.
The Soobehdar of the Carnatic,	1801	11,65,400	£1,404,343	£493,279	£911,064
Families of former Soobehdars, &c. *about*		9,00,000			
The King of Tanjore,	1798	11,83,500	450,049	197,374	252,702
The Soobehdar of Bengal, Bahar, and Orissa,	1770	16,00,000	3,862,258	364,517	*3,197,741
Families of former Soobehdars, and various stipends, *about*		9,00,000			
The Raja of Benares, &c.	1795	1,43,000	738,532	232,359	506,173
Families of Hyder and Tippoo,	1799	6,39,549	1,178,468	299,331	879,137
Rajas of Malabar,		2,50,000			
The Peshwa's family, — The Ex-Peshwa Bajee Row,	1818	8,00,000	1,746,219	776,249	969,970
Chimnajee Appah,	1818	2,00,000			
Vinaeek Rao and dependants,	1803	7,50,000			
Zoolfikur Ali, Nuwab of Banda,	1803	4,00,000			
Descendants of Himmut Bahadoor the Gosaeen,	1806	60,000			
Vinaeek Rao, manager of Sâgur, and Seeta Baee, widow of the late chief, &c.	1818	2,50,000	. . . .	. . . .	70,000
Nana Gowind Rao of Calpee, *about*	1818	1,00,000			
Nuwab of Masulipatam,	1771	50,000	846,365	195,557	650,808
		107,32,432			£7,654,595
Total at 2s. per rupee,†		£1,073,243			

* In this instance the land revenue only is shewn; with other sources, including the salt and opium monopoly, customs, stamps, &c, the net revenue in Bengal amounted in 1827–28 to about £6,500,000.

† The Calcutta sicca and Bombay rupees are valued at 2s. 3d. each, which would increase this total to £1,218,648.

‡ This column includes revenue and judicial charges, charitable allowances, and stipends chargeable upon the revenue, and in some cases provincial corps.

SUBSIDIARY AND PROTECTED STATES.

Introduction.

THE general terms of the treaties existing between the British Government and Subsidiary States are, protection on the one side against external enemies, and on the other the submitting of all its political relations with foreign states to the arbitration and final adjudication of the protecting power. A specific force is furnished by the former, and territory ceded by the latter, the revenue of which is equivalent to the maintenance of the troops. The subsidizing state is also bound to keep on foot a specific contingent force, to act in subordinate co-operation with the subsidiary. The protecting power is bound not to interfere in the internal administration; but in cases of exigency it reserves the right in most cases to assume the whole of the resources of the state protected for the time being. According to the stipulations, the subsidiary force is not to be employed in the disputes between the head of the state and his chiefs, or Zumeendars, but it is liable to be called out to protect the legal succession. Sindhia and the King of Oude cannot now be styled subsidiary princes, the former being wholly independent of, and the latter entirely dependent upon, the British Government; as, however, at one period subsidiary engagements existed with both, their proper place is in this division.

HIS MAJESTY THE KING OF OUDE.

SAADUT KHAN, the ancestor of the King of Oude, commenced life as a private horseman in the imperial service, in which humble station he was noticed by the Siyuds, who then controlled affairs at Delhi, and was by them promoted to the command of the fortress of Biana. He nevertheless joined a conspiracy formed against his patrons, and was one of three who drew lots which should first attempt the assassination of the elder Siyud. To the success of that plot he owed his elevation to the government of Oude, to which he was appointed by the Emperor during the same year 1722. He bore a large share in the troubles of the period, but the actions nearest his end are worthy of remark. Nadir Shah, the Persian invader, having defeated the imperial forces on his advance towards Delhi, and the Ameer-ool-Oomra being killed in the battle, the surviving nobles submitted to the conqueror, who appointed Nizam-ool-Moolk to the vacant dignity, to the disappointment of Saadut Khan, who seems to have expected it. The conqueror demanded an enormous ransom for the city, which Nizam-ool-Moolk, as chief of the nobles, was collecting, when the recreant Saadut Khan, to undermine his rival, and conciliate the conqueror, magnified the wealth of Delhi, and occasioned an additional fine, the difficulty in levying which brought on a quarrel between the inhabitants and Nadir's troops, and a few Persians being slain, the city was given up to indiscriminate massacre and pillage. Saadut Khan, finding that his ambition had brought on so much evil without any benefit to himself, took poison. He was succeeded by his nephew and son-in-law, Abdool Munsoor Khan, who in turn was succeeded by his son, Shuja-ood-Dowla, the first of the family who came in contact with the British Government.

Cassim Ali Khan, the deposed Naib of Bengal, after being driven out of the Bengal provinces by the British armies in 1762, took refuge in the dominions of Shuja-ood-Dowla, whom he found perfectly disposed to espouse his cause. The imperial arms, conducted by the heir-apparent, (now Emperor,) had failed in making any impression on Bengal some years before, but a different result was expected when guided by the experience of Shuja-ood-Dowla, whose bravery at the great national battle of Paniput, had obtained him the Vizarut of the empire. An immense armed multitude, in which, however, were the disciplined battalions of Cassim Ali, rolled on towards Bengal, before which the British detachment retreated, and intrenched themselves at Patna. Here, though too weak to act offensively, they repulsed repeated desperate assaults upon their position, and the Vizier, being himself wounded, drew off his army to Buxar.

Towards the end of September, when the season admitted of operations, the detachment, which had been greatly reinforced, began its march to Buxar, where it was two days afterwards attacked by the enemy. In this important battle, 40,000 troops, under the imperial banners, were arrayed against 7000 British. The former left 6000 on the field; and 130 cannon, with their camp, containing an immense booty, fell into the hands of the victors. The Vizier was the last to quit the field; and the Emperor, glad of the opportunity to separate from him, came over to the British camp. The Vizier, pursued for a whole year from place to place, repeatedly defeated, and having hazarded and lost his last stake at Furruckabad, resolved to throw himself on British generosity, and came into General Carnac's camp. A treaty was then concluded with him, dated 16th August, 1765, by which he was reinstated in his dominions, from which, however, the districts of Corah, Currah, and Allahabad, were alienated and formed into a royal demesne for the Emperor. The Zumeendary of Benares was restored to the Vizier, but he was made to pay the expenses of the war. This was the first treaty with the Oude state. The next treaty, arising out of a suspicion of the pacific intentions of the Vizier, is dated 29th November, 1768; it stipulates for the reduction of his army to ten thousand cavalry, ten thousand infantry, five hundred artillery, and fifteen thousand matchlock-men and irregulars.

The first subsidiary treaty with this state, is dated 7th September, 1773, by which the Company engage to furnish the Vizier with a force, termed a brigade, consisting of two battalions of Europeans, six battalions of Sepoys, and one company of artillery, the subsidy being fixed at 2,10,000 rupees per mensem. At the same time, the districts of Corah, Currah, and Allahabad, which had been abandoned by the Emperor of the Mahrattas, were sequestrated, and given over to the Vizier. Shuja-ood-Dowla died in 1775, and left his

Begums,* (wife and mother,) with the rest of his family, consisting of two thousand ladies, eighty children, and a host of eunuchs and domestics, under the guardianship of the British Government, with all his wealth for their support.

The alliance with Shuja-ood-Dowla was mutually advantageous to him and the Company. The marauding nation of Mahrattas, unsated with conquest, were gradually appropriating to themselves the whole of Hindoostan, and the position of his dominions, interposed between their acquisitions in Bengal, enabled the Company to assist him without exposing their own territories to much jeopardy. The Emperor, under pernicious counsels, having, in 1772, led the Mahrattas against the Rohillas, those gallant tribes were taken into the alliance; but on condition of their engaging to pay the Vizier the sum of forty lacs of rupees for the promised protection to their country. The Vizier, however, made no efforts against the Mahrattas, who were recalled by their domestic dissensions; but Holkur did not leave Rohilcund until he had exacted a bond of fifty lacs of rupees from the chiefs. This weakened the resources of the Rohillas, and their failing to pay the forty lacs to the Vizier, when due, was made the pretext for an unjust and cruel invasion of their country, which cast a stain on the British administration of the day, for countenancing this injustice. The alleged motive for British interference was to strengthen their western frontier against the Mahrattas, by adding Rohilcund to the Vizier's dominions. A British detachment co-operated with the troops of the Vizier in the invasion of the Rohilla country. The personal exertions and bravery of Hafiz Rehmut and the other leaders,

* The widow of Shuja-ood-Dowla, styled the Bhow Begum, died in 1815, at eighty-four years of age, leaving much real and personal property, to which she constituted the British Government her sole executor, and residuary legatee. Her coffers contained 89,48,916 rupees, exclusive of jewels, &c. which last, together with her Jagheer, valued at an annual revenue of eight or ten lacs of rupees, were made over to her son the King of Oude. Of the cash, three lacs were applied to build a mausoleum, and one lac in donations to the holy shrines at Kerbela and Nujuf. The remainder, amounting, in 1827-28, to 56,84,554 rupees, constitutes a stipend fund, from which 3,50,000 rupees are paid annually to the Begum's relations and dependents agreeably to her will.

could not prevail against a disparity of numbers joined to European discipline, which decided the day. Hafiz Rehmut, with many of the chiefs, and two thousand men, having fallen, the remainder retreated in order to the mountains, where they intrenched themselves, and obtained honourable terms from their inveterate enemy the Vizier, through the influence of their admiring opponents, the English, who alone fought the battle of Cuttrah, of which their dastardly allies were but spectators. Fyzoola Khan, who had succeeded as chief, became a feudatory of the Vizier, and had a Jagheer (Rampoor, &c.) value 14,75,000 rupees, allotted him, for the support of five thousand horse, to which number he was limited, and the great body of the Rohilla nation were expelled beyond the Ganges.

Asoph-ood-Dowla succeeded his father, and the subsidiary treaty was renewed with him on the 21st of May, 1775, when the districts of Benares, Ghazipoor, Juanpoor, Sekunderpoor, Chumah, &c. were assigned to the Company, to defray the expenses of the brigade. Shortly after his accession, he applied for and obtained from the Governor-general, a sufficient number of British officers to form a temporary brigade of infantry, and three regiments of native cavalry, which, in less than two years, he capriciously wished to disband. By extravagance, misgovernment, and oppression of his subjects, his resources were soon found to be unequal to the expense of these additional troops, and they became, therefore, in 1781, a charge upon the Company: in lieu of them, another battalion was added to the subsidiary force, to allow of sufficient reliefs for all duties. The Governor-general embraced this occasion to recommend to the Nuwab to introduce a better system of administration into his country,—to leave the management of his revenues with his ministers and the British Resident, and to assign a fixed sum out of them for his personal expenses. He was also advised to reduce his own inefficient troops, to dispense with the services of such of the contingents of his Jagheerdars as he thought fit, and to resume the lands assigned for their support. Permission was also given to him to possess himself of those of the Rohillas of Rampoor, who, by Moghul fraud and British valour, had become his feudatories in 1774, and who had now thrown off their dependence. The tribes which had been allowed to settle in this district, under their Chief, Fyzoola Khan, had, by a breach of the treaty of 1774, forfeited the protection of the Company it was, nevertheless, provided, should the Vizier be able to possess himself of their country, that he should pay their army, limited to five thousand men, from his own treasury, through the British resident.

In 1787 the politics of the day seem to have been directed to the formation and perfecting of our subsidiary alliances, suggested probably by the growing power of the Mahrattas in the north, and of the Mysoreans in the south, of India. In the former, the territories of the Vizier were in fact the barrier of our own, and their defence became our interest as well as duty. A treaty was concluded in March, 1787, by which the two brigades of cavalry, originally raised as temporary, were added permanently to the subsidiary force, and the whole subsidy fixed at fifty lacs of rupees, including the expenses of the residency, and certain stipends payable through the British resident. By the same treaty, the Nuwab of Furruckabad, his family and dependents, were provided for, and the interference of the resident in the details of the government restricted.

In 1704 Fyzoola Khan died, and his younger son, Gholam Mahomed, usurped the government, after putting his elder brother, Mahomed Ali, to death, the British were now called upon to aid in expelling the usurper, and restoring the son of the murdered prince to the Musnud. The British army was attacked on the march by the Rohillas, who were repulsed after a well fought battle, in which the British loss was 600 men, including 14 officers, killed and wounded. Gholam Mahomed afterwards surrendered. A treaty was now concluded between the other Rohilla chiefs and the Vizier on 31st December, 1794, to which the Company was guarantee. The provisions were, that a Jagheer, realizing ten lacs of rupees, including the town of Rampoor, should be conferred on the Nuwab Ahmed Ali Khan, the grandson of Fyzoola Khan, during whose minority the administration was vested in a regency.* The treasures of the late chief, amounting to fifty lacs of rupees, during the negotiations, were deposited with the Company, by whom they were afterwards paid over as a Nuzzurana to the Vizier, and in lieu of all rights of confiscation of the late chief's property, on the confirmation of his grandson in the Jagheer; of this amount the Vizier gave one-fourth as prize-money to the British army.

In 1797, the home authorities having noticed the great increase of their military establishment in Bengal, entertained equally for the protection of their possessions in that quarter, as for those of the Vizier, his Excellency was invited to relieve the Company of the expense of two regiments of cavalry, one European and the other native. To this he acceded, the amount being limited to five lacs and a half of rupees per annum. The geographical position of the French interests in the Delta of the Jumna and Ganges, so close to the Vizier's frontier, was not to be viewed with indifference, nor would it have been safe to disregard the means of defence. Asoph-ood-Dowla died shortly after, and was succeeded by his son, Vizier Ali,† who was deposed in four months, on the discovery of his illegitimacy; a suitable provision was nevertheless made for him, amounting to one lac and a half of rupees per annum, which he forfeited by his flagitious conduct shortly after.

The Nuwab Saadet Ali Khan, brother to the late Asoph-ood-Dowla, was now elevated to the Musnud; with him a treaty was executed, dated 21st February, 1798, by which the permanent subsidiary force was fixed at 10,000 men of all

* Seven years after, the whole of Rohilcund, with the exception of the Nuwab of Rampoor's demesne, came into the possession of the Company. The Nuwab, the son of Ahmed Ali Khan, bore the character, in 1828, of a drunkard and spendthrift; and owing to misrule, neglect, or ignorance of business, his Jagheer does not realize half what it is rated at, though capable of realizing a great deal more.

† He was allowed to reside at Benares, where, on the 14th January, 1799, he headed a faction, who murdered the resident, and three other English gentlemen, for which, on his capture being effected, he was confined in Fort-William until death released him in 1817.

arms, the subsidy, including stipends and pensions, increased to seventy-six lacs of rupees, and the Fort of Allahabad made over to the Company.

Saadet Ali found, on his accession, an empty treasury and an increasing debt, the consequence of the mismanagement of Asoph-ood-Dowla; the country had fallen into anarchy,—the Zumeendars paid their rents only when compelled by the sword,—the peasants had become robbers and plunderers, and the territories afforded an asylum to offenders fleeing from justice; it therefore became evident, that, in order to enable the Company to disburse with regularity the charges for which they were responsible by their connection with the Oude state, a source should be created from which a regular supply of funds could be drawn. On the 10th November, 1801, a treaty was executed at Lucknow, by which half the dominions of the Vizier were ceded in perpetual sovereignty to the British Government, in commutation of the subsidy for troops, and of all other claims chargeable to his Highness, for which the Company stood pledged. These cessions, amounting in gross revenue to 1,35,23,474 rupees, (though under the present improved management they now realize much more,) include the districts of Corah, Etaweh, Azimgurh, Goruckpoor, Furruckabad, Allahabad, Bareilly, Kelpory, &c. The Company charged themselves with the military defence of his remaining dominions, and the troops of the Durbar were reduced to five battalions of infantry and nujeebs, 2000 horse, and 300 native artillery, besides armed peons for revenue purposes. In the reserved territories, an improved system of administration was introduced, but the revenue management continues still very defective.

In 1814, when Saadet Ali was removed from this world, he left a treasury containing thirteen millions sterling money of Great Britain, accumulated during his reign, though perhaps not all of it in the most creditable way. He was succeeded by his son, Ghazi-ood-Deen Hyder, who advanced to the Company, from the hoards of his father, a million sterling, towards the prosecution of the Nepaul war. This debt was extinguished by the cession of a strip of territory called the

Turriana, contiguous to his dominions, recently conquered from the Nepaulese. From the same hoards he advanced another million towards the Pindarry war, for which the Company is now his debtor in the six per cent loan; the interest being applied to the payment of pensions, amounting to 6,51,000 rupees, due from the Oude state, under the guarantee of the British Government.

In 1819 he assumed the regal dignity, a step which had the concurrence of the British Government, being beneficial to their interests. It freed him from the necessity of manifesting submission to the house of Timour, which, as members of that family resided at Oude, was of daily recurrence when the parties met in the streets. It was important to release him from a dependence, which the general sense of his nobles, or prejudices of his people, might hereafter improve against us in case of war raised for the restoration of the ancient house of Timour.

On the decease of Ghazi-ood-Deen Hyder, in 1827, he was, on the 9th October of that year, succeeded by his son, Shah Zuman, who is styled his Majesty Aboo Nuseer, Kootub-ood-Deen, Solimon Jah, Zuman Padshah, King of Oude. He was, at the time of his accession, about twenty-six years of age, and is described in Captain Mundy's interesting "Sketches of India," as a plain, vulgar-looking man, above the middle stature, with a complexion unusually dark, and his mental endowments, pursuits, and amusements, by no means of an elevated or dignified order.*

The King of Oude is too dependent to be regarded as one of the political states of India; but as his surplus revenues are said to exceed half a million sterling, after defraying the expenses of his government and a court maintained in all the magnificence of eastern parade, he may be considered the richest prince in the world, and as such possessing a power to do much good or evil.

* His ancestor, Shuja-ood-Dowla, stood in high consideration throughout India, equally for his personal courage, talents, and address, while his martial figure, and expertness in manly exercises, made him a favourite with the soldiery.

GOVERNMENT OF HYDRABAD.

The present dynasty of Hydrabad originated with Nizam-ool-Moolk, a crafty and ambitious Ameer of the rigid school of Aurungzeb, who was deputed from Delhi as Soobehdar of the Deccan, in 1713. His sway, as viceroy, extended over the greatest portion of India, south of the Nerbudda, until October, 1724, when the battle of Shukurkhera* transferred in fact, though not in form, the sovereignty of this part of the Moghul Empire, from the house of Timoor to that of the victor. This career of fortune had, of course, its concomitant political difficulties; nor was it exempt from domestic infelicity, he having, so late in his reign as 1740, to put down a rebellion, headed by his son Nazir Jung. Nizam-ool-Moolk died in 1748, at a very advanced age, leaving, by different mothers, six sons and six daughters, not all of whom were legitimate. The sons will require to be particularly noticed. The eldest legitimate daughter married the Soobehdar of Lahore; and the younger an Oomra, to whom she bore Moozuffir Jung, who, being a favourite of his grandfather, it is supposed was left heir to the Musnud. Hence originated those contests for empire in the Deccan, in which the French and English first appeared in the service of native princes as rivals in arms.

Ghazi-ood-Deen, the eldest legitimate son of Nizam-ool-Moolk, at the death of his father, held the office of Ameer-ool-Oomra, or chief of the nobles, at Delhi, and, as such, was at the head of the army and department of finance. He proceeded towards the Deccan in 1752, to assert, by arms, his claim to the Musnud at Hydrabad, then occupied by his brother Sulabhut Jung; but having, on his arrival at Aurungabad, accepted an entertainment from the mother of Nizam

* Illustrative of the weakness of the imperial authority, it may be noticed, that Nizam-ool-Moolk sent to the Emperor, with a congratulatory letter, the head of the viceroy appointed to supersede him, who was slain in this battle, as that of a traitor.

Ali, he ate of a poisoned dish, and died in September of that year.

NAZIR JUNG, the second, and youngest legitimate, son, assumed the viceroyalty of the Deccan on the decease of his father, but was opposed by Moozuffir Jung. The defection of the French auxiliaries in the army of the latter, induced him to submit to his uncle, who, seven months afterwards, fell the victim of a conspiracy, by the carbine of the Nuwab of Cudapa, on the eve of a battle at Gingee, in 1750. Moozuffir Jung, who had been thrown into irons on his submission, was then liberated, and proclaimed Soobehdar of the Deccan by the conspirator chiefs, but fell by the hand of one of them, in single combat, only a few months after. He was the first prince in India that made a subsidiary engagement with a European power, having entertained a body of French troops, under Monsieur Bussy, and assigned the Northern Circars for their payment.

SULABHUT JUNG, the third, but eldest illegitimate, son, succeeded his nephew, and reigned till 1763. He owed his elevation to the Musnud, and support on it afterwards, wholly to the French. When deprived of their assistance, his brother, Nizam Ali, who officiated as minister, imprisoned him at Beder, where he was strangled, it is said, the following year. The first treaty between the Company and the Nizam* was concluded with Sulabhut Jung, in 1759, for the expulsion of the French from the Deccan, when Masulipatam, which had been already wrested from the latter by the British, was ceded to the Company in perpetuity.

NIZAM ALI, the fifth, but an illegitimate, son of Nizam-ool-Moolk, usurped the general administration of affairs in the Deccan in 1762, and was left undisputed master of it on the death of Sulabhut Jung, which he is accused of having accelerated, though he had been declared heir-apparent. Great political changes took place in India during his long reign, in which he experienced the benefit of British alliance.

* The Soobehdar of the Deccan is always called the Nizam by Europeans, and the title is therefore retained, as most familiar to them. His own subjects call him Bundeegan-i-Aalee, literally, Slaves of the Most High.

The connection commenced in 1766, by the Company consenting to hold the Northern Circars from him, at an annual rent of nine lacs of rupees, out of which a body of troops for his Highness's service was to be defrayed. The Emperor had conferred them upon the English by Sunnud, in November, 1765; but Guntoor did not come into their possession until 1788, six years after the death of Busalut Jung.* The rent,

* BUSALUT JUNG, the fourth son of Nizam-ool-Moolk, was appointed Soobehdar of Beejapoor in 1756, but that province being ceded to the Mahrattas in 1760, a Jagheer was formed for him, comprising the districts of Adoni, Rachoor, and Guntoor. With Adoni for his capital, he endeavoured to establish an independent principality, and his conquests at length gave him the Kistna for his northern boundary, and Tippoo's dominions for his southern. As has been noticed, the Company had acquired a right to Guntoor by a Sunnud from the Emperor, in the first instance, and by subsequent treaty with the Nizam. In 1779, the Madras Government agreed to hold that district at a fixed rent, out of which a body of troops, to be furnished by the Company, were to be paid, and he was to dismiss the French then in his service. A treaty to this effect having been concluded without the consent or knowledge of Busalut Jung's feudal superior, the Nizam, it was annulled next year by the Supreme Government. Busalut Jung died in 1782, and Guntoor was surrendered in 1788 to the Company, agreeably to an article of the treaty of 1766, which stipulated that he was to hold it during life. He was succeeded by his son, Mohubut Jung, who defended Adoni in 1787 against Tippoo Sultaun, until succoured; but the place being nearly reduced to ashes, he removed to Rachoor, where he died in 1794. A rebellion was raised in the following year, in the name of his son, against his feudal superior, the Nizam, but it was suppressed by the subsidiary force. The remaining territories held by Busalut Jung, were transferred to the East India Company in 1800.

MOGHUL ALI KHAN, the sixth son, never attained to any political importance. He took part with the Peshwa against his brother in 1761, but returned next year, and threw himself on his clemency. He was intrusted with the command of a division of the Nizam's army in 1786, in the war with Tippoo; was some time after incarcerated at Beder, and so remained, till enlarged in 1796 by his nephew, Ali Jah, then in rebellion, with whom, however, he would not take part, but returned to Hydrabad, where he was allowed to reside during the rest of his life.

Of the six sons of Nizam-ool-Moolk, descendants of two of them only are of any consideration in the Deccan: viz. of Nizam Ali and Busalut Jung. Ghazie-ood-Deen, however, left a son, named Meer Shabodeen, who succeeded to his father's posts and honours at Delhi; and, shortly after, became Vizier of the empire. He was equally remarkable for talents, ambition, and wickedness.

£72,000, continued to be paid until 1823, when it was redeemed by a payment of 1,16,66,666 rupees, or £1,201,201 sterling, being the value of the annuity, to relieve the Nizam from a debt due by him to the firm of Palmer and Co. at Hydrabad, contracted originally in 1819, to pay off an accumulation of arrears to an augmented military establishment, arising principally out of the war of 1817-18.

In 1767, Nizam Ali entered into an alliance with Hyder Ali against the English; but their joint troops having sustained a repulse from the latter at Caverypatam, which was followed up by an advance of a detachment into the Nizam's territories, he listened to terms of accommodation, and a treaty of peace was concluded on the 23d February, 1768. The provisions of it relate,—to the Northern Circars, the tribute for which was reduced to seven lacs—to the discharge of our ally, the Soobah of the Carnatic, from all dependence upon the Soobehdar of the Deccan—Hyder Ali was declared an usurper, and the Nizam, as viceroy of the Deccan, transferred the Carnatic Balaghaut, then forming part of the dominions of Mysore, to the Company—and, lastly, stipulating to furnish

After bearing a conspicuous part at Delhi in the troubles and crimes of the period, he is said to have visited the Deccan, and, as if to fill up the measure of his guilt, suggested to the ill-fated parent of the ex-Peshwa the murder of his nephew, Naraen Rao, as the means of his accession to power. He afterwards made a pilgrimage to Mecca, and, returning from thence, died at Kalpee, in Hindoostan, in 1800. He left a number of children, but two only of his sons were legitimate, and they receive a pension of 6000 rupees a-year from the Nizam.

Nizam Ali had eight sons by his different wives. ALI JAH, the eldest, raised a rebellion in 1796 against his father, which was suppressed by the French corps in the Nizam's service, and Ali Jah fell into their hands. On the route the minister directed that the Howdah in which the Prince rode should be curtained, when the Prince, either from shame or despair, took poison. SEKUNDER JAH commanded the Hydrabad contingent, which joined Lord Cornwallis in the war against Tippoo in 1791. The third son, FURREEDOON JAH, together with his brother JUMSHAID JAH, who was the fifth son, are both deceased, and their sister is married to the Nuwab, Shums-ool-Oomra. The fourth son, JEHANDUR JAH, and the sixth, AKBER JAH, brother to Sekunder Jah, by the same mother, are also dead. The seventh son is SOOLEEMUN JAH, and KYWAN JAH is the youngest.

the Nizam, when required, with a subsidiary force, consisting of two battalions of native infantry, and a company of artillery. Peace with Hyder Ali, in the following year, prevented the execution of the articles of this treaty; but the subject of them was agitated in 1789, when war was contemplated against Mysore.

In 1779, the Nizam confederated with Hyder Ali and all the Mahrattas against the English. The convention of Wurgaom had, throughout India, operated to effect a change of opinion as to English invincibility; but the treaty made by the Madras Government with Busalut Jung, his brother and feudatory, for the farm of Guntoor, and reception of a British detachment for his protection, in substitution for the French corps of Lally, was the avowed ground of offence. The obnoxious treaty was annulled next year by the Supreme Government, and he was, though the contriver of the coalition, detached from it; but the corps of Lally was received into his service, and became the nucleus of a power or influence in the centre of India, threatening to subvert the British interests.

In 1784, the Nizam concluded a secret treaty with the Peshwa, which had for its object, to make Tippoo restore the territories taken from each of the contracting parties; but the Nizam's design was frustrated by Tippoo's making demands upon him before he was prepared for war.

The Nizam was a party to the triple alliance against Tippoo Sultaun in 1792, and obtained as his share of the ceded territory, districts rated at 13,16,666 pagodas; besides a third of the cash, amounting to three millions sterling, levied upon Tippoo by the allies.

In 1798, the French had established so strong a party at Hydrabad, that as its growing influence excited the suspicion of the Nizam, so it could not be viewed with indifference by the British Government. They had a disciplined body of 14,000 men, to which 124 European officers were attached; it became, therefore, the policy of the Governor-General to disperse so formidable a force, before entering upon the projected war against Tippoo. The concurrence of the Nizam was prompt and cordial, accompanied by an express wish for an increase of the British troops serving under his Highness.* Accordingly, on the junction of the new with the old detachment, their first operation was to assist in disarming the French; and by a judiciously planned rapid march from different points, the French party were taken by surprise, and the desired purpose effected without bloodshed. The subsidiary force was fixed at six battalions of Sepoys, one regiment of cavalry, and the usual proportion of artillery.

On the subversion of the Mahomedan dynasty of Mysore in 1799, the Nizam acquired, by the partition treaty, a farther increase of territory, the clear revenue of which was rated at 5,37,000 pagodas. All the territories, however, acquired by his Highness under the treaties of Seringapatam, in 1792, and of Mysore, in 1799, were ceded by him in perpetuity to the Company in 1800, to defray the expenses of the subsidiary force, then augmented to 8000 infantry, 1000 cavalry, and a proportion of artillery. Of this force, it was stipulated by the treaty, that in the event of war, 6000 infantry, with the cavalry and artillery, joined by 6000 infantry and 9000 horse of his Highness's own troops, should march to oppose the enemy.

Nizam Ali died in 1803. His son and successor, Sekunder Jah, proved less favourably inclined towards the English, and afforded no assistance in the war of 1803, though allowed to participate in the conquests from Sindhia, Holkar, and the Raja of Nagpoor, which extended his northern boundary to the Indyadree hills and the Wurda river. His Highness acquired a farther increase of territory by the war of 1817-18, estimated at a revenue of 6,26,375 rupees. His whole revenue in 1821, was 1,89,33,550 rupees, and his expenditure, including interest of debt, 1,75,11,400 rupees; leaving a surplus of 14,22,153

* "The Court of Hydrabad had repeatedly and earnestly solicited an increase of the British detachment in the service of the Nizam, under an assurance that the French corps should be dismissed from his Highness's service, upon the arrival of the additional British force."—*Extract from Lord Wellesley's Minute, 12th August*, 1798.

rupees. The expense of the military force of the Durbar, officered by English gentlemen, (many of whom were lent from his Majesty's and the Hon. Company's service,) is estimated at forty lacs of rupees. Of this force, the returns in 1831 shewed it to consist of 1538 European officers, staff, &c. and 10,244 rank and file, and recruits, divided into six regiments of infantry, and four of cavalry, the former being disciplined and clothed like the troops in the Company's service. The contingents, or parties of the Jagheerdars, or Chiefs, form another force.

His Highness Sekunder Jah died on the 21st May, 1828, at the age of fifty-nine. His eldest son, Nazir-ood-Dowla, was immediately proclaimed his successor by the ministers and British resident, and three days after placed on the Musnud with the usual ceremonies. His titles are, Muzuffir-ool-Moomalik, Nizam-ool-Moolk, Meer Furkhunda Ali Khan, Bahadoor, Futih Jung.

The Nizam has essentially benefited by British connection: it has preserved him from the Mahrattas and Hyder Ali, either of whom might have subdued him unprotected. The contest for supremacy in India, south of the Nerbudda, would, in all probability, have rested with these two powers, had Europeans not been forced by circumstances into a place among the substantive states. The districts which the Nizam has ceded as the price of the protection afforded him, are those which had been previously acquired for him by the British arms.

It is doubtful whether the Nizam or the King of Oude is the richest Prince in India. Besides the portion of the public revenue assigned for his personal expenses, he has ample private emoluments; he is the heir of all his subjects, and death gives him entire and unconditionally whatever portion of the riches of his Jagheerdars his forbearance leaves them during life.

GOVERNMENT OF SINDHIA.

Ranoojee Sindhia,* the first of this family who attained eminence, was one of the Commanders under the Peshwas, in the early expeditions of the Mahrattas into Hindoostan. He is brought into prominent notice as one of the leaders in the Mahratta army in 1738, when its success against the Imperial forces, conducted by Nizam-ool-Moolk, led to the cession of Malwa to the Peshwa, and the foundation of the Mahratta states of Sindhia, Holkur, and Puar. He is again brought into notice as one of the securities for the observance of the treaty between his master and the Emperor, in 1743, a circumstance which indicates integrity of character, unless the being obliged to accept the guarantee of Chiefs serving in the army opposed to him, be attributable rather to the helpless condition of his Majesty. Nearly half the conquests in Hindoostan were made over to Ranoojee for the support of troops, and were held by him at his death, which happened about 1750. He had five sons, Jyapa, Joteeba, Duttajee, Mahadjee, and Tookajee, of whom the first four were distinguished leaders in their father's lifetime.

Jyapa succeeded his father in the Jagheer, and was present with the family contingent at the siege of Ahmedabad in 1755:

* The Sindhia family, to which the rulers of half Malwa trace their origin, were Patels of Kunnerkheir, near Satara, and, in the absence of other information, we may judge of their respectability from the circumstance of the Emperor Aurungzeb selecting a lady from the family to give in marriage to the Raja Sahoo, about 1706, before deputing him to claim his inheritance as sovereign of the Mahrattas. This lady died in 1710, when residing at Delhi with Sahoo's mother. It is said of Ranoojee, that in early life he was a domestic of very inferior degree in the service of the Peshwa, viz. the carrier of his slippers; a story repeated by almost all writers of his history. But as the family had always been Silahdars, (Cavaliers,) nothing can be more improbable than that any member of it should serve in a menial office, more especially at a period when the army afforded an ample field for the display of courage, talent, and birth. Ranoojee, moreover, must have been a near relation of one of the Raja Sahoo's wives, or princesses, and would, therefore, hardly be allowed to stand in the capacity of a domestic to the Peshwa, who was himself only the servant, or minister, of Sahoo.

in 1759 he was assassinated in his tent, when besieging Beejee Singh, the Raja of Joudpoor in Nagore, by emissaries of that Prince, who devoted their lives to accomplish the destruction of the Mahratta Chief, on the simple condition of their families being provided for. The conduct of the war then devolved upon Rugoonath Rao, the Peshwa's brother, and it terminated in the Joudpoor state becoming nominally tributary to the Mahrattas. The atrocity of Beejee Singh was afterwards avenged by Mahadjee Sindhia, when these chiefs were opposed to each other in the sanguinary battle of Mairtah, in which the Rajpoots sustained a severe defeat. Beejee Singh, independent of the tribute, was compelled to cede the district of Ajmeer as the price of the blood of Jyapa Sindhia.

Junkoojee, more distinguished as a leader than his father, became the head of the family; but his subsequent military career was likewise brief, for, after escaping from a field in which his uncles, Duttajee and Joteeba, were slain, he was among the captives at Paniput, who, after the battle, were put to death by the conqueror.

Mahadjee Sindhia, the fourth, but illegitimate, son of Ranoojee, was now the only survivor of the family, (for Tookajee had died a natural death,) and having established claims by his own services, he was confirmed in the Jagheer, then rated at sixty-four lacs of rupees. He had escaped from the fatal field of Paniput, but with a wound which rendered him lame for life. The distinguishing outline of his career may be traced in the talent by which he influenced the politics of Poona; in the extension of his possessions in Hindoostan by encroachments upon his neighbours; in his rendering most of the Rajpoot states tributary; in circumventing and mulcting Hyder Ali in the Carnatic; and in prosecuting a war of some duration with the English, which ended in a peace honourable to him. The military achievements of this veteran commander, and his influential position among the powers of India, during a long reign, must, however, be passed briefly over in a narrative confined to transactions more immediately connected with the British.

Mahadjee Sindhia was a member of the Mahratta Regency,

formed on the decease of Narraen Rao, and was the chief leader against the English army, when it was reduced to agree to the convention at Wurgaum in 1779. On this memorable occasion, a separate negotiation was opened with him, and to him in particular Rugoonath Rao surrendered himself, and the English gentlemen sent as hostages to the Mahratta camp were commended to his care.

His first treaty with the Company was in October, 1781, the provisions of which were, that the country taken possession of belonging to Sindhia, west of the Jumna, should be restored by the Company. The Maha Raja agreed, in return, not to molest the Rana of Gohud, to restore the Raja of Chunderee to his territory, and displace his Dewan, who had usurped it. But what will probably better illustrate Mahadjee's influence, is his engaging to use his endeavours for the restoration of peace with Hyder Ali, and also with the confederate Mahratta Chiefs, with both of which powers the English were at war. In the treaty of Salbey, concluded the following year, between the British Government and the latter, Mahadjee became mutual guarantee for the adherence of both purties to its conditions; either party deviating, the Maha-Raja was to join the other, and endeavour to bring the aggressor to a proper understanding. Shortly after, the fort and district of Broach, which had been continued to the Company by this treaty, were given up to Sindhia in 1782, to mark the Company's sense of the humane treatment experienced from him by the English hostages of Wurgaum.

Sindhia about this time introduced European discipline and tactics into his army, and being unmolested by the English, the only power in Hindoostan capable of checking his career of conquest, he made himself master of Delhi, Agra, and the person of the Emperor, by whom he was appointed alter-ego, rather than Vicegerent of the Empire. In 1785 he had the temerity to prefer a demand for the Chouth, or tribute, of Bengal, which had been fixed by agreement between the confederate Mahratta Chiefs and the Soobehdar of Bengal in 1751, at twelve lacs of rupees per annum, payable to the Raja of Berar. This claim, never realized from the English, and now become obsolete and forgotten, is only noticed here in proof of the fact, that Mahadjee's arrogance did not abate as he rose to good fortune.

Mahadjee Sindhia died at Poona in 1794, the most powerful of the native Princes of that day. His whole life, one of constant activity, was passed in the camp, and devoted to the improvement of his army. He formed his infantry and artillery upon the model of those of Europe; and for his cavalry, he adopted the more convenient, and comparatively graceful, dress and arms of the Rajpoots and Mahomedans. He was succeeded by his grand-nephew and adopted son, Dowlut Rao Sindhia, then only thirteen years of age.

Dowlut Rao married Bueza Baee, the beautiful daughter of the notorious Surji-Rao Ghatgay, who became minister at Gwalior in 1796, and by whose pernicious counsels and influence, the early part of the reign of his son-in-law was stained with various acts of rapacity, bloodshed, and gratuitous cruelty. For some years after the accession of Dowlut Rao, no intercourse of political consequence, on the part of the Company, appears to have taken place with Sindhia's camp. But in 1798, the rumour of another visit from the King of the Afghans, for the purpose of restoring the sovereignty of the Great Moghul in Hindoostan, suggested to the British Government the expediency of a defensive alliance with Sindhia. That Prince's advisers either saw no immediate danger of invasion, or did not choose to listen to overtures which might introduce a powerful stranger to participate in, and direct, their counsels.

The contests between Sindhia and Holkur, in 1801-2, terminated in the battle of Poona, which drove the Peshwa to solicit British protection. The treaty of Bassein followed in consequence, the construction of which imported serious disadvantages to Sindhia. His family had, for half a century, ranked first in influence among the Mahratta confederacy, and of late years had held a controlling power over its chief, the Peshwa. He could not, therefore, with indifference see the Peshwa seek foreign aid to restore him to, and support him on, his Musnud. And Sindhia's assertion, that he visited the Deccan on invitation from the Peshwa, may have truth for its basis, as it is not improbable that that Prince regretted his precipitancy in vesting the military protection of his dominions in a power with which he could not, at pleasure, shake off connection. The army of Sindhia, at this period, constituted a disciplined force of 45,000 infantry, divided into seventy-two battalions, under European officers, with a park of 500 pieces of artillery, and a numerous cavalry. Co-operating in the same hostility, the army of the Nagpoor Raja, though not so numerous, and without the advantages of discipline, was yet formidable; and the British had to fear in the progress of the war, lest Sindhia and Holkur should compromise their differences; in which event, the disciplined brigades of the latter might prove a powerful accession to the confederacy.

Sindhia, when advancing towards Poona, was apprised by the British Envoy, that as the Peshwa was now restored to the Musnud, and the tranquillity of the Deccan secured, he would be expected to recross the Nerbudda. Confident in his strength, he hesitated to comply, but promised not to ascend the Ghauts. He did ascend, nevertheless, and advanced to Assaye, where he was joined by the Raja of Nagpoor. Here their united forces were attacked and routed by Sir Arthur Wellesley, and again at Argaum. Sindhia's army in Hindoostan was also attacked and beaten by Lord Lake, at Delhi and Laswaree. His detachments suffered wherever they encountered the British; the fortified town of Ahmednuggur was carried by escalade, the strong fort of Aligurh by storm; many others of his forts on both sides of the Nerbudda, were taken; and after a variety of brilliant successes on the part of the British, the war terminated in the treaty of Surjee-Anjungaum, on the 30th December, 1803.

By this treaty, Sindhia was compelled to cede to the Company all his forts and territories situated between the Jumna and the Ganges, and northward of the countries of Jeypoor, Joudpoor, and Gohud. The Jagheer lands, however, to the amount of seventeen lacs of rupees, held in these cessions, by various members of the family of the late Mahadjee Sindhia, (one of whom was Bala Baee, his daughter, who held a Jagheer of two lacs,) and Sirdars late in his service, were continued to them under the British Government.

Broach and Ahmednuggur were also ceded to the Company, with farther lands in Khandes and Guzerat, which were afterwards restored to him. All his territories south of the Indyadree hills, were also ceded, and made over to the Peshwa* and Nizam. He renounced sovereignty over certain of his tributaries, who were taken under British protection, while the British engaged not to interfere with the rest. He relinquished farther interference in the affairs of the Emperor, and it was stipulated that envoys should be sent by each, to reside at the Court of the other. Out of the revenues of the ceded lands, a subsidiary force of six battalions of infantry was to be maintained for Sindhia's service. But how far he might consider advantageous a force furnished to him under such circumstances, is doubtful, the resources for its maintenance having, in the first instance, been alienated for ever from his dominions.

In the treaty of defensive alliance, concluded two months after, the contracting parties agree, in case of war, that 6000 infantry and 10,000 cavalry, of the Maha-Raja's own army, should join, or co-operate, with the subsidiary force against the enemy. But this treaty, owing to subsequent events, was never acted upon; and Sindhia is, at this day, one of the few substantive states without a subsidiary force.

Affairs went on tranquilly for some time, and Sindhia looked forward to a participation of the territories of Holkur, with whom the Company were then at war. But the violence of Ghatgay, who presided over the administration in Sindhia's camp, occasioned his master to join the declining cause of Holkur, even at the critical moment when that Chief was reduced to extremity. Regardless of the sacred character of an envoy, the Residency was attacked and plundered, and the person of the Resident placed under restraint.

The ground of offence,—an alleged obscurity in several articles of the late treaty of amity, was removed by a definitive

* It was discovered, after the settlement of the Deccan in 1818, that the cessions obtained for the Peshwa, from Sindhia, had been continued to the latter Chief, which is one proof that the Peshwa was personally well disposed towards him, though he joined in the war against him.

treaty, in November, 1805. The Sirdars who had taken part in the recent acts of hostility, were deemed to have forfeited their pensions, and compensation was made for the plunder of the Residency. The Chumbul was now made the boundary between the two states; and to relieve the Maha-Raja of a portion of the loss sustained, from this river being made the line of demarkation, an annual sum of four lacs of rupees was stipulated to be paid to him; while to his wife, Bueza Baee, was assigned a Jagheer of two lacs; and to his daughter, Chuma Baee, another of one lac of rupees, within the Company's territories. Gwalior, and part of the former possessions of the Rana of Gohud, were transferred to Sindhia, who took upon himself, in return, the payment of the pensions with which the cessions of Surjee Anjungaum were charged. The Rana of Gohud, an ancient ally of the British Government, had been dispossessed by Sindhia of his lands, some years before, and the desire to reinstate him, was one of the minor objects of the war. The Rana was compensated from the disposable lands on the north bank of the Jumna.

Though Sindhia had still a large territory, and an extensive power left to him in Rajpootana, he forbore to interrupt the tranquillity of India by any extensive military operations. The alienation of so large a portion of his dominions diminished his financial resources; and he fell into arrears with his army, which, whether impelled by vanity, or indulging in views of conquest, he still kept up, when the pernicious system of giving assignments on the revenues to commanders began to be severely felt. Their exactions knew no bounds, and many cultivated and populous districts were thus rendered waste and wretched.

Sindhia did not again come into any collision with the British power until 1817, when the reduction of the Pindarries became essential to the future peace of India. He was known to have been secretly one of their supporters, and to have entered into a combination, hostile to the English, with the other Mahratta states, so extensive in its nature that even the Raja of Nepaul was to have been included. When the British army, therefore, advanced to the Jumna, a demand, in conformity to treaty, was made for the Maha-Raja's co-operation with his stipulated contingent of 5000 horse against the Pindarries; at the same time his consent was required to the abrogation of that condition of the treaty of 1805, which bound the British Government to regard the tributaries in Rajpootana as subjects of Sindhia, which prevented alliances being formed with them. His plea of inability to restrain them, had virtually annulled the stipulation in question, which had been agreed to under the belief of his ability to coerce them. A union with the Rajpoot states was now indispensable for suppressing and preventing the revival of the predatory system. By having encouraged that system, and given protection to the Pindarry leaders, Sindhia had unquestionably been guilty of an infraction of the treaty.

After some procrastination Sindhia acceded to and ratified the treaty proposed to him on the 5th of November, 1817. The British Government reserved to itself the power of collecting and guaranteeing to Sindhia the tribute justly receivable by him from the Rajpoot states; the amount of which, with the stipends of seven lacs settled upon Sindhia and members of his family by the treaty of 1805, was applied to the payment of the contingent of 5000 horse stipulated to be employed with the British detachments. British officers are now stationed with each division of the contingent; and the rest of Sindhia's army being completely insulated by our military positions, his power of aggression is greatly diminished. Sindhia lost Asseergurh by his conduct in 1817-18. It having been discovered, on the capture of that fortress, that he had sent secret orders to the commander to defend the place, in contravention of his official and public instructions to permit its temporary occupation by British troops, the British Government resolved to retain it.

Dowlut Rao Sindhia died on 21st March, 1827, having about thirty years played a considerable part on the political arena of India. His military talents were certainly not of the first order, though he had always kept up a large military establishment. The expense of such a force far exceeded his financial means, and not unfrequently exposed him to the disagreeable necessity of listening to the clamours of tumultuous troops long in arrear; while, for the supply of personal demands, he was often obliged to have recourse to bankers, whose accommodations were obtained at high rates of interest.

He left territories capable of realizing a revenue of 140 lacs of rupees, under proper management. His dominions, with the exception of the exchange of Ajmeer, remain in the same state as they were left by the treaty of 1805. The acquisitions from Sindhia by the British Government at that period, comprise the principal part of the Delta of the Ganges and Jumna, from the source of the latter river in the mountains of Cashmeer, to near its confluence with the former. They included the ancient city of Delhi, which, with a tract of country round it, was continued under the nominal authority of the titular Emperor, the real authority being vested in the British resident. Ajmeer, with other districts and tributes, came into the British possession in 1818, by exchange with Sindhia, for part of the Veechoorkur's Jagheer in Malwa.

The late Maha-Raja having no prospect of a male heir, sent, shortly before his death, to the Deccan for the children of some of his distant relations, that he might select an heir from amongst them. The candidates, five in number, not arriving at Gwalior till after the Raja's death, the right of selection fell upon Bueza Baee, the Regent, who chose Moogut Row, a boy twelve years of age, the second of the candidates in regard to years. The ceremony of adoption took place on the 17th June, 1827, and of marriage on the same day to the grand-daughter of the late Maha-Raja, by his daughter married to Dhabarry, Rao Suenaputee. He was seated on the Gaddee on the following day, under the auspices of the British Government, and assumed the name of Junkoojee, in compliment to his distinguished ancestor of that name. The Regent, Bueza Baee, is vested with the conduct of the affairs of the state during the Maha-Raja's minority, assisted by her brother, Hindoo Rao, who is at the head of the military department, and Bapoo Rugoonath, formerly minister at Dhar, is the minister of finance.

The army of the state, at the period of the death of the late Maha-Raja, was, at the lowest computation, exclusive of the British contingent, and garrisons to forts, estimated at 14,000 infantry, 10,000 cavalry, and 250 pieces of cannon.

GOVERNMENT OF HOLKUR.*

Tookajee Holkur, who had held the command of the army of the Holkur state since the accession of the celebrated Ahilya Baee to the head of the government, in 1767, died in

* Mulhar Rao Holkur, who originated this once powerful family, was the son of a shepherd; and his father, to the hereditary occupation of tending sheep, added the more industrious one of weaving cumlies, a species of blanket. They lived in the village of Hol, or Hul, on the Neera river, from which, with the adjunct Kur, signifying inhabitant, the family derive their name of Holkur. The young Mulhar Rao, disdaining a shepherd's slothful life, sought the adventurous camp, and we find him with the army under Kantajee Kuddum, whom he followed to the plunder of Guzerat, where his services obtained him the command of 25 horse. While on duty on the family estate of the Kuddum, on the Taptee, a party of the Peshwa's troops, on their way to Malwa, attempted to pass over the Kuddum's lands; Mulhar Rao, with an inferior number of troops, resolved to dispute the passage. His conduct and courage on this occasion attracted the notice and admiration of the Peshwa, who prevailed on Mulhar Rao to quit the declining fortunes of the Kuddums, and enter his service. The family of Holkur has, however, retained to this day the banner of the Kuddums, under which their ancestor rose to notice.

Mulhar Rao appears to have joined the army of the Peshwa about 1724, and to have commenced his career at the head of 100 horse. In 1732, he was the principal leader under the Peshwa, when the fate of Malwa was decided by the defeat of the army of Dia Bahadur, the Soobehdar of the province, who fell in the action. Indore, with the greatest part of the conquered territory, was then assigned to Holkur for the support of troops; and in 1735, he was left by the Peshwa, on his return to the Deccan, in charge of the Mahratta interests north of the Nerbudda. In 1738, when the Imperial army, under Nizam-ool-Moolk, allowed themselves to be hemmed in near Bhopal, Mulhar Rao was the most active and enterprising of his assailants, and the convention which followed confirmed to the Mahrattas the sovereignty of the whole of the territories from the Nerbudda to the Chumbul.

In the following year we find him assisting at the memorable siege of Bassein, then held by the Portuguese; and after its reduction (which was not accomplished until, it is said, 5000 of the besiegers, and 800 of the defenders, had been numbered with the killed and wounded) he returned to Hindoostan, to join the Peshwa in defence of the Mahratta possessions against Nadir Shah; but that ruthless invader returned to Persia, after the plunder of Delhi, without advancing farther towards the south.

About 1751, Holkur assisted the Vizier in his war with the Rohillas,

1797, leaving four sons, Khassee Rao and Mulhar Rao by his wife, and Wittoojee and Jeswunt Rao by a concubine, the whole of whom were invited to Poona on the death of their father. Khassee Rao, weak, wicked, and deformed, the chiefs

between whom he mediated a peace. The heavy arrears incurred to the Mahrattas by this war, were discharged by Ghazi-ood-Deen from his private funds, and he, in return, received a Firman for the government of Hydrabad; and Holkur, with Rugoonath Rao and 40,000 Mahrattas, joined the immense army assembled to try, between the brothers, the right to the Musnud. On the death of Ghazi-ood-Deen by poison, Holkur returned to Hindoostan, where the distractions at the Imperial court soon found employment for the Mahrattas.

About this time arose that animosity between Holkur and the Peshwa's brother, commonly called the Bhow, which had so fatal an influence on Mahratta affairs eight years after at Paniput. The experience of Holkur proved useless against the obstinacy of the Bhow, when he tendered his advice on the eve of the battle, and Paniput became the grave of the largest army of their countrymen ever assembled to contest for religion and empire; a remnant only being led off by Holkur and a few other chiefs.

Mulhar Rao died in 1765, an active soldier for forty years, and the most distinguished of the Mahratta leaders of the day, leaving possessions rated at a gross revenue of 75,00.000 rupees. His son, Khundee Rao, had died before his father, but he left a son named Malee Rao, a minor, who was recognized by the Peshwa as successor to the Jagheer, but who did not live to attain his majority.

The administration was now conducted by Ahilya Baee, the extraordinary widow of the late Khundee Rao. Her regard to justice, and attention to business, rendered her a blessing to Malwa. For charity unbounded, and munificent liberality, her memory will ever be justly revered. She appointed Tookajee Holkur, an able officer, but no relation, to the command of the army.

Tookajee, by being placed at the head of the army, was virtually at the head of the state. In 1780 we find him, in conjunction with Sindhia, employed against Colonel Goddard in Guzerat; and in 1786 aiding the Nuwab of Savanoor against his liege lord Tippoo Sultaun, whose army he defeated. In 1792 he introduced European tactics and discipline among his troops, when he raised the four battalions of infantry under Monsieur Dudernaic. These battalions performed good service at the battle of Lukhairee, against Sindhia, in the same year, in which they were almost destroyed; and Holkur, though defeated, gave his attention to the improvement of this arm. The ruin of the Mahratta is, however, dated from the time that they introduced infantry and guns into their army, which often compelled them to engage to disadvantage; the genius and habits of the people being better suited to the seem to have contemplated setting aside,* but his cause was supported by Sindhia; and the troops of the latter having attacked those of Mulhar Rao in the night, the latter was slain, and his infant son, Khundee Rao, fell into the hands of Sindhia's general, the notorious Ghatgay. Wittoojee and Jeswunt Rao both escaped; but the former turned freebooter, and being captured while marauding in the Deccan, was carried to Poona, where he was put to a barbarous death by order of the Peshwa, being dragged through the city, tied to the foot of an elephant.

Jeswunt Rao sought protection with the Raja of Nagpoor, who treacherously imprisoned him. He again escaped, after a confinement of six months, and led a fugitive life of a year more. The energy of his character rose higher in the school of adversity, and the estimation in which the house of Holkur was held, soon enabled him to collect followers, and, by a succession of daring exploits, to increase his means and reputation. The whole of his brother Khassee Rao's army, which included the disciplined battalions and artillery of the Chevalier Dudernaic, with the Patan leader Ameer Khan and his troops, with all the Pindarries, rallied under his standard.

The Regency was assumed by Jeswunt Rao, in the name of his nephew, Khundee Rao, though the latter was in Sindhia's hands. Forced by his necessities to lead a predatory life, he subsisted his large army by indiscriminate plunder of friend and foe; and a large part of Sindhia's and the Peshwa's territories in Hindoostan were laid waste before those chiefs

rapid movements of cavalry, which could choose the field to fight, and the time to ravage and destroy the country and resources of their enemies. Tookajee died in 1797, leaving four sons, one of whom, Jeswunt Rao, first tried the strength of the house of Holkur against the British power. Ahilya Baee, to whom Tookajee had been faithful and grateful to the last, died two years preceding, in 1795.

* The son of a chief, or minister, was usually confirmed in his father's Jagheer, or employment; and if he were a minor, a manager was appointed till he became of age. When it happened, however, that the representative of a great family possessed neither merit or ability, it was not unfrequent to resume the Jagheer, or office, and confer it upon other persons, from whom the state had better expectations. Very ancient Jagheers, called Suwusthans, are never resumed.

took measures to stop the work of desolation. At length, Sindhia's army was encountered by Holkur's at Oujain, and a desperate battle ensued, in which the regular infantry of the former was nearly annihilated, four-fifths being numbered with the killed and wounded. Of eleven European officers, seven were slain, and three wounded and made prisoners. Jeswunt Rao was afterwards defeated at Indore by the army of Sindhia, and that place, which was his capital, was given up to be ransacked by the troops of the victor. The resources of Jeswunt Rao had now failed, and his army becoming clamorous, he led them to the plunder of the rich city of Rutlam. Here he proclaimed his regular resources at an end, but offered to lead those who were disposed to a predatory life. Consonant with this plan, he led off the remnant of his army to plunder Rajpootana, whence he retrograded, carrying devastation through Candesh, levying contributions, or committing ravages, down to Poona. On the 25th October was fought the battle of Poona, between Holkur and Sindhia, when a complete victory was the reward of the uncommon energy displayed by Jeswunt Rao, and occasioned the flight of the Peshwa, and subsequent treaty of Bassein on the 31st December, 1802, so important in its results to the Mahratta nation and the British Government.

Jeswunt Rao had procured from the Raja of Satara the investiture for a new Peshwa, for which honour the present Venaik Rao was intended, when the return of Bajeerow to Poona, escorted by a British force, induced all the discordant parties in the state to endeavour to reconcile their differences, and unite to oppose an alliance equally affecting all. Sindhia, in order to conciliate Jeswunt Rao, gave over in charge to him his nephew, Khundee Rao Holkur, during whose minority he was officiating as Regent; but Jeswunt Rao, though he promised co-operation against the British Government, nevertheless did not afford it in the war which followed in 1803, with Sindhia and the Raja of Nagpoor. Shortly after its termination, the Holkur state became itself involved in disputes with the British Government, and a detachment, too weak for the enterprise, under Colonel Monson, having advanced into Malwa, was compelled to a disastrous retreat,* followed and harassed during a long march, by Jeswunt Rao. This success imboldened Jeswunt Rao to attempt more extensive operations; and he invaded the Company's possessions in Hindoostan, at the head of an army said to consist of 90,000 men, of which 19,000 were in brigades of disciplined infantry, and 7000 artillery. Defeated in the battles of Furruckabad, Deeg, and his detachments in other places, he took refuge in Bhurtpoor, where his forces, united with those of the Raja, successfully repulsed the British in several assaults. On a separate peace being concluded with the Raja of Bhurtpoor, Jeswunt Rao marched off towards the Seik country, in expectation of inducing Runjeet Sing to join his cause. He was, however, overtaken by the British army under Lord Lake, when a treaty was concluded, which, while it deprived him of certain districts, dictated the route of his army back through Hindoostan to Malwa. But as Jeswunt Rao subsequently manifested a friendly disposition towards the British Government, the alienated districts were restored to him during the following year, leaving him in nearly the same condition as before the commencement of the war.

Jeswunt Rao, in 1806, that he might be rid of all fear of a rival in his brother, Khassee Rao, at that time his prisoner, employed persons to put to death both him and his wife, who was pregnant. His nephew, Khundee Rao, then about eleven or twelve years of age, died by poison the same year.

He now applied himself with extraordinary activity to the improvement of his army, his enthusiasm in forwarding which often indicated an aberration of reason. The native ferocity of his disposition, acted upon by most unbounded dissipation, which he had indulged in from his youth, settled at last into confirmed insanity, and obliged the members of his

* Monson's great error, next to advancing so far, without leaving posts to retire upon, was that of not acting upon the offensive, arising, it is believed, from a want of confidence in his own Sepoys, against whom this unquestionably brave officer, unfortunately for his own fame, entertained a strong prejudice, from ignorance of the native character. The Sepoys had no less a mistrust of him.

Government and family, in 1808, to place him in confinement, under which he remained till his death, in 1811.

The Regency, and care of Jeswunt Rao's person, was intrusted to Toolsah Baee, his favourite mistress. She adopted Mulhar Rao, the son of another mistress, and he succeeded to the Musnud, while she administered affairs in his name,—a regency controlled by a concubine, and one of most profligate habits, but whose beauty and talents fascinated all who approached her, could not prosper.

The Government of Holkur had been rapidly decaying since the death, or previous insanity, of Jeswunt Rao, its best provinces having been appropriated by overbearing chiefs; and the young Mulhar Rao, with the Princess Regent, were obliged to seek refuge in a fort from the clamours of the troops demanding their arrears. At this time, the advance of the British forces towards the rendezvous of the Pindarries, brought from the Princess Regent a spontaneous application for herself and the young representative of the family to be received under British protection. During these negotiations, hostilities with the Peshwa commenced, when the Holkur Durbar proclaimed its resolution to adhere to his fortunes; and funds having been provided by the Peshwa's agents, the arrears of the army were discharged, the chiefs became clamorous for battle, and thus put an end to the negotiations. The first decisive step of the Patan chiefs, who had usurped the direction of affairs, was to send the Princess Regent to the banks of the Seepree for execution, and throw the ministers into confinement. The battle of Mehidpoor was fought next day, which irretrievably broke the Holkur army. The treaty of Mundisoor followed on the 6th January, by which the Holkur state was deprived of nearly two-thirds of its territories. The principal terms of this treaty embrace the cession in perpetuity to the Nuwab Ameer Khan, and his brother-in-law, Ghufoor Khan, of the Jagheers then held by them of the Holkur family,—to the latter, however, for the maintenance of a contingent of 600 efficient horse; the relinquishment of all claims or conquests from the Rajpoot states; the cession to the Regent of Kotah, of four districts, formerly rented by him; and to the British Government, of Holkur's possessions within and south of the Sautpoora range of hills. In return, the British Government took the remaining provinces under its protection. The territory left to Holkur gave, at that time, an actual revenue of twelve or thirteen lacs of rupees, and being susceptible of great improvement, his income lately has been rated at twenty lacs, and the only military charge upon it is the maintenance of a body of 3000 horse. Mulhar Rao, is still at the head of the government, and the greatest tranquillity prevails throughout his country,—a contrast to the state of anarchy, misrule, and oppression, to which the wretched inhabitants were subjected during the eleven years which followed the confinement of Jeswunt Rao.

THE GOVERNMENT OF BARODA.*

THE Mahrattas seem to have commenced their incursions into Gujerat about the year 1720, but a formal grant of the Chouth was not yielded until 1729. The grant was for the

* The founder of this family was Dumajee Gaekwar, a distinguished officer under Dhabary, the Suenaputee, or Chief, in command of the Mahrattas: he died in 1720, and was succeeded by his nephew, Peelajee, who, with Kantajee Kuddum Bandy, continued, as lieutenant under the Suenaputee, to make annual inroads into Gujerat, each being at the head of a separate army. In 1724, a new Viceroy from Delhi being appointed over the province, to supersede Nizam-ool-Moolk, when Hamed Khan, his uncle, who officiated as his deputy, called in the Mahrattas under Kantajee Kuddum, and gave him battle, first near Ahmedabad, and afterwards at Bussoo. The Imperial troops were led by Shujaet Khan, Foujdar of Surat, the new Deputy-Governor of the province, and his brother, Roostum Ali Khan, Foujdar of Baroda and Pitlaud, who were considered the bravest officers of their time. They were both killed, and the Imperial army was annihilated. Peelajee Gaekwar, by whose treachery, in affecting to join Roostum Ali at Bussoo, the overthrow of the latter had been caused, received, as a reward, the Chouth of that part of the province east of the Muhee river, including the Mahals dependent on Surat; while Kantajee had conferred upon him the Chouth west of that river, each for the maintenance of a body of horse. The whole of the Mahrattas in the province proceeded afterwards to the siege of Cambay; where, a quarrel arising between the leaders Kantajee and Peelajee, a battle ensued. Trimbuck Rao

maintenance of 2500 horse for the Imperial service, and the cessions under it divided between the lieutenants of the Suenaputee, one of whom was Dumajee Gaekwar,* ancestor of the present reigning family of Baroda. The Mahrattas did not, however, obtain possession of the whole revenues until the capture of Ahmedabad in 1755, when the Imperial authority over the country ceased, and it was divided between

arrived shortly after from the Deccan; and, after reconciling his lieutenants, prepared to contest with the Peshwa whether Bramin or Mahratta ascendency should prevail in the empire. This was decided at Dhubboy, on the 1st April, 1731, where Trimbuck Rao was slain, leaving a complete victory to the Peshwa, with all but nominal supremacy over the Mahratta nation.

Ooman Baee, widow of Khundee Rao Dhabary, and mother of the infant Suenaputee, Yeswunt Rao, seems on this conjuncture to have been vested with the conduct of the family interests in Gujerat, with Kantajee and Peelajee as her deputies. The latter was assassinated in 1731, by emissaries of Abhee Singh, the Raja of Joudpoor, who had been appointed from Delhi, Soobehdar of the province; and in 1732, Ooman Baee displaced Kantajee Kuddum from collecting the Chouth of the Ahmedabad side of the Muhee, and placed the whole Chouth of the province under Dumajee Gaekwar, the son of Peelajee.

In this year Baroda, in which Momin Khan commanded for Sher Khan Babi, was besieged and taken, after a creditable defence, by Dumajee Gaekwar, and it became thenceforth the seat of government of the Gaekwar family.

The devoted province of Gujerat, which for so many years had been a perpetual field of bloodshed and oppression, arising out of the weakness and constant changing of the Imperial officers, and the absence of all principle in their annual visitors, the Mahrattas, who never sought a reason to justify an attack upon a weaker power, was destined to change masters. The combined Mahratta forces, under Rugoonath Rao, father of the Ex-Peshwa, and Dumajee Rao Gaekwar, laid siege, in 1755, to Ahmedabad, which, after a gallant defence, conducted by Juwan Murd Khan Babi, capitulated. From that day the royal authority over the province ceased.

* The Gaekwars assume the peculiar privilege of saluting with the left hand, a mode of salaam which would be considered an insult from any other native of India. The privilege arises from the following circumstance:—On the decease of Peelajee, some hesitation took place in confirming his son, Dumajee, as his successor, whereupon he repaired to the Deccan, at the head of a large army, which he was induced, by solemn oaths exchanged between him and the Raja of Satara, to disband. The Raja then directed Rugoonath Rao, who at that time held the reins of Government, as Peshwa, to plunder Dumajee, which induced him solemnly to swear, that he never would pay the compliment of a salaam with the hand which had been pledged in that of his prince in a false oath.

the Peshwa and Gaekwar. Dumajee commanded a division of the Mahratta army in the disastrous battle of Paniput, from which he escaped, and died at Baroda in 1768, leaving four sons, the eldest of whom, Syajee, was an idiot; the others reigned in succession. Two of these, Futih Singh and Gowind Rao, are intimately connected with this memoir.

The first agreement between the Baroda Government and the English, was with Futih Singh in 1773, for a participation of the revenues of Baroach, which had been reduced by a British detachment. At this time Futih Singh was only Regent, but being attached to the interests of the Poona Regency he was confirmed in the Government in 1778, in prejudice to his elder brother, Gowind Rao, who had espoused the cause of the exiled Rugoba. The successes of General Goddard's army in Gujerat, however, induced Futih Singh to enter into a treaty with the Company in 1780, and to espouse the same cause. By the treaty, the Peshwa's share of Gujerat was to be subdued and given over to Futih Singh, and the Gaekwar revenues south of the Nerbudda were transferred to the Company. The countries acquired by this treaty were, however, relinquished by that of Salbey in 1782, and Gaekwar reverted to his former relation to the Peshwa.

In September, 1800, Gowind Rao, who had succeeded to the throne of Baroda in 1792, died, leaving three legitimate, and a number of illegitimate, children. The eldest of the former, Anund Row, was of weak intellect, and the reins of Government were usurped by Kanhoojee, the eldest of the illegitimate, whose pretensions were supported by Mulhar Row, his cousin, the Jagheerdar of Kurree. But in a few months he was deposed by Rowjee Appajee, the minister of the late Gowind Rao. To support his authority he proposed an alliance with the English, and a treaty was in consequence concluded, which led to the present intimate connection. He agreed to take into his pay a force consisting of three battalions of Native infantry, and a company of European artillery. This force was first employed in establishing him in his government, against the joint pretensions of Kanhoojee and Mulhar Row, and in subsequently expelling the Arab mercenaries in their service. The conduct of Mulhar Row, as might be expected, produced the sequestration of his Jagheer; he was then settled at Neryad, on a stipend of 1,25,000 rupees, but afterwards removed to Bombay, where he died.

At this time there was a large body of Arabs in the service of Anund Row, which it was necessary to reduce; but they had claims for heavy arrears of pay. To effect the liquidation of these claims, it became necessary to raise a loan of 41,38,732 rupees, of which the Company was solicited by the leading men of the State to take a share, and become guarantee to the bankers who might advance the rest. Consequent upon this, the Company took about a half, and native bankers the remainder: this was to be extinguished, with interest at nine per cent, in three years; in failure of which, districts were to be assigned, and the revenues collected and applied by the Company to its extinction. No part of this advance having been repaid in April 1805, suggested the expediency of a definitive treaty, consolidating the stipulations of all former engagements. The subsidiary force, which had been augmented to 3000 men, in June 1803, was made permanent, and the Pergunnahs of Dholka, Neryad, Bejapoor, Moondha, Mahter, &c. together rated at 11,70,000 rupees, were assigned in perpetual sovereignty to the Company, to provide for its payment. Territorial funds were also assigned, rated at 12,95,000 rupees, for the liquidation of the loan and interest. The cession in perpetuity to the Company, of the districts of Chourassy, Chickly, Kaira, &c. was also confirmed.

In 1809 the affairs of the Baroda state were involved in much confusion, and encumbered with debt, accumulating under the steady operation of nine per cent interest. Fortunately at that time the Resident at Baroda was the late Colonel Walker, whose personal influence in the administration of which he was a member, did much towards removing the existing difficulties. That officer left India in 1811, much too soon for the country, which still acknowledges the value of his labours. His successors, though not restricted from interference, were not provided with powers of equal extent.

After his departure for England, Futih Singh was vested with the sole direction of affairs, with the Resident as an adviser. The famine of 1813 contributed, with other causes, to prevent the liquidation of the debt, which in 1816 had accumulated to fifty-five lacs.

The assassination of Gungadhur Shastry, the Gaekwar Minister, by an unprincipled favourite of the Peshwa, to whose Court he had been sent as a Commissioner, for the purpose of adjusting claims long pending between the Peshwa and Gaekwar, in which the British Government, by the provisions of treaties with both states, was bound to arbitrate, produced, ultimately, very important political changes in India.

The farm of the Peshwa's share of the revenues of Gujerat, under Ahmedabad, had been granted first in 1800 to Gowind Rao Gaekwar, for five years, at five lacs of rupees a-year, and had been renewed to Anund Rao in 1805, on a decennial lease, at four lacs and a half of rupees. The management of these revenues was resumed by the Peshwa on the expiration of the lease in 1815. It became, in consequence, desirable to avoid the inconvenience of two sets of revenue officers, those of the Peshwa and Gaekwar, having separate interests in the same districts or towns, coming into collision, and it had therefore been one of the objects of the mission, to get the farm of the Peshwa's share renewed to Gaekwar, together with his share of the tribute of Kattiwar. The negotiations, which embraced these and other topics of considerable delicacy and moment, were put a stop to by the assassination of the envoy; and the honour and interests of the British Government being directly concerned, involved the necessity of measures of interference. The assassin was reluctantly surrendered by the Peshwa, by reason of the judicious and persevering firmness of the Resident; but having escaped from his confinement, he appeared at the head of an insurrection, in which he was supported by the Peshwa against the British Government. After every effort at conciliation had failed, war was resorted to, but was concluded by the treaty of Poona, in June, 1817, which secured important benefits to Gaekwar. The Peshwa's claims upon him, as head of the Mahratta confederacy, were renounced for ever; his unadjusted pecuniary claims were settled for an annual payment of four lacs of rupees; the farm of Ahmedabad was renewed on the former terms, but the tribute of Kattiwar was transferred to the British Government, as part of an additional subsidy, leaving to the Peshwa no pretext for interfering in the affairs of Gujerat.

In November, 1817, an augmentation of the subsidiary force, corresponding to his Highness's fair proportion of the military charges of the province, took place. It now amounted to 4000 native infantry, and two regiments of cavalry, &c. for the increased charge of which his share of Ahmedabad, taken at 12,61,969 rupees, was ceded in perpetuity to the Company. In addition to this, his Highness's Government became bound to raise and maintain a body of 3000 horse, to co-operate with the subsidiary force.

During 1818, died Futih Singh Gaekwar, who had officiated as Regent, since 1805, during the imbecility of Anund Rao. The latter did not long survive his brother. Futih Singh, from habits of intemperance during the latter years of his life, was not better qualified than Anund Rao to conduct the affairs of an administration. Their younger brother, Syajee, succeeded to the Government, and his character gave promise of better management in his country.

In 1820, when the Governor of Bombay visited Baroda, Syajee complained of the hardship of being controlled in the administration of his Government by the Resident. The enlightened Governor heard and attended to the remonstrance; and, in consequence, the Gaekwar was vested with the uncontrolled possession of his dominions, on the condition, however, that the debt with which the state was encumbered, and for which the Company stood as guarantee, should be liquidated in seven years, at twenty lacs of rupees annually.

Syajee failed to perform his engagements. He anticipated the revenues of certain districts which had been set aside for his creditors, and failed to keep up the contingent at its stipulated strength. This occasioned a new arrangement to be forced upon him in 1828, when districts were sequestrated, and placed under separate management, the revenue of which was set aside for the liquidation of his debts, and towards defraying the expense of the contingent; leaving, after deducting pensions and other charges on the revenue, a clear income to the Gaekwar of about twenty lacs of rupees. These arrangements naturally engendered discontent against the British Government, until all differences were adjusted at Baroda, in April, 1832, by the Earl of Clare, the Governor of Bombay. The Gaekwar debts having been liquidated, the sequestrated districts were restored, and an arrangement being made for the payment of the contingent, the relations of the two states have been again placed on the most friendly footing.

The whole of Gaekwar's dominions, before the British alliance, produced a gross revenue of ninety-nine lacs of rupees, of which the territory ceded to the British Government in perpetuity for the subsidiary force, is only rated at twenty-seven lacs.

GOVERNMENT OF CUTCH.

The Rao of Cutch, Mirza Rao Shri Desuljee, styled Maha-Raja, was elevated to the Musnud in October, 1819, by the unanimous voice of the Jahrejah Chiefs, on the dethronement of his father, Bharmuljee. The tyrannous and oppressive conduct of Bharmuljee to the Jahrejah * Bhyad, (brotherhood of Chiefs,) after his accession in 1815, indicated insanity, which had no doubt been induced by inebriety; and his unprovoked hostility to the British Government obtained their concurrence to a spontaneous proposal of the Chiefs for his deposition. He is now a state prisoner, residing in Bhooj,

* The Jahrejahs were originally Rajpoots till they became proselytes to Mahomedanism, and lost caste. They still cling to their Rajpoot origin; but however high they may rank in temporal power or wealth, the lowest Rajpoot would not intermarry with them. Hence the chief cause of female infanticide among that class, as their daughters are not likely to meet with suitable matches in their own sect.

at large, with a suitable maintenance. The Rao was then three years of age, and during his minority, (which will terminate in his twentieth year,) the administration is in the hands of a Regency of six members, viz. four of the principal Jahrejahs, Lukmidass Wulubjee, the Minister, and the British Resident for the time being.

The first communications between the Company and the Cutch state, occurred between 1801 and 1804, when several deputations arrived from that Court at Bombay, but no connection was then formed. The celebrated Jemidar Futtih Madomed at that time held the reins of Government, with the title of Vizier. He had commenced life as a private horseman, and passing through the rapid career of a fortunate soldier, assumed the direction of the Government in 1792, while the lawful Prince was reduced to a pageant. The aggressions of his subjects, both as pirates and plunderers, led to a treaty with him in 1809; the objects of which were, to remove all pretext, grounded on pecuniary claims, for incursions of banditti from Wagur, that had periodically plundered Kattiwar, the territory of our allies, and to suppress piracy, of which the province was a hotbed.

Futtih Mahomed died in 1813, leaving two sons, one of whom was assassinated in public Durbar by a discontented officer; and the other, after a short and turbulent reign, in which he evinced a palpable incapacity, resigned the Government, when Bharmuljee, then eighteen years of age, was formally invested with it.

This country had long been the scene of disorder and misrule, and its government being too weak to prevent the constant irruption of banditti, or freebooters, from Wagur into the territories of our ally, the Gaekwar, a deputation was sent, in which the envoy was instructed to require compensation for the past, and a guarantee against future inroads. The mission having failed in its object, the British and Gaekwar troops advanced and reduced the fort of Anjar, and by consequence the whole country. This led to the treaty of Bhooj, in January, 1816, and subsequently to the subsidiary treaty in December, 1819. The latter guaranteed to the Rao the security of his dominions against foreign and domestic enemies, the internal authority therein being left to the Regency, and provided a sufficient British force for the protection of the country. The extent of the Rao over the Jahrejah Chiefs was also clearly defined by this treaty. The British connection with Cutch arose out of political rather than pecuniary motives, in order to curb the plunderers from Wagur, whose depredations had been carried on with a desolating vigour,—to check the Khosas, and keep at a distance the Sindians, who had formerly been the occasional invaders of the province.

The state subsidizes a battalion of native infantry, with artillery, for which the Rao pays to the Company seven lacs of kories annually, besides 88,000 rupees for the rent of Anjar and its dependent villages, which were retransferred to the Rao in 1822. The military force of the Durbar is very limited, consisting of about 500 horse, and 2,000 sebundy, principally employed in revenue matters, and as police of the country. A few Arab infantry are also maintained, for the defence of the forts of Luckput and Mandavee. The Jharejah Bhyad of the Abbrassia and Wagur, with their retainers, are obliged to attend at the Camp of the Rao, on a summons from the Durbar. The contingents of all the Chiefs may amount to 20,000 horse and foot; but it is only during their attendance that subsistence or pay is demanded. The annual income of these Chiefs, who exceed 200 in number, varies from a lac of kories to 400: there are not less than 50 whose income exceeds 5000, and who can bring 150 men into the field. Each Chief exercises an unlimited authority within his own lands, the tenants upon which are his kinsmen, or Bhyad. Disputes between the Chiefs are, however, referred for adjustment to the Durbar at Bhooj.

The revenue of Cutch, including the lands of the Bhyad, is estimated at fifty lacs of kories, (about sixteen lacs of rupees,) though of this sum not more than thirty lacs are realized upon the demesne to which the ordinary jurisdiction of the Rao is confined. After, therefore, alienating the villages assigned for the maintenance of the ladies of the Durbar, amounting to three lacs—charities and pensions, three lacs and a half—and the subsidy to the British Government, including the rent of Anjar, ten lacs, only thirteen lacs of kories (less than four lacs of rupees) are left to the Rao for his personal expenses. From the circumstance of the Rao's being in debt in 1820, coupled with the necessity, on several occasions since, of remitting part of the subsidy, it may be inferred that the amount stipulated is higher than the resources of the state can well sustain.

Since 1819, the country has been subjected to many misfortunes. In that year an earthquake took place, which destroyed many of the forts and principal buildings in Cutch, and occasioned a great loss of life. In 1823 and 1824, the periodical rains failed, necessarily causing much distress, and the emigration of a large portion of the population. With the return of plenty in 1825-26, the country was overrun by plunderers from Sinde, conducted by the emigrants from Cutch the year before, thus in a great measure renewing the calamities of former years. Since that period Cutch has been better protected,* confusion has given place to order, and its people have for the most part returned. The population is estimated at 500,000 families, of which about 10,000 compose the Bhyad. These latter derive their descent from the same common origin as the Rao, whose ancestor came from Thutha, in Sinde, about the middle of the sixteenth century. The census of 1827 exhibits 332,000 Hindoo families, and 153,000 Mahomedan. The famine and pestilence of 1812 deprived Cutch of a great portion of its population. Infanticide is suspected to prevail in the country, and particularly among the Jahrejahs, notwithstanding all the measures taken by the British Government for its suppression. The Rao is, by the treaty of 1819, bound to use his utmost endeavours to suppress it, and especially to abolish it in his own family.

In the district of Wagur, a tribute was formerly levied from the Chief, of forty kories upon each plough of their

* About the beginning of 1832, a body of about 500 marauders, from the north, entered Cutch, and drove off a number of cattle, the only foray of any consequence for a number of years; and measures were immediately taken to guard against a repetition.

cultivators; subsequently this was commuted for a fixed tribute, agreeably to the supposed number of ploughs in each village. The deposed Rao had endeavoured to establish a similar tribute from the rest of his Chiefs in other parts of the country, but the attempt was one of the immediate causes of his deposition.

The soil of Cutch is principally of a sandy description, but it contains extensive tracts of land, such as the plain of Abbrassa, and some districts in Wagur, of an extremely rich and productive nature, particularly favourable to the growth of cotton, which may be considered the staple of the province. It possesses, likewise, on its northern boundary, extensive pastures, which are resorted to by numerous tribes of wandering Rehbaries and Jhuts.

The Rao attained his fourteenth year in February, 1830, when the ceremony of his marriage took place with four wives at the same time.

GOVERNMENT OF NAGPOOR.*

THE state of Nagpoor, or government of the Eastern Mahrattas, first came into communication with the English in 1779, when Moodajee Bhonslay held the Regency, during the

* The ancestors of this family were Patels of Hingun-Berdee, near Poona, and Deoor, near Satara. Early in the eighteenth century, Pursoojee Bhonslay, styled Soobehdar of Berar, though probably only an agent for collecting the Chouth, had a nephew, Rughoojee, serving under him with four horse, but of whose remarkable talents the uncle was jealous. Rughoojee in consequence deserted, plundered some villages, and, collecting a body of 100 horse, entered the service of the Raja of Chanda, brother of Bukht Boolund, Raja of Deogurh, or Gondwana. About this time a merchant named Putwurdhun, on his way from Benares to Poona, had heavy transit duties levied upon his merchandise by the Raja of Gondwana; and Pursoojee, when solicited, declined interference to get them remitted. This refusal of justice rankled in the mind of Putwurdhun, who finding, on his arrival at Poona, that Pursoojee's withholding for a number of years the Chouth of Berar, (3,00,000 rupees per annum,) was a subject of public discussion, chose the opportunity to avenge his private wrong, by bringing Rughoojee to the knowledge of the Durbar, and suggested that the nephew should supersede the uncle. Rughoojee was thereupon sent

minority of his son Rughoojee. Janoojee, his predecessor, died without issue in 1772, after having adopted Rughoojee

for to Poona in 1734, and invested as Soobehdar. The contingent was fixed at 5000 cavalry, but he was to repair to the Peshwa's standard with double that number, in case of war. Putwurdhun became security for Pursoojee's arrears; and it was made a farther part of their concerted designs, that the youthful warrior should assail, in order to subdue, the Raja of Gondwana. Rughoojee, alive to present circumstances, and looking to prospective fame, attacked his uncle, took him prisoner, and sent him to Satara. Bukht Boolund having died without issue, Meer Buhadoor, an illegitimate son of the Raja of Chanda, usurped the government of Gondwana, though three legitimate sons were living, viz. Boorahan Shah, Akber Shah, and Wulee Shah. The latter having been put to death by the usurper, his mother called upon Rughoojee to avenge it, at the very moment that the crafty Mahratta was assembling troops for the invasion of the province, agreeably to his engagement with Putwurdhun, who had provided funds for the payment of 10,000 horse. The Mahrattas entered the province, and encountering Meer Buhadoor, a drawn battle ensued. Meer Buhadoor was afterwards seduced to an interview, and treacherously put to death by Rughoojee, who restored the surviving brothers, and having received the districts of Pownee, Brimapooree, &c. he annexed them to Berar.

In 1739, he was appointed leader of the army for the invasion of the Carnatic, with the title of Sena-Sahib-Soobah, and his successes rendered the Mysore tributary to the Poona state. On his return to Satara in 1740, he at first opposed the succession of Balajee Bajee Rao to the office of Peshwa.

An expedition during this year, under Rughoojee's general, having entered Bahar, its weakness and wealth were at once laid open. Two years after, two large armies, respectively led by Rughoojee and Balajee Bajeerow, entered from different points, and laid waste the provinces of Bengal, Bahar, Lucknow, and Orissa, under pretext of collecting the tribute, to which they claimed a right on a grant in 1717 from the Emperor. In 1744 a Sunnud for the undivided Chouth of these provinces was obtained by Rughoojee, and they were periodically invaded for the purpose of realizing it, until it was redeemed by a cession to Rughoojee in perpetuity of all the province of Orissa.

In 1742, on the occasion of a quarrel between the two Princes of Deogurh, Akber Shah wounded his elder brother, and made him prisoner. In this dilemma, the captive Prince entreated assistance from Rughoojee, who prepared to afford it; and on his entering the province, he was met by Akber Shah at the head of a strong force, which, nevertheless, Rughoojee contrived so to divide, that he gained an easy victory. Akber Shah escaped to Hydrabad, where he died three years afterwards. Deogurh and Chanda were added to Rughoojee's former conquests.

In 1742 also, Mundela was taken by assault by the united Mahratta armies; and the Raja having fallen in its defence, his son Seoraj was invested by the as his heir, leaving his widow as Regent during the youth's minority, assisted by the counsel of his brother Sabajee. Moodajee, indignant at this arrangement, engaged in perpetual conspiracies to effect its overthrow, till at length, in January, 1775, a battle ensued between the brothers, and Moodajee was defeated; but at the close of the battle, Sabajee fell by a pistol shot, discharged in the moment of excitement by his brother, then a prisoner, towards whom he had advanced, to confer with him. This occurrence gave a new turn to affairs, and left the fratricide in undisputed possession of the Regency, in which he was confirmed by the Poona Durbar, on the presentation of a Nuzur of ten lacs of rupees.

In 1778-9, during the war with the Poona state, the Supreme Government sent an embassy to Moodajee, in order to effect an alliance, and to detach him from the Mahratta confederacy. The ill success of the British arms at this time in Western India, retarded the alliance, which did not take

Peshwa as his successor, and an annual tribute fixed, of three lacs of rupees, which was assigned to Rughoojee. On the death of Seoraj in 1749, the Chouth was commuted for territory realizing that amount. The whole of Gurrah-Mundela was conquered by the Mahrattas in 1778, and was made over to Khundoojee Bhonslay in 1793, for his services in the Carnatic in 1786, agreeably to a promise given him by the Peshwa. The gross revenue of Gurrah-Mundela was then rated at 15,02,905 rupees.

After having governed Berar seventeen years, Rughoojee died about 1753, leaving four sons, Janoojee, Sabajee, Moodajee, and Bembajee, between whom he divided his possessions, but made the whole dependent upon the eldest. Janoojee reigned twenty years, and died, after adopting Rughoojee, a son of his brother Moodajee, during whose minority his widow officiated as Regent, with the assistance of Sabajee. Moodajee, conceiving that he had the best right to the guardianship of his own child, collected troops, and, giving battle to Sabajee, on the 27th January, 1775, sustained a defeat. The victor approached his brother, and was in the act of uttering some conciliatory expressions, when Moodajee drew a pistol, and shot him through the head. By this atrocity he became guardian of his child, and ruler in Berar. He died in 1788, and was succeeded by Rughoojee.

By the treaty of Poorundhur, concluded in 1776, between the Company and Poona Regency, the latter engaged to render the Nagpoor state no assistance in recovering the Chouth of the Bengal provinces, a Mahratta mode of shewing that, though its realization had never been attempted from the Company, yet, nevertheless, the Nagpoor state had a right to claim it.

place until late in 1779, when pecuniary aid was secretly afforded by the British Government, to enable Moodajee to reduce Gurrah-Mundela, an extensive province in the valley of the Nerbudda, then in possession of the Peshwa, but which Moodajee had long coveted, as being contiguous to his own dominions. These districts, though reduced by Rughoojee, were not formally confirmed to his successor by the Peshwa until 1793, when they were made the reward of former services of the Nagpoor contingent in the Carnatic. It will hence be observed, that though the Rajas of Nagpoor usually acted as a branch of the Mahratta confederacy, that they nevertheless maintained their independence, framing treaties, remaining neutral, or acting either with or against the Peshwa, as it suited their interest or their policy. The plea of duty, therefore, in this state joining the Peshwa during the last Mahratta war, cannot be sustained.

Moodajee died in 1788, and Rughoojee succeeded to the uncontrolled administration of his dominions. It was his policy not to interfere with the quarrels of his neighbours, as his army had sufficient employment against the half-subdued Rajas of the wild and extensive territory over which he nominally reigned. Moreover, he was jealous of his brother Khundoojee, whom he was afraid to send with the army on foreign expeditions, and not less fearful, by accompanying it himself, of leaving Khundoojee in charge of the Government at Nagpoor. On this account, when called upon, agreeably to his engagement as one of the feudatories of the state, to join in the war against Tippoo, in 1790, he purchased the absence of his contingent, by a payment of 10,00,000 rupees, towards the expenses of the war. The contingent, by the Sunnud of the Raja of Satara, in 1734, granting the Chouth of Berar, was 10,000 horse, with which he was liable to be called upon to serve, by the Raja or Peshwa, in case of war.

Rughoojee had enjoyed a long peace, but in an evil hour he united in 1803 with Sindhia, to oppose the objects of the treaty of Bassein. The victories obtained over the united armies of these Chiefs, at Assaye and Argaom, led to the treaty of Deogaom with Rughoojee, by the provisions of which he was deprived of a great part of his territories. The province of Cuttack, with the port and district of Balasore, were ceded to the Company, and all territories west of the Wurda river, of which he and the Nizam had participated in the revenues, together with part of the districts south of, and depending upon, Nehrnalla and Gawilgurh, were ceded to the Nizam, giving to the latter a better defined northern boundary in the Indyadree hills and Wurda river. He was obliged, moreover, to renounce future adherence to the Mahratta confederacy.

In 1806, the provinces of Sumbhulpoor, Patna, and other districts, were restored, and re-annexed to the Nagpoor dominions, with the exception of the territory of Joojar Singh, a petty Raja, to whom the protection of the British Government was continued.

In 1809, the Nagpoor state refused to enter into the British proposals for a subsidiary alliance, which might have retarded rather than advanced its own views upon Bhopal, with which it was then at war. Shortly after this, Ameer Khan concluded an alliance with the latter state, and together they advanced upon Nagpoor. They would probably have succeeded in subverting the dynasty, had not British detachments marched from two different points and prevented them.

Rughoojee died in 1816, and his son, Pursoojee, who was blind, and labouring at the same time under a paralytic affection, was raised to the throne; but the Regency was intrusted to his cousin, Appah Sahib, the son of his late uncle, Khundoojee. On the 26th May a treaty was concluded with the Regent, by which the Company engaged to furnish the state with a subsidiary force of one regiment of cavalry, and six battalions of native infantry, the charge for which was fixed at 7,50,000 rupees, being merely the additional expense of the field establishments of the force. The Regent engaged on his part to maintain an efficient contingent of 3000 cavalry and 2000 infantry, to co-operate with the subsidiary force.

There falls to be noticed, among many of the like sort with which the history of Asiatic dynasties teem, another sanguinary deed,—the murder of Pursoojee by the Regent. Not content with the eminence of his post, and impatient to be freed from all check to paramount authority, on the night of the 1st of February, 1817, he sought to prevail on the Prince to take poison; but not succeeding in that endeavour, he in a few hours after procured his victim's death by strangulation. The act was planned and executed with all the adjunctive precautionary measures to ensure concealment, and no question arising after its commission, he was proclaimed successor to the Musnud. It was in fact some time before the affair was sufficiently bruited to bring upon the criminal any portion of retributive justice, as will be seen in the sequel.

During this year Appah Sahib, in common with the other great Mahratta Chiefs, cherished secret plans of hostility against the British. Co-operating with the proceedings at Poona, he, while the most amicable intercourse existed, treacherously attacked, on the 27th November, the British troops stationed at his capital. After a trying contest of eighteen hours, during which the British lost more than one-fourth of their number in killed and wounded, and a large proportion of officers, victory declared for them; the assailants being repulsed at all points. The arrival of reinforcements on the 15th December, enabled the British to assume the offensive. Accordingly, next day the Nagpoor army was attacked and defeated, and the city fell on the 30th following; but previously Appah Sahib had surrendered himself to the Resident.

A forbearance was shewn towards the discomfited Chief, which a farther development of his character proved him unworthy of. He was allowed to retain his Musnud, but compelled to cede territory equivalent to the former subsidy, and the maintenance of the contingent; but effectually to prevent his hostile designs in future, some of his forts were required to be given up to the occupation of British troops.

It was found, however, that Appah Sahib still continued his intrigues for the overthrow of the British power, insomuch that it became a measure of necessity to place him under restraint; and his atrocious murder of his cousin Pursoojee having now transpired, it became the less objectionable to send him under arrest to Allahabad. On the route, he escaped from his escort; and, after a variety of adventures on his part, and operations against him, he was reduced to the situation of a powerless, unregarded fugitive, till at length, totally deprived of means of injuring the tranquillity of India, he made his way to Lahore, near which, according to the latest accounts, he was residing, on a scanty allowance from Runjeeth Singh.

The intended measures for the succession, provided in the event of Appah Sahib's defection being repeated, were in the meantime carried into execution. A son of Nana Goojur, by a daughter of the late Rughoojee, was, after the ceremony of adoption into the family, raised to the throne by the name of Rughoojee; and Buka Baee, the widow of the late Pursoojee, was appointed alike his guardian, and Regent of the state. The unsettled parts of the country were also, during the minority, placed under the superintendence of British officers. The Raja attained his majority on the 1st December, 1826, when he was put in possession of a territory yielding a net revenue of twenty-six lacs of rupees; the remaining portion, equal to seventeen lacs, being reserved for payment of his army, which is officered by British. The reserved districts were also made over to him on the 27th December, 1829, when the contingent was reduced to a force of 1000 horse; the Raja's army was also disbanded, with a tribute to the British Government of eight lacs of rupees substituted.

GOVERNMENT OF MYSORE.

The territories of which this state was composed, at the beginning of the eighteenth century, included the districts of Mysore proper, Coimbcttoor, and Baramahl, and it was tributary to the petty Mahomedan principality of Sera, which had arisen out of the ruins of the kingdom of Beejapoor, and was, in turn, rendered by Hyder Ali tributary to Mysore. In 1704, during the reign of Chick Deo Raj, the revenue is registered at 13,81,571 pagodas. In 1792, the dominions of Mysore produced a revenue which exceeded six times this amount. On the subversion of Tippoo's power, in 1799, the state being deprived of most of its acquisitions, territories were allotted, equal to its original extent, calculated to realize a revenue of 14,00,000 pagodas, and formed into a separate government, in which was placed a descendant of the ancient Rajas, Kistna Raja Oodiaver, then six years of age. His revenues were charged with a subsidy of 7,00,000 pagodas to the East India Company, for the maintenance of a subsidiary force for his defence and security. By the third article of the subsidiary treaty, the Raja was bound to contribute assistance, in proportion to his means, in the event of hostilities against any other state. On the occurrence, therefore, of the Mahratta wars of 1803, 1804, and 1805, the Government of Mysore, being called upon, raised a body of upwards of 4000 Silahdar horse, which was sent to serve with the British army in the field. Their services during the war gave them claim to consideration at its termination; and, by articles supplemental to the treaty of 1799, concluded in 1807, the undefined contribution of assistance during war, was commuted for the fixed maintenance of 4000 effective horse. Very efficient aid is reported to have been rendered in the wars of 1817-18, by this body of cavalry, when they accompanied the army of the Deccan.

The commencement of the Company's transactions with the Mysore state may be dated from the operations before Tritchinopoly in 1752, 1753, and 1754, wherein the Mysore army, under Nunjraj, the Regent, was at first acting in conjunction with, and afterwards in opposition to, the British troops. In 1755, the Regent led his division back to Mysore, and, in 1761, he was deposed by the celebrated Hyder Ali, to whom he had been a benefactor. A pension of one lac of pagodas was assigned for his support, but of this he was deprived in 1767, and made a state prisoner. He died shortly after, and his wealth was converted to the supply of the Government's necessities.

The history of the pageant Princes of Mysore from this period is soon told. On the nominal Raja who occupied the Musnud in 1761, Hyder settled a pension of three lacs of pagodas for his maintenance. He died in 1766, and was succeeded by Nunjraj, a boy of eighteen years of age; but the sum allotted for the support of the Raja's dignity was reduced, and none but the dependents of Hyder allowed to serve in the palace. This young prince having been discovered, in 1772, in communication with the Mahrattas, was strangled while in the bath by Hyder's orders, and his brother elevated to the dangerous distinction. The latter died in 1775, when another was set up, who was father to the Raja restored in 1799 by the British Government.

On the establishment of the Government of Mysore in 1799, its administration was placed under Poorniah, the celebrated Dewan, or chief minister of finance, under Tippoo, one of the parties in the treaty of Mysore. He resigned his charge in 1812 to the Raja, then in his nineteenth year, who had evinced a maturity of judgment, from which the most favourable expectations were formed, but which riper years has unfortunately failed to realize. In 1831, the affairs of the state had got so much into disorder, that a civil war and rebellion ensued, and it became requisite to put in force the fourth and fifth articles of the treaty of Mysore, which empower the British Government to bring the Government of Mysore under the direct management of the Company's officers, with full authority to introduce such regulations and ordinances as shall be expedient for the better ordering of any branch of the revenue. In the event of a contingency of this kind, the treaty makes suitable provision for the Raja, namely, that his income shall never be less than one lac of star pagodas, in addition to one-fifth of his net revenues. The gross revenue of Mysore exceeds 80,00,000 rupees, and the subsidy amounts to 24,50,000 rupees.

GOVERNMENT OF TRAVANCORE.

The British connection with the Raja, or King, as he was then styled, of Travancore, originated in mutual commercial advantages from a very early period; but subsequently, on the rise of the power of Hyder Ali, the alliance was highly valuable to both parties. The Travancore possessions formed a barrier to the more southerly of the British, while the British was a powerful ally to the Raja in the event of war with Hyder. The Raja proved that he understood the value of the connection. In 1783, when the war with Tippoo Sultaun was at its height, and we had scarcely the credit of a single ally in the south of India, the Raja, confiding in the ultimate success of the English, stood forth their avowed friend. His troops contributed their share to the victory obtained by Colonel M'Leod at Panani, at that time important in its consequences. His zealous co-operation having entitled him to the distinction of being ranked as an ally of the British Government, he was included as such in the treaty with Tippoo of 1784. The earliest transaction of a political nature, and by which he gave offence to Hyder Ali, had occurred six years prior to this, when a free passage through his territory was allowed to the detachment sent to attack and occupy the French settlement at Mahé.

When the whole of Malabar and Canara had been subdued by Hyder Ali and Tippoo, the little independent principality of Travancore became insulated by the possessions of the Mysore state, and Tippoo obviously wished to bring it also under his dominion, and this the late treaty only prevented his accomplishing. He, however, sought every opportunity of disturbing the neutrality which the Raja had endeavoured to maintain, who was at length alarmed by the frequent movement of the troops of Mysore through the contiguous territories of Paulghautcherry and Calicut. He was therefore induced, as a precautionary measure, to apply to the Government of Fort St George, in June, 1788, for four officers and twelve sergeants, to discipline six battalions of infantry. Their reply, dated 12th August, 1788, states, that "it was contrary to their system to lend officers, except such as are in their pay; but if the Raja would suggest any means by which two or three battalions of the Company's army may be employed in securing the Travancore territory against any sudden attack of its enemies, it would be taken into consideration." In consequence of this communication, the Raja agreed to entertain a subsidiary force of two battalions, the subsidy for which, during peace, was fixed at 1755 pagodas a month each, to be paid for in cash or in pepper. This force had hardly reached its station on the island of Vipen, before Tippoo found a ground of offence against the Raja, for having purchased from the Dutch the town of Cranganore, to which he laid claim, as being situated on the territory of his tributary, the Raja of Cochin. Regardless, therefore, of the defensive alliance subsisting between the British Government and this state, Tippoo attacked the Travancore lines in December, 1789, in which he sustained a defeat; but the reverse only led to more formidable preparations. The British Government now interfered in favour of the Raja. But Tippoo, though he continued to make protestations of a pacific tendency, was too confident in his own strength to be constrained by any consideration of justice, in carrying into effect a favourite object of ambition,—the annexation of Travancore to his conquests in Malabar. His preparations being completed, in April, 1790, he began operations by breaching, or rather laying open a passage which extended half a mile in breadth through the famous barrier wall. The Travancoreans, panic-struck, were easily defeated, and the whole country was immediately laid waste. The British troops rendered no assistance on this occasion, and the pacific policy of the Madras Administration of the day would certainly have allowed Tippoo to complete his conquest, had they not been ordered by Lord Cornwallis to oppose him.

This unprovoked attack on an ancient ally, amidst profound peace, placed the English and Mysore Governments in a state of hostility, and a declaration of war ensued, by the result of which Tippoo lost half his dominions, and the Raja of Travancore had restored to him those districts which had been previously wrested from him.

The next regular treaty upon record with the Travancore state, was a commercial one, distinguished by the name of the Pepper Contract, in which the Raja engaged to furnish 3000 candies of pepper, at 115 rupees a candy, for ten years, in exchange for broadcloth, and other articles. It is dated in January, 1793.

The next treaty arose out of a proposal on the part of th Raja, in September, 1793, to subsidize three battalions of the Company's army. This does not seem to have been attended to until 1795, when a temporary engagement was concluded by the Bombay Government for one battalion, to be employed against external enemies. A permanent treaty, of the same date, 17th November, 1795, obtained confirmation in England, in 1797. The principal provisions which this treaty embraces are, the restoration to the Raja of three districts, ceded by Tippoo, in 1792, to the Company, and the payment by him, in return, of an annual subsidy, equal to the expense of three battalions of Sepoys, with artillery, to be stationed in his territory. By the seventh article, the Raja was bound to furnish troops, when required, to serve between Madras and Calicut, at the Company's expense.

In the following year the Raja Palpenaben died, and was succeeded by his son, of the same name, with whom a treaty was concluded, on the 12th January, 1805. Until the downfal of the Mahomedan dynasty of Mysore, the alliance with Travancore was mutually beneficial, and treaties were entered into with the Raja, as an independent Prince. The alliance upheld the Travancore state against its powerful neighbour of Mysore, whose possession of it would have endangered our own southern provinces. On the fall of their common enemy, when the Raja might reasonably have looked for a reduction of the expense of protection, he found himself compelled, by this treaty, to make a virtual surrender of his country to his ally. The 3d article requires him to pay the expense of one regiment additional, in consequence of the Company's relieving him from the obligation of furnishing troops, stipulated by the 7th article of the former treaty, above adverted to. The 4th provides that, if more force be wanted to protect Travancore, the Raja should pay a share of the expense. The 5th, in order to secure the Company against failure of funds to meet permanent or extraordinary military charges, concedes to them the power of regulating the administration of all branches of public affairs, and of bringing them under the direct management of the servants of the Company, whenever it shall appear necessary to their Governor-General. The Raja was, in such case, to be allowed, for his maintenance, one-fifth of the whole net revenue, and two lacs of rupees, annually. The 9th article stipulates, that the Raja is to attend to all such advice as the British Government may offer him respecting the management of his affairs. It will be observed, by a comparison of this treaty with that of ten years before, that the Raja had, in the interim, by some means, forfeited his independence.

Discontent had become so strong that, regardless of their obvious military inferiority, a hostile faction, headed by the minister, resolved, in 1809, to try an appeal to arms, when 30,000 troops of the Durbar surrounded the subsidiary force, but after several actions the commotion was suppressed. On the restoration of peace, the Raja, awakened to a sense of the evils attendant on the late mal-administrations, earnestly requested the Resident to take upon himself the direct management of affairs, as provided for in the treaty of 1805. The consequent assumption of the office of Dewan, or minister, by the British Resident, led to the introduction of an efficient system for the administration of justice, and an effectual reform in the revenue and financial departments, which, in the course of a few years, freed the state from all its encumbrances.

In 1812, an attempt was made by the ex-minister, to recover his rank and power, in which he contemplated the expulsion of the English. He succeeded in seducing a native officer, and a few men, from their allegiance, who were tried by court martial and executed.

In 1812 the Raja died, and on the 16th April, 1813, the Queen was delivered of a son; and a white elephant being caught in the mountains shortly after, the colour indicating an auspicious reign, his inauguration took place in July following. This Prince attained his sixteenth year in April, 1829, when his investiture in the sovereignty took place, agreeably to the proclamation issued at his birth. When the country had become insulated by the British possessions, it could have no external enemies; but the presence of the subsidiary force was considered necessary for the prevention of internal commotion, until the maturity of a better system of administration, which had been introduced by the Resident, made it safe to withdraw it from the country, and this was done last year, (1832,) when all responsibility was left to the

Raja. The subsidy, however, amounting to 7,83,110 rupees annually, is considered due to the British Government, which is still bound to afford protection and assistance to the Raja, should occasion arise to require it. The net revenue, in 1826-27, amounted to 40,42,645 rupees, and the expenditure, including subsidy, to 37,68,392 rupees.

Some peculiarities to Travancore may be noticed. The rule of succession, whether to the government or to private property, is through the female line, that is, the eldest son of the eldest daughter succeeds. The Nairs, or military class of the country, a brave but turbulent race, degraded by the worst vices, are ever ready to join an insurrection. Marriage is unknown among them; nor is any other contract entered into between the sexes, but such as can be dissolved at the pleasure of the parties.

THE RAJA OF COCHIN.

THE Raja of Cochin had been since 1776 a tributary of the Mysore state, for certain districts, which had been wrested from him by Hyder Ali about that time. The war of 1790, with Tippoo, commenced, by the British Government taking possession of those districts, and confirming the Raja in possession of them, on condition of his transferring his allegiance, and becoming tributary to the British for that portion of his territory only. An annual tribute of one lac of rupees was settled by treaty, 6th January, 1791, and is the same as used to be paid to Mysore.

The town of Cochin was taken possession of in 1795, in consequence of war with the Dutch; but wherever the Dutch law had force, the exercise of it was continued under the British authorities. Until the downfal of the Mahomedan dynasty of Mysore, the British alliance was essential to the political existence of the Raja of Cochin, but after that event, the coalition was no longer necessary, and the Raja expressed a desire to modify the connection. In 1809, a faction sprang up, headed by the minister, which had this end in view. The malcontents raised troops, and making common cause with the Travancoreans, commenced an absurd and unprovoked war against the British; previous to the commencement of which, an attempt was made to assassinate the Resident. These occurrences led to a new treaty with the Raja, who, it was supposed, had given his countenance and sanction to the hostile designs of his minister, by which he was obliged to accept a subsidiary force of one battalion of native infantry, to protect himself and his country against the recurrence of these insurrections.

The subsidy on this account, in addition to the former tribute of one lac of rupees, made an aggregate annual payment of 2,76,037 rupees. This increased amount of tribute tended to prevent the authority and the resources of the Cochin Government from being employed in designs inimical to the British interests, since the whole revenue, estimated at 4,80,000 rupees, left a balance hardly sufficient, with the charges of collection and of police, to maintain the Raja and his court. The embarrassments of the Cochin Government, shortly after, rendered it necessary for the British Resident to act as Dewan, or minister of the state, when one of his first measures was to effect the reduction of the tribute and subsidy to a fixed sum of 2,40,000 rupees, or half the revenue.

By the fourth and fifth articles of the last treaty, it is provided, that, if the Company should have reason to apprehend a failure of the funds destined to defray the expense of the permanent military force, agreed upon by the second and third articles, they are at liberty to assume, and bring under their direct management, the revenues of the country. On this contingency, a fixed sum of 35,000 rupees, besides one-fifth of the surplus revenues, is to be allotted for the support of the Raja and his family; but it has not yet been found necessary to exercise this reservation.

A portion of the country is attached to Malabar, and subject to the British code of regulations, while the rest is under the immediate administration of the Raja. Great part of the population of the town are descendants of the Dutch, who (after ousting the Portuguese, who were the earliest European settlers there) first settled at Cochin in 1663. It subsequently became one of their principal eastern settlements, but all their rights therein were finally ceded to the English, in 1814.

LIST OF PRINCES,

The military protection of whose territories has been undertaken by the Honourable the East India Company, with the AMOUNT of SUBSIDY paid by each, or the REVENUE on the Territorial Assignment, in lieu of Subsidy.

Princes and their Capital Cities.	First Treaty.	First Subsidiary connection.	Subsidiary Forces.		Gross Revenue	Charges, &c.*	Net Subsidy.
			Cavalry.	Infantry			
The King of Oude, (Lucknow,) . .	1764	1773	undefined	undefined	£1,813,562	£506,222	£1,307,340
The Soobehdar of the Deccan, (Hydrabad,)	1766	1795	1000	8000	610,000	120,000	490,000
H. H. the Gaekwar, (Baroda,) . .	1773	1805	2000	4000	382,796	147,170	135,626
Sindhia and others, (Gwalior,) . . .	1781	1803	. . .	. . . .	2,398,104	836,825	1,561,278
Holkur and other Chiefs, (Indore,) .	1805	1817	undefined	undefined	273,574 }	87,299	420,995
Raja of Nagpoor, (Nagpoor,) . . .	1779	1816	undefined	undefined	224,720 }		
Rao of Cutch, (Bhooj,)	1816	1819	. . .	1 Battalion	. . . .	. . .	32,400
Raja of Mysore, (Mysore,)	1799	1799	undefined	undefined	. . . .	. . .	280,000
Raja of Travancore, (Travancore,) . .	1784	1795	. . .	3 Battalions	. . . .	. . .	89,498
Raja of Cochin, (Cochin,)	1791	1809	. . .	1 Battalion	. . . .	. . .	22,857
							£4,339,994

* The column of charges includes, 1*st*, Pensions chargeable on the revenues; 2*d*, Revenue charges collection; 3*d*, Political charges; 4*th*, Judicial salaries; 5*th*, The charges of police, and diet of prisoners; 6*th*, The maintenance of provincial battalions; 7*th*, The customs' charges, and expense of the mint. The balance remaining, after these deductions, is applicable to the purpose for which the territories were originally granted, viz. the military protection of the state which assigned them.

PROTECTED STATES.

Introduction.

The states comprehended under this description are those with which no subsidiary engagements have ever been formed. They are perfectly independent in their internal rule, but acknowledge the supremacy of the British Government, and benefit by its protection against the aggressions of any foreign power. Engagements or treaties have been concluded with these states, framed agreeably to the peculiar circumstances of each; but the stipulations which have general application to all are: That the protected state maintain no correspondence of a political tendency with foreign powers, without the privity or consent of the British Government, to whom the adjustment of its political differences is to be referred: That on all occasions in which the interests of both states are concerned, the troops of the protected state take the field, and act in subordinate co-operation with the British: The protected state to use its utmost endeavours to defend the passes, or roads, through its country, in any part of which the protecting power is at liberty to station its own troops when necessary: No asylum to be afforded to criminals or defaulters, and every assistance to be given to effect their apprehension; in like manner, criminals or defaulters fleeing from a protected state, will be apprehended and given up if found in the British territories: Europeans not to be employed without the permission first obtained of the British Government. Agreeably to the peculiar means or resources of the protected state, a tribute is demanded for the protection afforded; or a contingent force is maintained by it, liable to be employed on being required by the protecting power; but where neither tribute or military service is specified in the engagements, these states render service according to their means.

GOVERNMENT OF SATARA.

SIVAJEE, the illustrious founder of the Mahratta nation, and gallant assertor of Hindoo independence, was born in 1627, and derives his pedigree from the family of Oodipoor.* His father, Shahjee, was one of the principal military officers under the Mahomedan dynasty of Beejapoor, and held extensive Jagheers. They included Poona and Satara on the western frontier of the kingdom, and Tanjore on the southern, where respectively his sons, Sivajee and Venkajee, laid the foundation of sovereignties. A disagreement between his parents deprived Sivajee of a father's care during his youth,

* By the legend it appears, that the family trace their pedigree from the famous Bappa Rawul of Chitoor, who reigned over Rajpootana in the year 134 of the Christian era. But as any accounts of his very early descendants do not belong, or are immaterial to the Mahratta history, it may be briefly observed, that one of the descendants of Bheemsee, a son of Bappa Rawul, who had settled in Nepaul, returned to the land of his forefathers in 1442, and founded the principality of Doongurpoor and Banswara. The thirteenth ruler of this race, at Doongurpoor, named Abheesee, and styled the Maha Rana, left the Government to his sister's son, in prejudice of his own children. One of the latter, named Sujunsee, came to the Deccan, and entered the service of the King of Beejapoor, who conferred upon him the district of Modhul, comprising 84 villages, with the title of Raja. Sujunsee had four sons: Bajee Raja, in whose line descended the Modhulkur estate; the second died without family; from Wolubsye is Ghorpuray of Kapsee; and Sugajee, the youngest, had a son, named Bhosajee, from whom is derived all the Bhouslays. He had ten sons: the eldest settled at Deoolgaom, near Patus, the Patel of which, Maloojee Raja, was an active partizan under the King of Ahmednugur, and had a Jagheer conferred upon him, which descended to his son, Shahjee, afterwards a principal Mahratta leader, under the Beejapoor dynasty. He acquired, in Jagheer, nearly the whole of what now forms the Collectorship of Poona, together with part of the territory now under Satara; and it was in these valleys that his son, Sivajee, matured his plan of Hindoo independent sovereignty. The second settled at Hingnee; the third, at Bherdee, from which the Rajas of Nagpoor are descended; the fourth, at Sawuntwaree; the fifth, at Wavee, out of which family the father of the present Raja of Satara was adopted; the sixth, at Moongy, on the Godavery; the seventh, at Shumboo Mahadeo; the eighth, at Boregaom; the ninth, at Jeentee; and the tenth at Khunwutta, out of which family the present Raja of Kolapoor's father was adopted.

but it was supplied by that of a guardian, into whose hands the family interests in the west were intrusted. By him he was thoroughly educated in the usual accomplishments of an Asiatic cavalier,—archery, horsemanship, the spear, and the sword. He began very early to practise these acquirements, in exploits more daring than creditable, and his enterprises at length bore the character of rebellion. He obtained possession of various forts by means either of stratagem or courage, and laid the foundation of future sovereignty. The Hindoos, who had long borne a foreign yoke, rallied round him, and the slaughter of the unprepared Mahomedan army of Beejapoor, after the assassination of their General in the treacherous embrace of Sivajee, gave earnest of the future hero, agreeably to the rude notions of the times, and gained him a great accession of followers and resources. His contests with the Mahomedan kingdoms of Beejapoor and Ahmednugur, contributed to enlarge his own dominions, and to the final overthrow of these dynasties by Aurungzeb, with whose armies he was himself always at war till his death in 1680.

He left the sovereignty he had formed to a worthless son, Sumbhajee, and institutions, judicial, civil, and fiscal, for his guidance, which continued in practice as long as the Mahratta sovereignty endured. Sumbhajee, during the lifetime of his father, had given promise of future fame, but he commenced his reign inauspiciously, in the seizure and unnatural execution of his mother-in-law, and also the confidential ministers of his deceased father. After an inglorious reign, chiefly marked by tyranny towards his subjects, and sensual indulgence, he was surprised, and, together with his son, Sivajee, taken prisoner in 1694, and carried to the camp of Aurungzeb. The former having grievously provoked the emperor during his confinement, was made to suffer a cruel death, and the latter being spared on account of his youth, grew up under the protection of the accomplished Fuez-ool-Nissa Begum, Aurungzeb's daughter. This princess changed the name of Sivajee to that of Sahoo. Raja Ram, the younger son of Sumbhajee was raised to the throne in 1695, and died in June, 1698, leaving two sons, Sivajee and Sumbhajee, by his two wives, Tara Baee and

Rajis Baee. The former succeeded his father, but evincing symptoms of insanity some years after, he was deposed and confined by his own mother in 1703, who raised his half-brother Sumbhajee to the Musnud at Kolapoor, which had become the seat of government of the Mahratta empire. Aurungzeb died in 1707, but previously gave Sahoo liberty to go to Satara and claim his inheritance. He was for some time opposed to his aunt Tara Baee, a talented, violent, and ambitious woman, but Sahoo Raja at length consented to share the possessions of the family with Sumbhajee, who was permitted to retain Kolapoor, and all the country south of the Warna and Krishna, while to Sahoo was left all to the north of these rivers. Tara Baee retired to Kolapoor, and lived to an extreme old age, both she and her step-son dying in the same year, 1760.

Sahoo Raja having been bred in all the effeminacy of a Mahomedan seraglio, was of too indolent and luxurious habits to manage affairs of government. Happy to be freed from its drudgery, he left it to his ministers, of whom the Peshwa, then Balajee Wiswanath, was the chief, both in rank and talent. He was succeeded by Bajeerow Bullal, to whom succeeded his son Balajee, denominated Nana Sahib. Sahoo Raja died without issue, 27th December, 1749, and by his will empowered the Peshwas, in hereditary succession, to conduct in future the affairs of the Mahratta empire, on condition of keeping up the dignity of his house. From that day the subversion of the power of the house of Satara was complete, and that of the Peshwas established. The Peshwa then brought forward Ram Raja, the son of Sivajee, and nephew of the reigning Raja of Kolapoor, and caused him to be adopted as the son of Sahoo, agreeably to the understood intention of the latter prince. Ram Raja, having no children, after being married many years, adopted, in 1777, at the suggestion of Nana Furnawees, a youth of the family of the Desmookhs of Wavee, and, dying in the following year, this youth was raised, in 1778, to the Musnud of Satara, by the name of Sahoo the Second.

The semblance of respect was still maintained towards the

reigning, or rather pageant, princes, and a guard of honour, consisting of five hundred horse, was appointed by the Peshwa to escort and to watch him, but his expenses were limited, as well as the range of his excursions in the neighbourhood of his capital. All reports of war, and peace, and the result of campaigns, however, were regularly submitted to him; and while the creation of new, and the nomination to the succession of hereditary, offices and estates, derived confirmation from him alone, the Peshwa himself was not deemed exempt from accepting this token of homage.

The revolution which succeeded on the death of Madhoo Rao, at Poona, in October, 1795, afforded the Raja an opening to emancipation, of which he did not fail to avail himself, and seizing the person employed to control him, encouraged his brother, Chutr Singh, to raise troops and seek for foreign aid. The troops which the Raja had collected were attacked by superior numbers under Purusram Bhou, an experienced and popular commander, when many of his highness's gallant kinsmen were killed and wounded maintaining a hopeless resistance. Sahoo the Second became henceforward a close prisoner in the fort of Satara, and died 4th May, 1808, leaving three sons, of whom the eldest was Purtab Singh, who now reigns. The war of 1817-18 having placed the whole of the dominions of the Peshwa at the disposal of the British Government, a tract was reserved sufficient for the maintenance, in comfort and dignity, of the Raja of Satara. Purtab Singh was therefore raised to the throne in February, 1818, but as he was wholly ignorant of business, from the seclusion in which he had been brought up, the reserved territories were, in the meantime, placed under the management of British agents. The Raja, who had been taught to expect the control of his affairs, as soon as he was qualified to exercise it, by his assiduity soon became so, and the entire powers of the state were formally delivered over to him, in April, 1822.

The whole territory under the authority of the Raja yields a revenue of thirty lacs of rupees, of which about half is assigned to Jagheerdars, Enamdars, &c. and the rest, realizing a net revenue of sixteen lacs, is under the Raja's own management, assisted by the Resident. His military force, besides the contingents of his Jagheerdars, consists of seven hundred horse, Mahrattas and Mahomedans, of which two hundred form the Paga, or household troop, and four thousand infantry, which are employed in revenue and police duties, and as garrisons to forts. These are, exclusive of the Shetsundee, a hereditary militia, which may be reckoned two thousand more. They serve by turns six months in the year, and only one half of the whole is, therefore, effective. His domestic expenses cost four lacs of rupees annually, including five thousand five hundred a-month to his brother, Appa Sahib, and a like sum to maintain the surviving members of the family of his late brother, who died in 1821. The civil establishment exceeds three lacs of rupees at Satara, and a sum of one lac and a half is devoted to the improvement of the country in public buildings and roads. The hill forts in which garrisons were maintained at Satara, Purlee, Wusuntgurh, Purtabgurh, Nandgeree and Wurdungurh, and seventeen other forts within the same territory, have been dismantled.

The Jagheerdars who furnish contingents, are the descendants of the chief leaders under Sivajee, and the number of horse they are required to serve with is as follows :—

	Horse.
The Raja of Akulkot,*	100

* RAJA OF AKULKOT. The first Raja was the son of the Patel of Parud, in the district of Sewnee in Gungthuree, who closed his village against the troops of the Raja Sahoo, and fell in its defence; this occurred in 1707, when Sahoo was on his way to Satara to claim his inheritance. The Patel's four sons, with their mother, were, on the capture of the village, carried to Sahoo, who took one of the boys, then twelve years of age, under his protection, giving him the name of Futih Singh, in allusion to the victory which occasioned it. He afterwards was adopted by Sahoo, assumed the title of Raja, and had Jagheers conferred on him for the support of 500 horse. He died in 1760, without issue, and his widow was allowed to adopt one of the nephews of her husband from Parud, who succeeded to the estates of Akulkot only, and died in 1789, leaving two sons, the eldest of whom, Futih Singh, succeeded his father, and died in April, 1823, and his son, Mallojee Rao, died in 1828. The elder son of the latter, named Shahjee, a child then eight or nine years of age, now possesses the estates of Akulkot.

In 1827, a census was taken of the Perguna of Akulkot, when it was

	Horse.
The Chief of Phultun,*	75
The Chief of Jhut,†	50
The Punt Suchew, commuted for a money payment,‡ .	15
Khan Mahomed, descendant of Shaikh Meeran of Waee,	25
Total of the contingents of Jagheerdars,	265

found to contain 12,740 families, distributed into 101 towns and villages, exhibiting a clear revenue of 1,50,000 rupees. Mallojee Raja was not above bettering himself by traffic; but he does not appear to have left much wealth. Besides the Akulkot Perguna, the family receive 35,000 rupees from various sources,—the customs of Poona, and the Chouth of certain villages in the Satara and Nizam's districts. The expenses of the contingent are 30,000 rupees per annum, so that a large balance remains for personal expenses.

* BUJABA NIMBHALKUR, styled Naik, and Phultun Rao. The districts, called Phultun Des, situated on the south bank of the Neera River, have been held by this family in Jagheer for probably some centuries: its revenue is about two lacs of rupees. The Naiks of Phultun were enterprising leaders, under the kings of Beejapoor, and among the most active opponents that Sivajee had to contend with. Nor did this family join the cause of their religion till many years after Sivajee's death, though connected with him by marriage. The late chief, Jan Rao, died in 1825, at an old age, without heirs, but leaving two widows. He left a paper of adoption in favour of Bujaba Naik, the present chief, which was confirmed by H. H. the Raja, with the concurrence of the British Government.

† DUFFLAY, Ram Rao Chohan, the Jagheerdar of Jhut. An ancestor of this chief was an active partizan in the service of the kings of Beejapoor, in the time of Sivajee. It does not appear at what time he joined his countrymen. The present chief has, besides his hereditary freehold estates, which are rated at 19,162 rupees, Jagheers rated at 1,48,101 rupees; including, however, alienations, on account of religious establishments, amounting to 9,115 rupees, and money payments to relations, amounting to 11,250 rupees.

‡ The PUNT SUCHEW. Chimnajee Shunkur died in October, 1827, leaving three widows, who were allowed to adopt the present Punt, Rugonath Rao Chimnajee. The family are of the Yejurwedee sect of Bramins, and lineally descended from Sunkrajee Narraen Gaudèkur, the Suchew of the great Sivajee. The Jagheer comprises about five hundred whole villages and shares, situated principally in the mountainous country west of Poona. A line drawn, commencing a few miles west of Poona, through the forts of Toong and Tenkona down to Nagotna, and thence running south, passing through Roh-Astummee, and along the bottom of the hills to Rohira, thence east by north to Seerwul, and thence north to Poona, will define it. The tract contains five forts belonging to the Suchew, viz. Rajgurh, Torna, Rohira, Teekona,

THE GOVERNMENT OF KOLAPOOR.

On the execution of Sumbhajee, as noticed in the account of the Raja of Satara, his son, Sahoo, was declared his successor by a council of the nation, and his uncle, Raja Ram, the son of Sivajee by another wife, was appointed Regent during the minority and absence of his nephew. Raja Ram died about 1698, leaving two widows, Tara Baee and Rajis Baee, the former of whom assumed the powers of Regent, and declaring Sahoo an impostor, prepared to resist his claims to the succession. Tara Baee retained her usurped power until 1712, when her own party, at the head of whom was the Amat, or prime minister, put her in confinement, and raised Sumbhajee, her step-son, the son of Rajis Baee, to the Gadee.* It was no doubt the policy of Aurungzeb to foster distractions among the Mahrattas, as contributing to the strength of the Mahomedans, to whom they would become an easy conquest. He, therefore, liberated Sahoo, and sent him to contest for his inheritance. The nation was divided upon the claims of the rival cousins, and both had also their supporters among the neighbouring princes. At length, in 1730, the camp of Sumbhajee was surprised under Panalla, by the army of his

Toong, and Bhorup; and the following valleys,—Rohir Khoreh, 42 villages; Heerdus Mawul, 53; Velwur Khoreh, 32; Goonjun Mawul, 81; Seerwul, 40; Kanund Khoreh, 33; Moosee Khoreh, 71; Mooté Khoreh, 19; Pawun Mawul, 52; Khereh-Barreh, 39: total in the mountains, 462 villages. In the Konkan he has Nagotna, and four other villages. The amount of the Suchew's revenue, including a hereditary claim of six per cent upon the revenues of the original territory of Sivajee, which alone realizes to him about 70,000 rupees, is about four lacs of rupees per annum. He has no other service to perform besides attending the Raja at the Dussera; but he pays an annual sum of 15,000 rupees instead of his party of horse, as settled at his adoption and investiture; besides, 5500 towards the Feel Khana, (elephant stud,) which was settled during Chimnajee Shunkur's time. The duty of Suchew was that of Secretary of State.

* The same transactions are differently related in the Annals of Satara:—the reader must determine the preference.

rival, and many of the chief persons of his party being captured, a treaty was the consequence, by which the Mahratta territory was divided into two distinct States, and the boundaries specified.

Sumbhajee died in 1760 without issue, and with him the line of the great Sivajee became extinct. His wife was made to adopt a son, who was named Sivajee, from the family of Khunwutta,* and she continued to conduct the administration in his name. During this minority, piracy by sea, and plundering excursions by land, rendered this State a scourge to its neighbours. The first being principally practised against English vessels, an expedition from Bombay, in 1765, proceeded against and reduced the fort of Malwan, which was restored to Kolapoor, on receiving indemnification for the past, and security for the future. To stop their disposition to predatory excursions, the Peshwa invaded the Kolapoor State, and deprived it of several districts, which were added to the Jagheer of the Putwurdhuns. These lands were afterwards restored, when a rival party at Poona gained the ascendancy in the administration; but from this period may be dated the commencement of that petty warfare with the Putwurdhun family, in which they had been engaged until British ascendancy put a stop to them. At a later period, Nana Furnawees found no difficulty in inciting the Raja of Kolapoor to attack the Putwurdhun possessions, and the Putwurdhuns acted with vigour against Kolapoor, at the instigation of the Peshwa. The latter, however, was, notwithstanding, the inveterate but secret enemy of the Putwurdhun family; and on the death of Purusram Bhow, its principal chief, in battle against the forces of Kolapoor, the Peshwa prepared to crush that powerful family. This discovery being made by the son of Purusram Bhow, who had succeeded his father, had nearly reduced the Raja of Kolapoor to extremity, and saved the political existence of the latter.

The Kolapoor State had carried on war with its neighbour of Sawunt Waree during twenty-three years; but both these

* See note at page 130.

States practised piracy to a very great extent, and though the former was punished for it in 1804, it did not seem disposed to relinquish the advantages derived from it, until 1812, when the British Government felt obliged to fit out an expedition against Malwan, the principal seaport of Kolapoor, which was captured, and has since been retained.

By the articles of agreement, dated October 1, 1812, the British Government, in consideration of the cession of the harbour of Malwan, with the lands and forts dependent upon it, takes the Kolapoor State under its protection. At the same time, the districts of Chikoree and Menowly, the claim to which had been the cause of a long war between the Poona and Kolapoor Governments, were relinquished to the former. When, however, the war broke out between the British and Poona Governments, the Raja of Kolapoor remained faithful to his engagements, and these districts were given over to him on the restoration of tranquillity.

Shahjee, the present Raja, succeeded his half-brother, Sumbhajee, styled Abba Sahib, who was shot in July, 1821, by a chief of the family of Mohitay. They were both sons of Sivajee, adopted from the Kunwutta family. The present Raja has married six wives, of whom five are still living, but he has no family. His brother left a son, during whose minority the Government was to have been carried on by his mother and the minister; but he is since dead. The oppressive conduct of the Raja towards certain of his Jagheerdars, who held their Jagheers under guarantee of the British Government, and various aggressions, led to a campaign against him in 1827, when the former were better secured in their Jagheers, and the Raja ceded Chikoree and Menowly, which he had forfeited by his conduct, to meet the expenses of the war. His military establishment was limited by the treaty to 400 horse and 800 infantry, exclusive of weak garrisons to forts. The revenues are rated at thirteen lacs of rupees, exclusive of the Jagheer lands, which may be half as much more.

The unsettled disposition of the Raja, however, did not permit him to remain quiet; he again raised fresh levies, commenced aggressions against his neighbours, and a British force was again sent to oppose him. On the 15th October, 1828, he was obliged to surrender the forts of Kolapoor, and four others. He was allowed to retain his government, but hereafter a British force is to be stationed in the vicinity of his capital, which, by checking his naturally turbulent disposition, may preserve him on his Musnud.

THE GOVERNMENT OF OODIPOOR.

The Oodipoor family boasts an antiquity of some thousand years, and a descent from the celestial Ramchunder. But though the highest in rank, it is but the third in power or resources, of the states of Rajpootana. It is fruitless to seek for any accurate information respecting a people whose history is founded in a great measure upon the enthusiastic narratives of bards, who, by their marvellous traditions, draw largely on the credulity of wondering auditors. The story of the existence of Bappa Rawul of this line, who reigned at Chitoor over the whole of Rajpootana, about A. D. 134, is also found in the legends of the south of India, some of the princes of which boast the same proud origin as the Rajpoots. His father having been murdered, Bappa Rawul owed his preservation in infancy to the fidelity of a Bheel, who carried him away, and bred him up in his cave. In boyhood, like Timoor, or like young Norval in the fiction of our own country, he shewed himself to be the first in enterprise among the shepherd youth, who elected him their king. The ceremony of investiture was performed by a young Bheel associate drawing blood from his own finger, and using it to mark the Teeka upon the forehead. This remarkable ceremonial is still kept up, a Bheel being the principal actor in the investiture, and the material used for the Teeka being his own blood. But a more remarkable circumstance is, that when the Rana of Oodipoor has occasion to pass the Muhee river, an individual of a tribe descended from a Chohan Rajpoot, by a Bheel mother, is sacrificed, his throat being cut, and his body thrown into the river. This sacrifice, it is said, has once been performed during the lifetime of the present Rana.

When Bappa Rawul attained manhood, he sought a wider field for the operation of his valour and talent. After establishing his fame, he became connected by marriage with the royal race of Malwa, and having founded an extensive empire, died at the patriarchal age of a hundred years.

Samarsi, the twenty-third king of his race, joined the army of the Prithwi-Raja, (who was his father-in-law,) in opposing the Tartar invaders, and fell in battle, with all the chiefs of his family and nation, about 1193. He left two sons, Bharatsee and Bhemsee, who lived and died in exile, but the son of the former was restored to Chitoor, where his descendants reigned through a long uninterrupted line, till the parricidal murder of the reigning prince by his illegitimate son, who usurped the throne, in the sixteenth century, brought about a new era in its history. Oodee Singh, a posthumous child of the murdered Rana, was reared in exile; but in the school of adversity he learned the lessons which directed his native valour to success, and enabled him to recover his throne, and to restore freedom to his country, whence he drove the usurper, who afterwards established himself at Serowi, where his descendants now reign. Oodee Singh founded the city of Oodipoor about 1541, and made it the seat of his government, after the capture and destruction of Chitoor by Akbar, in 1567. Such is the legendary history of Oodipoor.

The repeated invasions of Mahadjee Sindhia to levy tribute on his own account, or by invitation from the Rana to coerce his powerful feudatories, first depressed his authority. These potent chiefs had not only assumed independence, but usurped the Rana's own lands, and the measures taken to reduce them by foreign aid, which, from the strength of their castles, was not always successful, dissolved the connection between them and their superior—the struggle terminating in the degradation of the Rana's authority, and his becoming a tributary to the Mahrattas. In 1768, Sindhia obtained from the Rana, in commutation of tribute, the half of the revenues of the districts of Jawud, Jeerun, Neemuch, and Morwun; but in 1774 he ejected the Rana's officers from the management of these districts, and retained them for himself. About the same time, the districts of Bampoora, Rampoora, Mulhargurh, and the tribute of Purtaubgurh were given to Holkur. The revenue of the lands thus alienated by Sindhia and Holkur, amounted to thirty lacs of rupees, to which may be added seven lacs, being the aggregate tribute of the collective body of feudal chiefs which was at a later period levied by the officers commanding the troops of these states for themselves. But this was not the worst feature of the Mahratta alliance, as Ameer Khan and Sindhia had billeted their Patan and Rohilla auxiliaries on the country. These concurrent causes had reduced the Rana to comparative poverty, his revenues being quite insufficient to meet his ordinary expenses. This state of anarchy prevailed throughout the country, in which fields were wasted and cities ruined, when the British army approached it in 1817, and the Rana's personal character being little adapted to take full advantage of the favourable turn of affairs, which the overawing attitude of the British power at that time gave to all the depressed states of Rajpootana, a decided interference was requisite to enable this state to recover itself. The Thakoors, or nobles, were convened and prevailed on to restore the territories usurped from the Rana's demesne, and the Rana engaged on his part to respect and maintain their hereditary lands, and preserve to them all their constitutional privileges.

No regular tribute was payable either to Sindhia or Holkur, and the usurpations of the latter, amounting in annual revenue to 14,75,000 rupees, reverted to their original state by the treaty of Mundissoor.

The superiority of the family continues to be admitted, and all matters of cast or precedence being referred to them, their decision on these points is absolute. When the legitimacy of a successor to the Gadee of any of the neighbouring princes or chiefs is disputed,—a very common case in central India,—the Rana is referred to, and if he consents to eat with the individual in question, his legitimacy and consequent right to succeed is considered as fully established. The Rajas of

Joudpoor and Jeypoor, and all the neighbouring petty Rajas, were originally dependent on the Oodipoor family, and presented at the Dusserah their Nuzurs, either through a Vakeel or in person.

An alliance by marriage with the family is the highest honour to which a Rajpoot prince can aspire; and the war which commenced in 1806-7 between the Rajas of Jeypoor and Joudpoor, both of whom advanced pretensions to the hand of Kishen Koour, a princess of that family, too celebrated for her beauty and tragical end, made Rajpootana for some years equally the prey of foreign invasion and civil war. To restore peace, her parents were obliged, in 1810, to consent that poison should be administered to her, which the victim, for the sake of her country, unhesitatingly drank. The sacrifice was, however, useless, as it brought no peace to Rajpootana.

By the treaty dated 13th January, 1818, one-fourth of the revenues are payable to the British Government for five years, and three-eighths from that time forward. The territory is fertile, and as rich as the same space in any part of India, but great part is mortgaged to Shroffs.

In January, 1832, the Governor-General invited the princes of Rajpootana to a general congress at Ajmeer, at which, among the rest, appeared the Rana of Oodipoor, whose ancestors never had attended upon the emperors, though forced to yield an unwilling submission. He did not consider his honour compromised by taking this opportunity of evincing his gratitude to a government which had raised him from a state of misery and destitution, to the enjoyment of a considerable revenue, and to nearly the whole of the territories possessed by his immediate ancestors.

FEUDAL CHIEFS OF OODIPOOR.

THE constitution of all the Rajpoot states resembles the feudal system, and an account of one is an account of all. The Rajpoot feudality has arisen out of the custom of allotting lands to the support of younger sons, and individuals of merit, who hold them on the common feudal tenure of military service, and as, while they continue faithful, the lands so alienated cannot be resumed, the crown lands continue to decrease. There are sixteen superior chiefs, or nobles, belonging to Oodipoor, who are entitled to take precedence of all the rest, but there are three others who have acquired greater power, and two of them are royal Rajas, *i. e.* they or their predecessors were created by the emperor. These are the Rajas of Shahpoora and Buneera, both possessing fortified towns of considerable extent, especially the former ; the third is Surdar Singh, a nominal nephew of the Rana, his father and the Rana having been cousins. He is heir to the Gadee after Jowan Singh, the son of the present Rana.

LIST of the Sixteen principal Chiefs of Mewar, arranged according to their Families.

Family.	Chief Towns.	Title.	Names.	Revenue.
Chundowut,	Saloomber,	Rawut,	Puddum Singh,	84,000
———	Deoghur,	———	Nhar Singh,	80,000
———	Baygoo,	Sawai,	Keshow Singh,	2,00,000
———	Arnait,	Rawat,	Salem Singh,	60,000
Suctowut,	Bheendur,	Maharaj,	ZoorawurSingh,	64,000
———	Bhansee,	Rawul,	Nhar Singh,	40,000
Rhatore,	Bednore,	Thakoor,	Jhod Singh,	80,000
———	Ganowra,	———	Ajeet Singh,	1,00,000
Jallah,	Doulwarra,	Raj,	Kullain Singh,	1,00,000
———	Gogoonda,	Raj,	Chutter Singh,	50,000
———	Burra Sadree,	Raj,	Keerut Singh,	92,000
Chowan,	Palsora,	Rawul,	Lall Singh,	40,000
———	Kotario,	———	Mokun Singh,	80,000
Poohur,	Beejolia,	Sawai,	Karsoodas,	45,000
Rhanowut Surungdeo,	Kanore,	Rawul,	Ajeet Singh,	95,000
Chowan,	Baidla,	Rawul,	Kesree Singh,	1,00,000
			Total Rupees,	13,10,000

The chiefs of inferior rank are thirty-two in number. The principal of these is Doolee Singh, adopted son of Ajeet Singh, chief of Askeena, who figured as the instrument of

Ameer Khan in proposing to the Rana the murder of his daughter, Kishen Koour, in 1810: the others are Ameer Singh, and Jowan Singh. All these belong to the tribe of Chundowut, and are cadets of the Saloomber family. The last mentioned family is descended from an elder brother of one of the Rawuls of Chitoor, called Chundoo Singh, and hence the name of the tribe. He was disinherited, by consenting to an arrangement to enable his father, one of the former Rawuls of Chitoor, when far advanced in years, to marry a daughter of the Jeypoor Raja. This was, that the issue by this marriage should succeed to the Gadee, and that the claims of his son by the former marriage should be set aside. From the very advanced age of the father, there was but little chance of a child being born; but a son, nevertheless, made his appearance, and as his legitimacy was not questioned, he succeeded to the Gadee. This is noticed to shew how the line of succession is sometimes managed.

In 1822, the fiscal lands were rated at Rupees 10,00,000
The lands now held by the sixteen nobles were,
sixty years ago, rated at 13,00,000
The inferior feudal chiefs, *about* 30,00,000

The feudal chiefs are obliged to send three horsemen to join the army for every thousand rupees of land revenue, so that the feudality alone can furnish twelve thousand cavalry.

THE GOVERNMENT OF JEYPOOR OR AMBER.

THIS state is the most considerable of the Rajpoots. The family is the next in rank, and equal in purity of blood or antiquity, to that of Oodipoor, from which it is originally descended, but it now possesses greater temporal power than the latter. The legends of the family record a long line of ancestors, but this account of them shall commence only with Mirza Raja Jeysingh, the founder of the city of Jeypoor. This Prince, equally celebrated as a statesman and a soldier, was selected by Aurungzeb to command the army of the Deccan, against Sivajee, then in the full career of success, and who had thwarted the imperial leaders then acting against him. The skill of the Mirza Raja, and the strength of his army, proved too much for Sivajee, who, after a few unsuccessful actions, entered into a treaty, by which he yielded up a great part of his conquests, acknowledged himself a vassal of the empire, and agreed to visit the Emperor at Delhi. Jeysingh then proceeded to reduce Beejapoor, in the first invasion of which he received the co-operation of his late antagonist, Sivajee, along with his Mahrattas.

While the operations proceeded against Beejapoor, Sivajee visited the Emperor, who received him not so warmly as the pledges given warranted him to expect. He therefore contrived to effect his escape from Delhi, and returning to the Deccan, succeeded in recovering all his former possessions, the re-occupation of which the Mirza Raja had not a sufficient number of troops to prevent. The bad success of Jeysingh, at this juncture, made his fidelity to be suspected, and he was, in 1667, recalled to Hindoostan. He became discontented, and his boasting and murmurs of unrequited services, induced the Emperor to tempt his youngest son with the offer of the succession, on condition of despatching his parent. This he did in 1693, by poison, but he was disappointed in the expected reward, as he only received a small Jagheer. The two elder sons of the Mirza Raja succeeded each other on the Musnud, and died after short reigns.

In 1699, Jeysingh II, the celebrated astronomer, came to the throne, and founded Jeypoor in 1728, from which time the principality of Amber became known by the name of Jeypoor. Jeysingh was appointed by the Emperor to the viceroyalty of Agra and Malwa, but forming an intimacy with the great Bajerow, he was induced, in 1734, to transfer to him the latter province, with the concurrence of the Emperor. He also successfully used his influence to obtain for the Mahrattas the Chouth and Surdeshmookhee of the whole imperial territories, which were formally surrendered to them by the Emperor Mahomed Shah in 1743, in which year Jeysingh died. The Mahrattas, from this time, acquired a pretext for the periodical invasion of Rajpootana, but Jeypoor was preserved from their visitations during the lifetime of Bajeerow.

These annual visitations established at length a right to tribute, which was fixed with this state at 1,60,000 rupees, and assigned in equal shares to Sindhia, Holkur, and Puar. This continued to be levied until 1761, when the battle of Paniput broke, for a season, the strength of the Mahrattas. Holkur had become the assignee of the tribute, and in 1768, he entered the Jeypoor territory, to levy the arrears. The amount received by him on this account was sixty lacs, together with a cession of various districts, including Rampoora.

Mahadjee Sindhia appeared suddenly at Jeypoor, in 1786, and demanded the arrears of tribute due to the Emperor, whose authority he produced, fixing the first instalment at sixty lacs. The Rana being unprepared for resistance, paid part of the demand and promised the rest. In the meantime, the principal Rajpoot chiefs confederated, and when Sindhia's army appeared to claim the balance, it was attacked and defeated. This led to more formidable preparations on both sides, and an obstinately contested battle ensued, in which the Rajpoots were again successful. Mahadjee Sindhia, however, persevered in his attempts to bring the Rajpoots again under the Mahratta subjection, and the sanguinary battles of Patun and Mairta so far effected this object, that the states of Jeypoor and Joudpoor became thenceforth his tributaries.

The first British intercourse with the Jeypoor state was in 1798, when an envoy was sent to the Raja, Purtaub Singh, to procure the surrender of the notorious Vizier Ali, who had taken refuge at Jeypoor. This was effected only under the stipulation that he should not be put to death. The next intercourse was during the operations in 1803 against Sindhia, when a treaty was concluded with the Raja, Dheeruj, by Lord Lake, in December of that year, by which Jeypoor was taken under British protection. The terms guaranteed his territories against external enemies, exempted him from tribute to any state; in return for which his troops were to co-operate with the British when required. Favourable though this treaty was to the Jeypoor Raja, he nevertheless failed in his engagements shortly after its conclusion, by preparing to join a general confederacy of the Mahrattas against the British Government, and was consequently excluded from the pale of its protection. Subsequently he performed some essential services, and rendered himself obnoxious to the great Mahratta powers, but the policy of the times did not admit of continuing the alliance, or renewing engagements with him.

Three years after this, the countries of Jeypoor and Joudpoor were torn by civil commotions, which continued several years, in which Sindhia, Holkur, and Ameer Khan, took part on one or other side, and subjected the country to unceasing ravages. After the termination of this war, Ameer Khan's lawless bands of Patans were quartered upon the Jeypoor lands, under pretext of collecting the tribute payable to Holkur. They occupied every position of consequence in the country, and there was no where any protection against their merciless exactions. This state of anarchy induced the Raja to endeavour to renew the connection with Britain, and in 1816 the authorities in England, regretting the policy which had abandoned the Rajpoot states to their own resources, were desirous of acceding to the views of the Raja of Jeypoor, and of taking him again under protection. Negotiations, having this object in view, were therefore commenced, and a fixed tribute of fifteen lacs was offered to the British Government. But though at this time the Raja had evinced so much solicitude for the alliance, he was, nevertheless, from the distracted state of his councils, the last of the Rajpoot chiefs to accede to the confederacy, or to send agents to Delhi, in 1818. At length, the fear of being excluded from the same benefits that had been accorded to the neighbouring Rajpoot states, which had readily accepted the alliance, induced the different factions severally to send an envoy to Delhi, and a treaty was at length completed, on the 2d of April, 1818, with that party which was in possession of the government. The articles embraced, as usual, protection against external enemies, acknowledgment of supremacy, and tribute. The latter was fixed with reference to the state of the country, and its prospective improvement. Having been afflicted with a dreadful scourge for many years, in the annual visitation of the Pindarries and Ameer Khan, and the insubordination of the feudatory chiefs, who had usurped many of the crown lands, payment of tribute was excused for the first year. The second year the amount was fixed at four lacs, increasing every year, until, in the sixth year, it was agreed to be eight lacs, and to continue at that sum annually ever after, with the addition of five-sixteenths of the excess revenue above forty lacs, being the estimated amount which the crown revenue might attain to, and by progressive improvement exceed. The feudal and ministerial lands amount to nearly as much more, and the tribute payable by lesser states to Jeypoor amount to four lacs. The revenue of the fisc was formerly reckoned at one crore of rupees, and it is supposed capable of being increased to eighty lacs under proper management. The military force of the Durbar is reckoned at 8000 infantry and 10,000 cavalry. The contingents of the feudatories form another force.

On the conclusion of the treaty, a British agent proceeded to aid in the restoration of order and tranquillity in the country, a task of no ordinary difficulty. The conquests of the Mahrattas, and annual visitations of the Pindarries, left the Raja no power beyond the walls of Jeypoor, the whole country being in the occupation of the lawless bands of Ameer Khan, and the feudatories living independent in their fortresses. An article of the treaty with Ameer Khan stipulated for the surrender of his cannon and other arms, and it was necessary to move a force against the commander of his troops to enforce its observance, and his evacuation of the Jeypoor country. This being effected, the feudatories were convened, and agreements were entered into securing them in their legitimate rights and possessions, while the lands which they had usurped were restored to the Raja.

The Raja Juggeth Singh died in December, 1818, and a successor was placed upon the Gadee by one of the deceased's profligate companions; but the British Government interfered in favour of the rightful heir, and hence the first benefit which resulted from the British connection was a permanent settlement of the succession without appeal to arms.

GOVERNMENT OF JOUDPOOR, OR MARWAR.

The Joudpoor state is one of the three of the first class in Rajpootana. Tradition ascribes its foundation to Joda, a scion of the house of Oodipoor, who, about 1460, made the city his capital which now bears his name. His successors carried their dominion over neighbouring lands, and Joudpoor had become a considerable state, when the Emperor Akbar, about 1570, invaded Rajpootana, and compelled the Rajpoots to become tributaries to the empire. The independence of Joudpoor was not, however, completely annihilated until 1584, when the Raja was obliged to furnish his contingent to serve with the imperial forces.

Raja Jeswunt Singh, of this house, was one of Aurungzeb's best generals. He was sent into the Deccan with a strong reinforcement, in 1660, to aid in the war against Sivajee, whose continued success in his efforts to achieve Mahratta independence called forth, as his opponents, the best leaders of the empire. Jeswunt Singh was appointed commander-in-chief under the Viceroy Sultaun Mauzim; but not being more successful in the conduct of the war than his predecessors, he, as well as Sultaun Mauzim, were recalled, when Raja Jeysingh of Jeypoor was sent to supersede the former in 1665. A doubt of the loyalty of Jeysingh having taken possession of the Emperor, he was recalled also, when Jeswunt Singh was reappointed, in 1667, together with Sultaun Mauzim, in the same relative situations as before; but the continued success of Sivajee occasioned their final recall in 1671. Jeswunt Singh died while on an expedition to Cabul, in 1681, when the Emperor Aurungzeb directed that the children of this most able and attached of all his officers should be circumcised. The horror which the measure created roused the Rajpoots, and numbers perished in the contests which ensued. The family were in the end exiled from their country until the death of Aurungzeb, when the distractions which followed that event enabled Ajeet Singh, the grandson of Jeswunt, to recover his hereditary possessions. This gallant prince, whom the imperial forces could not overcome in battle, fell a victim to the ambition of his own children, the two elder of whom, instigated by the wicked administration who guided affairs at Delhi, conspired against him, and compassed the death of their parent. The elder son, Abhee Singh, was rewarded for the parricide with the viceroyalty of Gujerat, in addition to his paternal possessions; and the second son, Bukht Singh, by whose hand the dagger was struck into his father's breast during sleep, had a grant of Jalore, a district of five hundred and fifty villages on the southern frontier of Marwar, the revenue of which was equal to the possessions to which his brother succeeded.

Abhee Singh entered upon the government of Gujerat in 1731, and commenced it inauspiciously by the assassination, at a conference, of Peelajee Gaekwar, who at that time was commander-in-chief of Mahrattas in the province. The benefit which he had calculated upon did not ensue from his treachery, as Dumajee Gaekwar, the son of the murdered chief, proved equally as enterprising a leader as his father. Dumajee being unable to make head against the imperialists in Gujerat, invaded and laid waste the country of Marwar, up to the gates of Joudpoor, a scheme which fully succeeded, as it obliged Abhee Singh to return for the defence of his own dominions. Subsequently he continued to hold Gujerat by deputy until 1736, when he was superseded by the ancestor of the present Nuwab of Cambay. About 1750 Abhee Singh died, and his two sons quarrelled about the respective allotments of their father's property. The Peshwa being invited by one of the brothers to arbitrate their dispute, Jyapa Sindhia was deputed for that purpose, but was cut off by assassins employed by the rival brother. This atrocity was avenged by the Peshwa, but more effectually thirty years after by Mahadjee Sindhia, the brother of the murdered chief, when the state of Joudpoor became tributary to the Mahrattas. It would not consist with the nature of the present work to enter into a detail of all the anarchy and misery which were heaped upon this portion of Rajpootana during the next fifty years.

In 1804, when the British army operated in Hindoostan, Raja Bheem, the descendant of Abhee Singh, who had destroyed, by poison or steel, all his other relations, died while besieging Raja Maun, in Jalore, and the latter in consequence succeeded to the throne of Joudpoor.

The British alliance was offered to Raja Maun by Lord Lake, but as he refused to ratify the treaty concluded with his agent, he was left to his own resources, and his country became a prey for many years after to lawless bands of faithless allies, as well as of open enemies. The Princess of Raja Bheem had been left pregnant, and was secretly delivered of a child who was named Dhokul Singh, whom she sent to the chief of Pokurna, who two years after presented him to the assembled feudal chiefs. This party did not prove sufficiently powerful at this time, and he was therefore sent for concealment to the chiefs of Shekhawuti in the desert. There Dhokul Singh remained until 1807, when the war between the Rajas of Jeypoor and Joudpoor for the hand of the Princess of Oodipoor gave another opportunity of bringing him forward in aid of the cause of the former. He was, however, cut off; and his principal adherent, the chief of Pokurna being assassinated, Raja Maun was established, without a competitor to dispute his title, in the government of Joudpoor, in 1809.

Shortly after, Raja Maun, dreading conspiracies, it is said, against his life, became at first abstracted, and afterwards assuming imbecility, the resentment of his enemies was neutralized, and his son was associated in the government under the title of Regent: he was a dissipated youth, and a fit tool in the hands of a faction which ruled in his name. Great part of the Marwar territory had been alienated in commutation of tribute by the Mahratta states of Sindhia and Holkur; but since the Rajpoot war of 1806-7, in which the military leaders of these states took opposite sides, the whole of Rajpootana for eleven years became the prey of a lawless soldiery. Such was the condition of Marwar in 1817, when the British army advanced towards the haunts of the Pindarries, and invited the Rajpoot States to accept the protection of the British government, and assist in the annihilation of predatory power. The Regent of

Joudpoor, with whom, as the acknowledged head of the state, the negotiations had commenced, died before the treaty was signed, and his father Maun Singh threw off the mask of insanity and resumed the government. The treaty, by guaranteeing to him the uncontrolled administration of his country, and security against any internal interference, had an effect which was not anticipated. The Raja, who had performed a part for a number of years, in order to save himself from being the object of conspiracies, now gave loose to all his smothered passions, and proved himself revengeful, vindictive, and avaricious. In eighteen months after his resumption of the government, he had used his power to cut off, by poison or otherwise, all the civil and military chiefs whose disposition towards him had been unmasked during his assumed part, and whom he had distinguished as his enemies. He confiscated property to the amount of one million of English money. The British alliance, while it secured him against external enemies, did equally so without specification against his own subjects, who would otherwise have done themselves justice.

The government revenues of Marwar amount to ten lacs of rupees. The feudal lands may realize three times this amount, though the former are rated on the old records of the government at 29,45,000 rupees, and the latter at 50,00,000 rupees. If, therefore, the feudal array is to be calculated at one horseman and two foot soldiers for every 1000 rupees of revenue, the feudal contingents alone should form a body of 5000 cavalry and 10,000 infantry. The Raja's own troops are principally Rohillas and Patans, for his policy is to have foreigners as a counterpoise against the native levies of his own feudatories. His household force consists of 3500 foot, and 1500 horse, and a park of 25 guns. He has also a body of Bishen-Swamees, consisting of 700 foot and 300 horse, with a small rocket corps. The Raja, by the treaty, is bound to furnish a contingent of fifteen hundred horse to serve with the British force; but when necessary, all his forces would be called upon, excepting such a portion as might be requisite to secure the internal tranquillity of the country. No tribute is paid by the state to the British government for itself; but it receives the former tribute due to Sindhia, amounting to 1,00,389 rupees, and pays it over to that chief, preventing thereby all occasion for his interference. A closer connection with Joudpoor is not of any political importance, its remote situation and its restricted foreign relations rendering a general control over its political measures quite sufficient to ensure the preservation of tranquillity.

THE GOVERNMENT OF KOTA.

The territories of Kota and Boondi were at a former period under one dominion, until the ambition of a younger brother, supported by the Rana of Oodipoor, apparently the feudal superior of the state, obtained half the lands; and hence the State of Kota, the ruler over which was allowed to assume the title of Maha-Rao, or great prince. By another account Rao Ruttun, who flourished as Raja of Boondi in 1342, left four sons, between whom he divided his possessions, which in the next generation resolved into the states of Boondi, Kota, and the twelve fiefs of the former. The legendary history of Kota is immaterial in this sketch, and is passed over until the succession of Oomed Singh, the first of its princes, who resigned the power or essence of sovereignty, and became contented with the name.

Oomed Singh had been reduced by the encroachments of his rebellious feudatories to such a state of distress, that he was unable to pay his fixed tribute to Sindhia, which amounted to 75,000 rupees. At this time Zalim Singh, the son of an old officer in his family, had, as a young man in Sindhia's service, been distinguished for a precocity of intelligence and energy of character, which induced the Maha-Rao to invite him to take on himself the office of minister. Zalim Singh, on proceeding to assume the office, prevailed on Sindhia to afford him the aid of a body of troops, by which he settled the country, and increased Sindhia's tribute to one lac of rupees. From this time the Maha-Rao allowed Zalim Singh exclusively to manage the affairs of his government; and Kota prospered under his administration, while he, as its minister, or regent, bore the highest character for wisdom and integrity among the surrounding chiefs. It was before entering the service of Kota that he had obtained the title of Raj-Rana.

The earliest communication which the British had with this state took place in July, 1803, when Colonel Monson's detachment passed through the territory of Kota, and every aid was afforded to facilitate its progress towards Gujerat. But on the retrograde of the detachment towards Hindoostan, followed by Holkur, the Raj-Rana denied him admittance into his capital, an apparent defection for which he has been blamed; but whether he would have been justified to his country in exposing it to the certain vengeance of a victorious army, to favour its enemy which had not the instant means of saving him from the misfortune of the moment, is questionable. The aid which Kota had already afforded was dearly purchased, by a fine of ten lacs of rupees, which Holkur exacted.

In 1817, the Raj-Rana, sagaciously perceiving the utility of the coalition, set an example to the other inferior states in Rajpootana, and consented to put his territory under the protection of the British. On the advance, therefore, of the army under the Marquis of Hastings, he proceeded to cooperate in the extirpation of the Pindarries, and bestirred himself in the blockade of the various mountain passes leading through Harrowtee. He sent a body of 1500 troops, infantry and cavalry, to join the British Deccan army, strained his influence with his neighbours, and employed his whole energy in furtherance of the common cause.

On 26th December of the same year, he concluded the treaty with the British, by which the tribute formerly exigible by the Peshwa, Sindhia, Holkur, and Puar, is now paid to the British Government, though Sindhia's share is accounted for to that Chief; the British, on the other hand, confirming to the Maha-Rao and his heirs his hereditary possessions.

After the conclusion of this treaty, Zalim Singh naturally felt desirous of perpetuating his influence in his descendants, and his conduct, whether as Regent of the principality for more than half a century, or as having contributed by his influence and example to the tranquillization of India, having given him claims to consideration, two supplemental articles were added to the treaty, by which the functions of general administration were confirmed as heritage to him and his descendants. These articles were concluded at Delhi, two months after the treaty with the Maha-Rao, who, it is said, died in ignorance of their existence. They reduced the Maha-Rao to an entity, and gave to the Raj-Rana every attribute of sovereignty without the name, and a title to improve or abuse, for perpetuity, the resources of the state. Though a line is drawn between the titular and executive authorities, it has not been sufficient to prevent continual and petty jealousies, by which the state has been racked by factions.

This was the state of affairs when Kishore Singh succeeded his father, about 1822. Finding himself stripped of all but the semblance of sovereignty, he appealed to arms in 1827, to vindicate his right to the whole functions of the government. But after a vain contest with the British, who co-operated with the troops of the Regent, he was necessitated to succumb in the unequal struggle; and, through the advice of the British agent, he subsequently returned to the capital, to grace the principality with the phantom of royalty.

Kota had, in 1822, an efficient force of 20,000 men, besides a fine park of artillery. The revenue was rated at 25 lacs of rupees, and the tributes to the British Government and to Sindhia, were respectively 1,00,000 rupees, and 1,02,430 rupees.

THE STATE OF BOONDI.

Boondi and Kota having a common origin, the early history of the former has been noticed in the sketch of the latter. The first Raja of Boondi with whom the British Government had any intercourse was Omeda, the grandfather of the present Chief. Omeda, or more probably his father, had been obliged by a faction to flee his country when he was very young, but he recovered his Musnud from the usurper who had been raised to it, by the assistance of the

Mahrattas. For the service rendered, he ceded the town and districts of Patun, which were divided between Sindhia and Holkur. Omeda died in 1804, after a reign of upwards of half a century, and was succeeded by his son, Bishen Singh. It was during the reign of the former that the British army, in its disastrous retreat under Monson, were aided so efficiently by this state; and as its fidelity and attachment is believed to have exposed it to much severity from the Mahrattas, it established peculiar claims on the British Government, to which it subsequently owed its regeneration.

During the period of anarchy, when all the states of Central India were subject to the visitations of predatory armies, this state became unable to pay its tributes. The officers of Sindhia and Holkur, therefore, assumed the management of the revenues, which had so much deteriorated as to leave a mere pittance to the Raja, after payment of the tributes and expenses of collection. From this lamentable condition he was raised again by the British Government to his place among the princes of India. Holkur's share of Patun, with other lands which had been usurped, was relinquished to him by construction, though not by specification, in the treaty of Mundisoor, together with the tribute heretofore payable to that state. A gratuitous restoration of the lands formerly ceded to, or usurped by, Sindhia, was not in the power of the British Government, but the share of the district of Patun held by that Chief, and to which the Raja of Boondi had an hereditary attachment, was obtained for him by exchange, for a portion of the lands which had been usurped by the Pindarries, and which were ceded to Sindhia. For these lands, however, an annual tribute of 80,000 rupees is paid by the Boondi state to the Company.

The Raja Bishen Singh died in 1821, and was succeeded by his son, Rao Ramsingh, then a minor, eleven years of age. The fiscal revenue cannot be estimated at more than three lacs of rupees, but sometimes fiscal and feudal revenues together may produce five lacs. The household and feudal array together may amount to 700 horse, and, inclusive of garrisons and police, 2700 infantry, with a park of twelve guns.

STATE OF BHURTPOOR.

This petty state, so remarkable in the annals of British India for the stout defence of its principal fortress in 1805, and for the operations which became necessary against it in 1828, deserves a lengthened notice.

The Jaths, or Jauts, are Hindoos of the Shoodr tribe, who migrated from the vicinity of the Indus about one hundred and fifty years ago, and settled in the country which now forms the principality of Bhurtpoor. They were, at that time, peaceable renters of land, but during the reign of Aurungzeb, Chopramun, the ancestor of the present Rajah of Bhurtpoor, became the leader of banditti. His first enterprises were directed against the baggage of Aurungzeb's army; and subsequently, during the contests between that Emperor's sons, Chooramun hung on their rear, and plundered both their armies. The Nurwar hills afforded him a refuge, his local knowledge of which enabled him to baffle and harass his pursuers in their unavailing efforts to overtake him. At length, he found it necessary to conciliate and bribe the Soobehdar of Agra, who allowed him to build the fortress of Bhurtpoor.

On his decease, his possessions went to his son, who became tributary to the Raja of Jeypoor, and, after him, to his grandson Soorujmull, who was created a Raja by the Emperor Mahomed Shah. Soorujmull joined one of the factions which at this period distracted the empire; but it proved the unsuccessful party, and he had to sustain a long siege in Coombheer, which his enemies were obliged to raise. Soorujmull joined the Mahrattas in 1761; but on their taking post behind intrenchments at Paniput, he made his peace with the Mahomedans, and, withdrawing his division from the Mahratta army, returned to his own country. Such of the Mahrattas, however, as escaped that disastrous day, and reached his territories, found kind treatment. When the conqueror quitted Hindoostan, he left Soorujmull as Soobehdar of Agra; but his ambition made him aspire to still greater influence in the empire. He levied an army with this view, but, having one day quitted the camp on a hunting excursion, he was attacked by a party of his enemies and slain.

Soorujmull was succeeded by his son, who rebelled against the Jeypoor state, and was defeated. He was afterwards assassinated by a person he had offended, and was succeeded by his brother, who met his death from a Faqueer, who was unfolding to him the secret of the philosopher's stone. A child of one year old now succeeded to the Musnud under the Regency of the third son of Soorujmull. This Regent was a very able chief; but his enemies were too powerful in the field, and he took shelter in Deeg, where he died of dropsy in 1773. The Regency now fell into the hands of Runjeeth Singh, in whose time the principality was reduced to the possession of Bhurtpoor and a small district round it.

At an early period of the war with Sindhia, the Raja of Bhurtpoor was the first of the petty chieftains of Hindoostan who evinced a desire to connect their interests with those of the British Government. A treaty was, therefore, concluded in September, 1803, by which the Raja was guaranteed in the independent possession of his territories, and was permanently relieved from the payment of his accustomed tribute to the Mahrattas, and from the apprehension of exactions or encroachments of any foreign state. Lord Lake was afterwards joined by the Bhurtpoor contingent of horse, which continued to serve with the British army, until the end of the campaign, and was present at the battle of Laswaree. In addition to the advantages which the Raja acquired by the treaty, a voluntary and gratuitous cession of lands, yielding seven lacs of rupees per annum, was granted to him by the Company.

Shortly after the conclusion of the treaty, a treacherous correspondence commenced between the Raja and Holkur, the object of which was directed to the subversion of the British power. As no interference had taken place with the concerns or administration of the state, its defection was unjustifiable. On the commencement of the war with Holkur, the Raja was called upon to send his contingent to the army, which he at first evaded, and afterwards refused. This contingent joined

Holkur, and, as was afterwards discovered, was present at the battle of Deeg, in November, 1804. His first act of open hostility occurred at this battle, when the routed troops of Holkur were pursued to the glacis of that fortress, a destructive fire was unexpectedly opened from it upon the British army.

From this time, Holkur and the Raja of Bhurtpoor were identified as confederates, and the British army proceeded to reduce the territories and forts of the latter chief. Deeg was carried by storm on the 23d December, 1804, and such of the garrison as escaped took refuge in Bhurtpoor, which the British proceeded to invest. The Raja Runjeeth Singh, foreseeing his downfal in the loss of his principal fortress, evinced a skill and resolution equal to the exigency, which was well seconded by the devotion of his people. The British were repulsed in four successive assaults, with a loss of 3203 men in killed and wounded. Dreading, however, the consequence of British perseverance, and his treasures, which had been the chief support of Holkur's army as well as his own, beginning to fail by protracted operations, he made overtures which led to a treaty, and, by the conditions, he engaged to pay twenty lacs of rupees towards the expenses of the war, and acknowledged the supremacy of the Company.

The defence of Bhurtpoor was a subject of admiration throughout India for many successive years; and it was a taunt that the British had not been able to prevail there as in other places. The Raja himself could not be ignorant of his power when placed in comparison with the British Government; but in discussions, it suited his policy or disposition to irritate to the full extent of forbearance, and to concede when he could not safely risk farther provocation. Nothing farther, however, occurred to disturb the relations of amity with this state, which readily furnished its contingent of horse in aid of the operations against the Pindarries, until 1826, when this fortress, hitherto deemed impregnable, was destined once more to prove British skill and valour.

The Raja Bhunder Singh died without children on the 7th October, 1823, and was succeeded by his brother Buldeo

Singh, who died on the 26th February, 1825, leaving a son, named Bulwunt Singh, then six years of age. His succession was recognized by the British Government, but opposed by his uncle Doorjun Lall. The Resident at Delhi, who was at the same time the agent for Bhurtpoor, promptly and properly assembled a force to reinstate the rightful heir; but it was not allowed to proceed to operations, in the expectation of an amicable adjustment of their family differences among them selves. The necessity of interference becoming at length unavoidable, an army of 25,000 men, with an ample train of artillery, proceeded, under the personal command of Lord Combermere, then Commander-in-Chief, to reduce the fort, and expel the usurper. The siege was begun in December, 1825; but as the mud walls were of great height and sixty feet thick, fronted by a deep wet ditch, mining operations were resorted to. These commenced on the 23d December, and the mines were sprung on the 17th January following, when a sufficient breach was effected, and the fortress was carried by assault. Doorjun Lall was made prisoner, and the young Raja Bulwunt Singh was duly installed on the 5th February, 1826.

THE RAJA OF MACHERI.

Purtaub Singh, the ancestor of this prince, was the revenue manager, under the Jeypoor state, of the districts which formed the original lands of this petty principality. While Jeypoor was torn by factions, he took part in rebellion against his prince, when the lands under his management were not only alienated from the parent state, but he took advantage of circumstances to usurp others, which were confirmed to him about 1774, by Nujeef Khan, who held the control of affairs at Delhi. The strong hill fort, and fortified town of Alwar, however, which is now the capital of Macheri, was a conquest from the Raja of Bhurtpoor.

Buktawur Singh, who first brought the state into connection with the British Government, was the son of the founder of the principality. Prior to this period, it is affirmed, that his policy was to discourage cultivation, that the poverty of his country might present no temptation to the invader, while he rendered it stronger by fortified positions.

A treaty was concluded with him in 1803, by Lord Lake, on the usual terms of protection and service. No tribute was demanded; but he furnished his contingent for the campaign of the following year. In reward for his fidelity, the lands which had been granted to the Bhurtpoor Raja, and afterwards forfeited by his treachery, were resumed, and conferred upon this chief.

The Raja was seized with a religious frenzy in 1811, which was displayed in a strange persecution of his Mahomedan subjects. He destroyed their mosques; and apprehending some of the devotees, mutilated them, and sent their noses and ears to a neighbouring Mahomedan Prince. His savage zeal did not stop here; and, among other exploits, he caused the bodies of Mahomedans to be disinterred, and sent their bones out of the country. The interests of humanity, and the discovery that he had given powerful support to a rebellious subject of the Jeypoor Raja, which was altogether inconsistent with the subsisting relations of amity with the British Government, called for its interposition. This circumstance led to a new treaty, in 1812, by the terms of which the Raja is prevented from entering upon any engagements with foreign states, without the knowledge and consent of the British Government. Toleration was also secured to his Mahomedan subjects.

Raja Bukhtawur Singh, of Macheri, or Alwar, died in 1815, leaving a nephew, named Reney Singh, and a son, Bulwunt Singh, both minors, who were made joint rulers, by the authorities of Macheri. In 1824, when the former was seventeen years of age, and the latter ten, Reney Singh attempted to get the whole power into his own hands; but, after the capture of Bhurtpoor, he made his submission to Lord Combermere, and the territory was divided between them. The revenue, before this division, was sixteen lacs of rupees.

AFGHAN CHIEFS.

NUWAB OF BHOPAL.

BHOPAL now ranks as the principal Afghan state remaining in India. Dost Mahomed, the founder of this family, commenced life as revenue manager of the district of Bairseeah, during the reign of Aurungzeb. In this situation, he obtained a reputation for integrity, and was left by a neighbouring Hindoo Prince in the charge of his territory and family, while he was absent at Delhi, where he died. Dost Mahomed afterwards acquired a title to the possessions of which he had been only appointed the manager. These he extended, by talent, courage, and successful treachery, till he had acquired all the lands now forming the possessions of the family, in which he was confirmed by Nizam-ool-Moolk, about 1721. He died about 1723, after an adventurous career of thirty years; during which, it is said, he had received as many wounds.

His eldest son, Yar Mahomed, though illegitimate, was supported in his claim to the succession by Nizam-ool-Moolk, and he was seated on the Musnud accordingly. On his demise, contests arose between his son, Fuez Mahomed Khan and the legitimate son of Dost Mahomed, which ended, after some desperate conflicts, in favour of the former. The Peshwa, Bajee Row, being appointed Soobehdar of Malwa, in 1739, summoned the Bhopal Afghans to restore all the lands they had usurped in Malwa, by which they lost half their original possessions: the remainder, however, situated in Gondwana, was confirmed to the Nuwab, by treaty. During the reign of Fuez Mahomed, three ministers were successively cut off, by poison or assassination. On the murder of the last, a Hindoo, his wife destroyed herself and her family by gunpowder laid under the chamber in which she ad assembled them for the sacrifice. On the death of Fuez Mahomed, each of his brothers reigned in succession, the last of which, Hyat Mahomed, being indifferent about governing, set aside lands, yielding five lacs of rupees, for his own support, and left the rest of the revenues, fifteen lacs, with the minister, for the expenses of the state. The adopted son of the Nuwab was the first minister; and it was during his time, in 1778, that General Goddard's detachment, in passing from Bengal to Bombay, experienced such cordial and essential assistance from this state, which established claims for his descendants upon the British nation.

The interesting history of this petty state, the able administration of Chuta Khan, and the romantic and highly interesting history of Vizier Mahomed, who returned from exile in 1797, to preserve, by his talents and courage, the political existence of his country, against powerful neighbours, who had confederated for its annihilation, are not matters for this brief sketch. In 1809, Sindhia and the Raja of Nagpoor had reduced the whole country, and obtained possession of Bhopâl itself. At this low ebb of his fortune, Vizier Mahomed re-captured the city; and recovered, with the aid of Ameer Khan and the Pindarries, all his possessions. In retaliation he carried a predatory war into the Nagpoor dominions, and a British force, in consequence, prepared to act against him; when he would have suffered, had circumstances, unnecessary to be here specified, not saved him.

The operations of Sindhia and the Raja of Nagpoor, were renewed against this state in 1812; and Vizier Mahomed had to sustain a siege in his capital, during nine months of 1812-13, which is as remarkable for the skill of the chief and devotion of his people, as any on record, in any age. In the following year, his enemies again prepared to act against him, when he earnestly repeated his solicitations for British protection. The Residents at Nagpoor and Gwalior interposed their mediation in consequence; and the hostile designs of those courts were abandoned. Vizier Mahomed died in 1816, having ruled as Dewan nineteen years—constantly at war; but during seven of which, the state was on the verge of annihilation.

His son and successor, Nuzzur Mahomed, endeavoured to effect what had been the earnest desire of his father,—an alliance with the English. Having cordially co-operated against the Pindarries, though his possessions were situated in the midst of their positions, his proposals were fully acceded to, and a treaty concluded with him on the 26th February, 1818. By one of the articles, he engages to furnish a contingent of six hundred horse and four hundred infantry; and by another, for the maintenance of this contingent, the Pergunnah of Ashta, Itchawur, Sehore, Doraha, and Deveepoora, commonly called the Punchmahals, with Shujawulpoor, being part of the lands which had been usurped by the Pindarries, and being situated contiguous to his other possessions, were made over to him, in perpetual sovereignty. Islamnugur was also obtained for him, from Sindhia, in return for part of the forfeited Jagheer of the Veechoorkur; and, by these several annexations, he has now a compact territory, which is calculated to realize between twenty and thirty lacs of rupees. The military force of Bhopal consists of about 2000 horse and 4000 infantry; which, with all the resources of his government, may be depended upon in any emergency. Nuzzur Mahomed was killed by an accidental pistol-shot, fired by a child, in 1818, leaving an infant daughter married to his nephew, who succeeded to the chiefship.

THE NUWAB AMEER KHAN.

This Chief commenced his military career with one of the parties which divided the Bhopâl state, in which service he remained twelve months. He afterwards connected himself with the ex-chiefs of Ragooghur, who, expelled their country by Sindhia, subsisted themselves and followers by plunder. He quitted this predatory life for Sindhia's service, and that again for the service of the celebrated Nuwab of Bhopâl, Vizier Mahomed, who, discovering his true character, dismissed him in six months. At no period of his career as a military leader, prior to his making overtures to be received under the protection of the British Government, can Ameer Khan be considered in any other character than that of a leader of mercenaries, who might be hired and discharged at pleasure.

About 1798, the desperate fortunes of Jeswunt Rao Holkur, gave employment to Ameer Khan, and brought about a connection between these Chiefs which proved beneficial to both, but essentially so to the latter, as will be seen in the sequel. They were fit associates,—the one meditating usurpation, the other subsistence of his party, which consisted of 1500 Patans, by any means whatsoever. Ameer Khan was, however, distinguished for his ability and enterprise, during all the vicissitudes of that predatory Chief in his operations against Sindhia, the Peshwa, and the British. On Jeswunt Rao becoming insane in 1808, he assumed a control over the Regency formed for the government of the Holkur state, of which he appointed his brother-in-law, Ghuffoor Khan, a member. But two years prior to this he may be considered as pursuing views distinct from those of the state he nominally served, from which his Jagheer was in effect from this time irrevocably alienated. His army consisted of 35,000 men, with 115 pieces of field artillery, to support which his Jagheer was unequal, and it was necessary to subsist them upon other countries. His bands ranged over every part of Rajpootana, Malwa, and Boondelcund, the disputes between the petty chieftains of which provinces presented a fine harvest for a predatory chief. Though he sometimes found it convenient to prosecute his own views under the sanction of the Holkur name, it was perfectly understood, that as that state had no power of control over his actions, it was not responsible for them.

In 1806-7, he entered the service of the Raja of Jeypoor, who was then contending with the Raja of Joudpoor for the hand of the Princess of Oodipoor. When the rival chief could no longer keep the field, and was compelled to take refuge in Jeypoor, Ameer Khan who was the partisan of that faction which paid him best, changed sides, and reversed the probable issue of the contest, while he plundered indiscriminately the country of both princes. The horrible deeds perpetrated during the Rajpoot war, by the cool-blooded policy of this chief, are unsuited to this sketch. It is supposed that, in 1809, he contemplated the subversion of the Mahratta dynasty of

Nagpoor, and the erection of a Mahomedan in its stead, in his own person and family; but whatever were his intentions in invading Nagpoor, they were frustrated by the prompt interposition of the British Government.

When the British army advanced, in 1817, towards the frontiers of the Pindarries, the offer was made to Ameer Khan, in common with all the other petty states of Hindoostan, to accept the protection of the British Government, under the conditions that he should reduce his army to a certain specified number, and surrender his artillery at a valuation. In return, the assignments for the payment of troops, which he held under grants from the Holkur state, to which he was only nominally subject, were to be guaranteed to him in sovereignty; he relinquishing all the conquests made during his predatory career. The terms were hard, but as he could not be considered in any other light than as a principal supporter of the predatory system, which the British Government were now putting forth their whole strength to annihilate, this chief may be considered as too liberally dealt with. He procrastinated in ratifying the treaty, until information reached him of the result of the battle of Seetabuldee, when, considering the Mahratta game lost, he completed the treaty, and resolved to contribute to the maintenance of tranquillity, or to support the new order of things.

His Jagheer lands are supposed to yield about nine lacs of rupees, but they are scattered all over Malwa and Rajpootana, and are in some cases one hundred and fifty miles distant from each other. They comprise the districts of Seronj, Peerawa, Gogul, Tonk-Rampoora, and Neemahera. Such of his old retainers as were not taken into the British service have settled on his lands, and he keeps in pay a great number of them, for the purposes of revenue and police; but his regular military establishment consists of only about 500 or 600 horse.

He has grown devout in his old age, being now in his sixty-fifth year, dresses in sackcloth, reads the Koran, is surrounded by *religieuse*, is extremely rich, and has twelve thriving children, whom he is at particular pains to educate. In January, 1832, when he went to pay his respects to the

Governor-General at Ajmeer, six of his sons accompanied him. Five of them were in chain armour, which is sufficiently indicative of their inheriting a portion of their father's *esprit militaire*. This interview was marked by a spirit of frankness and cordiality; and the Nuwab, who is particularly distinguished for his acuteness and powers of conversation, left a very favourable impression upon his entertainers.

THE NUWAB GHOUS MAHOMED KHAN, a minor, has succeeded his father, the late Ghuffoor Khan. His Jagheer comprises the districts of Sunjeet, Mulharghur, Tal, Mundawur, Jowra, and Barrode, which are computed to yield him a revenue of about seven lacs of rupees per annum. His contingent, which he is bound to keep up for the service of the Holkur state, consists of 500 cavalry, 500 infantry, and four guns, with which he is liable to be employed on the requisition of the British Government. Ghuffoor Khan owed his first elevation to his connection with Ameer Khan, who, in 1808, caused the Holkur regency to confer a Jaedad upon him, the continuance of which is guaranteed to him by the treaty o Mundisoor.

THE BEGUM SUMROO.

OF all the petty States which have started into existence, since the dilapidation of the Moghul Empire, that of Sirdhana is one of the most remarkable. It is now held by the wife of the founder, whose real name was Walter Reignard, a German by birth, though he afterwards assumed that of Summers, corrupted by the natives into Sumroo. Reignard purchased the Begum when she was a young and handsome dancing girl, married, and made her, in name, a Christian. He commenced his career in India by deserting from a company of Switzers in the British service at Calcutta, in which he was a common soldier, and entering that of the Nuwab-vizier of Oude, as a private horseman, and was afterwards in the service of different princes. While in that of Cassim Ali, of Bengal, he was instructed to put to death all the English, nearly 200 in number, who had been surprised and taken prisoners at Patna.* He commanded eight battalions in the service of Cassim Ali, on the decline of whose fortune he was engaged by Shuja-ood-Dowla, whom he quitted, and successively served the Raja of Bhurtpoor, Raja of Jeypoor, Raja of Bhurtpoor again, and lastly, Nujif Khan, who conferred Sirdhana upon him, for the support of a specified force. He had his own foundry for cannon, and possessed a good arsenal. After his death, in 1776, the Jagheer was continued to his widow, now known by the title and name of Begum Sumroo, for the support of three battalions of infantry. These battalions were officered by Europeans, of whom she had in employ a great number. In her service the celebrated Irish adventurer, George Thomas,† first rose to notice. The Jagheer yields ten or twelve lacs of rupees per annum, and the old lady has amassed great

* The deliberate manner in which this atrocious murder was perpetrated is worthy of notice. As the English gentlemen unsuspectingly proceeded, one at a time, through a passage to a room where a banquet, to which they had been invited, was said to be prepared, two of the assassins seized the victim, and a third cut his throat. The soldiers, and other persons belonging to the English party, were afterwards placed in a court yard, and deliberately shot.

† George Thomas ran away from a ship of which he was a cabin-boy, and found his way to Hydrabad, where he entered the Nizam's service as a private soldier. He afterwards entered that of the Begum Sumroo, into whose favour he ingrafted himself, and marrying her adopted daughter, was appointed to the management of a district. The expenses of his mistress exceeded her income, and Thomas, feeling his influence sufficiently established, began a reform, by attempting to reduce the Europeans. At this time the Seiks having invaded the Begum's lands, Thomas went to repel them, but during his absence his enemies poisoned the mind of his mistress, and he quitted her service. This occurred in 1795. He entered the Mahratta service, soon attained independence, and his former mistress having been ruined and imprisoned, he marched to her relief, and reinstated her. The territory he formed for himself was on the banks of the Sutledge, and his capital, Hansi, was made by him one of the strongest places in India. His army consisted of 10,000 infantry, 1000 good cavalry, and 50 pieces of cannon. His territories and army he proposed to annex to the British dominions, but at this time his views could not be acceded to by government. His antagonist, Perron, was too powerful, and after numerous battles, with alternate success, he took refuge in his fortress, which he defended until he obtained favourable terms of capitulation.

treasure, which she has deposited in the Company's funds. She is now seventy-eight years of age, and possesses all the powers of sovereignty within her own territory, a power which she has exercised in a very cruel way on many occasions. She has, however, by the persuasion of her domestic chaplain, who is a Roman Catholic, built a church on the model of St Peter's at Rome.

The troops of the Begum are commanded by her son-in-law, Mr Dyce, to whom she has given the rank of Colonel, but formerly she used to head them herself. In an attempt lately (1832,) to place her cavalry on half-batta, they mutinied, and she ordered her body-guard to fire on them, which they refused to do, when she dismissed both the mutineers and body-guard from her service.

LESSER STATES OF RAJPOOTANA.

THE RAJA OF BICKANEER.

THIS petty State was founded by a son of the Raja of Joudpoor, named Beeka, some centuries ago, by the union of a number of small communities or republics. Its independence has been preserved till this time, from its position in the desert, and its extreme poverty presenting nothing to tempt the avarice of a conqueror. The father of Soorut Singh, the present Raja, usurped the Musnud in 1801, upon the death of his infant nephew, the rightful heir, who is supposed to have been murdered at his instigation. His ambition led him to attempt the extension of his territories at the expense of the Bhatties, great part of whose country he subdued, together with their capital, Bhatneer, in 1805. The government revenues of this territory do not exceed six lacs of rupees, nevertheless, maugre such limited resources, its Chief keeps on foot a large body of household forces, amounting to 679 cavalry, and 1700 infantry, with twenty-nine guns. The dependent feudal Chiefs could bring into action 5000 fighting men, of whom 1200 would be mounted on good horses. In the war with the Bhatties, his household array exceeded three times the amount of his present force. A treaty of protective alliance was concluded with this State on the 9th March, 1818, by which the political influence of Britain was extended up to the banks of the Sutledge. The connection was calculated to promote the trade between the English and the north-western countries, the roads to which lay through the Bickaneer territories. The merchants and travellers were subject to be plundered by highway robbers, or banditti, from the Bhutty country; and as the fifth article of the treaty engages the Raja to afford assistance for their suppression, and, besides, binds him to restore all plundered property, it cannot otherwise than prove beneficial to commerce, in affording such security to it on its transit. This was the chief object sought in the engagement.

At the time of the alliance, several of his subjects had revolted, and had wrested from him certain forts and territories, which it was necessary to employ a British force to recover for, and restore, to him.

RAJA OF KISHENGURH.

THE family of this chief is derived from a younger branch of that of Joudpoor; and his subjects, except some of the lowest cultivators, who are principally Jauts, are of the same tribe. The government is patriarchal, and the Rajpoot subjects, of which there are supposed five thousand fit to bear arms, are under feudal obligations to follow their chief to the field in all his quarrels. The present Raja, Kulleean Singh, however, from his violent attacks on the liberties of his subjects, has forfeited all claim to their respect and confidence, and is hence supposed to be labouring under an aberration of intellect. He has abandoned his country, and was living, in January, 1832, at Ajmeer. The administration was ably conducted, during his minority, by his mother and a eunuch minister, and by their prudence it suffered less during the

Pindarry times than its neighbours. When Kulleean Singh attained his majority, he attempted to seize the minister, who escaped out of the country. But his efforts afterwards against some of his powerful feudatories, led to himself also becoming an exile. Since he abandoned his dominions, the administration has been carried on in the name of his mother and son, whose authority is respected throughout the country. The government revenue is something less than four lacs of rupees, and the feudal revenue is about as much more. As this state had never paid tribute to any of the predatory powers, none was demanded by the British Government, when it was admitted into the federal alliance in March, 1818.

This small principality is situated between Jeypoor and Ajmeer.

THE RAJA OF JESSULMEER.

THE early history of all the Rajpoot principalities furnishes subjects sufficiently interesting to both the general reader and philosopher; but no part of that of Jessulmeer is suited for the present sketch, which commences from the reign of Moolraj, the first of its princes which formed a connection with the British Government.

Moolraj, styled Maha-Rawul, succeeded to the Gadee of Jessulmeer in 1762. He had three sons; but his unfortunate selection in a minister, brought eventually ruin upon his family. This minister had rendered himself so obnoxious, that Rae Singh, the eldest son of Moolraj, a haughty and passionate youth, conspired against, and put him to death. The associates in his crime, in order to secure their own safety, compelled Rae Singh to ascend the Gadee, and to confine his own father. During confinement, a counter revolution took place in favour of Moolraj, who was reinstated, and the usurper was exiled. Salim Singh, the son of the murdered minister, succeeded to his father's posts and influence over the Raja, and he used it for the gratification of his revenge more than the benefit of his country.

In the meantime, Rae Singh resided at Joudpoor, where his bridle being one day seized by a creditor, he drew his sword and laid him lifeless. The deed led to his returning to Jessulmeer, where he was incarcerated, and afterwards, with his two sons, poisoned at the instigation of Salim Singh. This person possessed so much influence as minister, that the remaining sons or grandsons of his master, who escaped poison or assassination, fled their country for safety. On the death of Moolraj in 1820, after a reign of fifty-eight years, his grandson Guj Singh succeeded to the Gadee, himself the submissive pageant of the minister, on whose bounty his family became dependents.

A treaty was concluded with the Raja of Jessulmeer on the 12th December, 1818, by which his heirs were secured in the succession. The minister endeavoured to obtain an article guaranteeing the functions of administration to his posterity, in the same manner as that conceded to the Raj-Rana of Kota, though no two characters, or their claims, could be more dissimilar. The tyranny of Salim Singh has driven all wealthy and respectable people from the reach of his influence: the well ordered government of the Raj-Rana made Kota a refuge to the oppressed from other countries.

This state is situated deep in the desert: it may be said to be beyond the limits of India, and a connecting link of the British dependencies in that quarter, with Sinde, and the nations beyond the Indus. The revenue is about four lacs of rupees.

THE RAJA OF KEROWLEY.

This petty State became tributary to the British Government, by virtue of its treaty with the Peshwa of June, 1817; and, on the 9th November, 1817, an engagement was concluded by the British government with the Raja, when the tribute of 25,000 rupees, which he had heretofore paid to the Peshwa, was remitted. The other articles of the engagement embrace protection on the one side, and service on the other; and, conformably thereto, the Raja sent a body of horse to act with one of the British detachments during the war of 1817, and undertook to guard the passes of the Chumbul within his jurisdiction.

RANA OF DHOLPOOR AND RAJAKHERA.

The ancestors of this chief, about a century ago, were Zumeendars of Gohud, then a petty village, until raised into a town and capital of a principality, by their warlike disposition and industry conjoined. During the first intercourse of the British with this state, it was tributary to the Mahrattas, when a treaty was concluded in December, 1779, by which the British Government agreed to afford military aid to the Rana, at 20,000 rupees a-month for each battalion, to defend his country and make conquests from the Mahrattas, the acquisitions being shared in the proportion of nine-sixteenths to the Company, and seven-sixteenths to the Rana. The service to be performed was to be prescribed by the Rana; but the mode of executing it was left to the English officer commanding. Gwalior, a fortress deemed impregnable, which formerly belonged to the Rana, was recovered for him during the following year from the Mahrattas, by one of the brightest exploits in the annals of Anglo-Indian warfare. It was again wrested from him by Sindhia, and the Rana became his tributary.

On the 17th July, 1804, another treaty was concluded with the Rana, by which he was to be established in all his hereditary possessions, together with other districts, and as a compensation, he was to maintain a subsidiary force of three battalions, at 75,000 rupees a-month, and the British were to retain Gwalior. This arrangement led to discussions with Sindhia, and, in consequence, a new treaty, by which the Rana relinquished all the possessions previously guaranteed to him; and the districts of Dholpoor, Barree, and Rajakhera, were made over to him in exchange. The revenue of his present possessions realize about five lacs of rupees.

ANCIENT CHIEFS OF BOONDELCUND.

CHIEFS OF BOONDELCUND.

THE British connection with the chiefs in this province originates in the supplementary treaty of Bassein in 1803, by which territory was ceded in Boondelcund, yielding a revenue of thirty-six lacs of rupees, to be selected from such parts as were most convenient. Those Bondela chiefs, who were feudatories of the Peshwa, were by this treaty transferred to the British Government, and had their lands confirmed to them in perpetuity, by engagements separately entered into with each. The other chiefs, descendants of the ancient Rajas, were also secured in their possessions by treaties, similar in conditions to those concluded with other protected states, by which they are allowed to govern their territory as they please, interference never being exercised, except in the event of a minority or obvious misgovernment, when a temporary manager is appointed by the British Government.

THE RAJAS OF BANDA AND PUNNA.

CHUTURSAUL SINGH succeeded a long line of ancestors to the Government of Boondelcund; and, availing himself of the distractions which ensued after the demise of Aurungzeb, he perfected the independence of his country. To secure his posterity against the encroaching power of the Mahrattas, he entered into a close alliance with the Peshwa Bajee Row, adopted him as his son, and bequeathed him a third of his possessions, under the express stipulation, that his posterity should be protected by the Mahrattas in independent possession of the rest, which were divided into two governments.

The Peshwa's share comprised the districts of Calpee, Hutta, Sâgur, Jhansi, Seronj, Koonch, Gurakota, and Hurdeenugur. The revenues were rated at 30,76,953 rupees.

The share which fell to Hirdee Sah, the eldest son of

Chutursaul, denominated the government of Punnah, included the fortresses of Punnah, Kalinjur, Mahun, Ereech, Dhamoney, &c. estimated at 38,46,123 rupees.

The division which fell to the share of Jugguth Raj, the second son, comprised the fortress of Bhondagurh, Bhooragurh, Bursa, Adjeegurh, Rungurh, Jytpoor, Churkharee, &c. supposed to yield, annually, 30,76,950 rupees. This was denominated the state of Jytpoor.

Hirdee Sah had two sons, the eldest of whom, Subha Singh, succeeded him in the government of Punnah; and the younger, Prithee Narayen, was appointed by the Peshwa manager of Gurakota, with a tract of territory around it, yielding six lacs of rupees.

Raja Subha Singh had three sons, of whom the second, named Hindooput, assassinated his elder brother, put his younger into confinement, and assumed the government.

Hindooput left several children; but his heir being a minor, he appointed by his will the Dewan, or minister, and his brother, who was Governor of Kalinjur, to be his guardians, and managers of the Government. But the political impossibility of having two persons in a state, swaying the same dominion with equal powers, was exemplified in these guardians. Each, or either, claimed the ascendancy, and a jealousy ensued which divided them. The Governor of Kalinjur, the least influential of the two, set up a rival to the throne—a number of sanguinary battles ensued—and, in the end, the guardians adjusted their own quarrel, set aside both princes, and agreed to establish a third, named Dhokul Singh, on the Musnud, who was also a minor, by which they retained their own power. The surviving disappointed candidate applied for succour to his cousin, the Raja of Banda, who espoused his cause; and war ensued between the descendants of Chutursaul, in which there were a number of battles; but that of Chuch-hurreea, in 1779, the last fought between the states of Punnah and Banda, is stated to have been the most obstinate and sanguinary of any on record. The principal chiefs of both armies were numbered with the slain, and the warriors of Boondelcund were annihilated. Dhokul Singh lost a great part of his dominions, which were annexed to those of

Banda; and his rival Surmedh Singh retired to his Jagheer Rajnugur.

A short period after the accession of Juggut Raj to the Musnud of Jytpoor, his territories were invaded by the Nuwab of Furruckabad at the head of a powerful army. Juggut Raj, being defeated in several battles, was obliged to take refuge in the hills, when he received assistance from the Mahrattas, agreeably to the stipulations of an agreement between the Raja's father and the Peshwa. The Nuwab was in turn reduced to solicit terms, and was allowed to quit the country. Juggut Singh died in 1758; and his son, Puhar Singh, assumed the succession, though his claims were contested by two nephews, the sons of an elder brother deceased; and the country became, in consequence, a prey to civil war and foreign invasion. At length, Puhar Singh consented, in 1765, to divide the territory with his nephews. To Gooman Singh he assigned the Jagheer of Banda, assessed at 16,25,000 rupees, when that chief assumed the title of Raja. Gooman Singh died about 1778, and left the succession to his nephew, Bukht Singh, then a minor, under the charge of guardians.

During the disturbances which ensued, Raja Bukht Singh was living in great indigence, and, in the latter part of the reign of 'Ali Bahadoor, received from that chief two rupees a-day; but on the occupation of Boondelcund by the British troops, he was restored to the Gadee of Banda, and now resides at Adjeegurh, enjoying a Jagheer, yielding four lacs of rupees per annum.

At the same period, Raja Kishor Sing of Punnah, who obtained no allowance during the reign of Ali Bahadoor, joined the freebooters, who plundered and despoiled the province,—a life from which he was reclaimed by the liberality of the British Government, and restored to the territory of his ancestors. He is now in possession of a Jagheer, estimated at the annual sum of seven lacs of rupees. Kishor Singh is the illegitimate son of the Raja Dhokul Singh.

The province of Boondelcund is valued at eighty-five lacs of rupees, of which the British Government realizes about thirty-six lacs. The rest is held by petty chiefs, of which the following are descendants of Chutursaul:—

Raja Kishor Singh, of Punnah, Rupees,	7,00,000
Raja Bukht Singh, of Banda or Adjeegurh,	4,00,000
Raja Bijee Buhadoor, of Churkaree, .	4,00,000
Raja Arjoon Singh, of Gurakota, . .	1,50,000
Raja Prithee Singh, of Bujour, . .	2,00,000
Raja Pareech-hut, of Jytpoor, . .	60,000
Raja Doorjun Singh, of Myheer, .	1,50,000
Raja Tej Singh, of Tundela, . . .	25,000
Raja Moorut Singh, of Jussah, . .	15,000
Rao Prithee Singh of Jignee, . . .	15,000

Surmed Singh, before mentioned, retired to Rajnugur, where he died, leaving a son, named Hurrah Singh, by a Mahomedan woman, under guardianship, during minority, of his minister Sonah Sah. This person had been originally a private soldier, but, availing himself of the anarchy of the times, he assumed the sole management of the country, for his own behoof; and the rightful heir, Hurrah Singh, was obliged to take refuge with the Nuwab Ameer Khan. On the death of Sonah Sah, these possessions descended to his son Purtab Singh, who now holds them, and resides at Chuturpoor, possessing a tract, said to yield a revenue of seven or eight lacs of rupees.

THE RAJA OF DUTEEUH.

THE principality of Duteeuh* seems to have been of much greater extent in the time of Aurungzeb, when its chief,

* The chronicle of the Raja of Oorchha and Tehree exhibits seventy-two generations, from the first Raja, the Celestial Ramchunder, who reigned at Ayodya, (Oude.) He was succeeded by his second son, Ankoosh, from whom Gungrukh, who founded some splendid temples at Gayah, in Behar, is the sixteenth in lineal descent. The twentieth Raja, Buldeo Rukh, founded those at the Pruyag, in Allahabad; and his son, Indradumun, built the celebrated temples of Juggernath. It is from Raut Singh, the second son of the thirty-second Raja, that the Burgoozur Rajpoots derive their origin. The thirty-fourth Raja, Kurmshya, conquered the province of Benares. Kemkurn, the second son of the forty-sixth Raja, having performed some religious austerities on the summit of Hinda-Chul, succeeded in propitiating Bedrao-

styled Dulput Rao, served in the imperial army. Chutursaul, the hero of the annals of Boondelcund, seems, at a subsequent period, to have wrested some of the lands of Duteeuh from its

sheny Bhowanee, the tutelary Dewee of the mountain. He was about to sacrifice himself, but, when in this act of devotion, the Dewee appeared, in all her glory; and a drop of blood having fallen from the wound which he had inflicted on himself, she conveyed to it a portion of the water of immortality, and it assumed the form of a child, afterwards the famous Beer Singh, who called his people Boondelas, from *boond*, a drop. He soon acquired a dominion, and ruled his subjects with justice. The sixtieth Raja, Prutab Roodra, having founded the city of Oorchha, intrusted the government to his son, while absent on an expedition, from which he never returned. Mudhookur, proverbial for his justice, power, and charity, was the sixty-second Raja, and reigned in the time of Akber. His eldest son, Ramasa, was appointed to the government of Ayodya, while the younger son, Nursingh Deo, was confirmed by Jehangeer in Oorchha, and the district of Chunderee was given to Ramasa, to reconcile him to the loss of a hereditary demesne. Nursingh Deo had twelve sons: the third, Pahar Singh, accompanied the Emperor Aurungzeb to Aurungabad, and founded a Suburb, which now bears his name. With Bhugwandass, the fourth son, originated the tribe of Koorers. The sixty-eighth prince was Chumput Rae, who, refusing to pay the usual tribute to Shah Jehan, Boondelcund was twice invaded by the imperial armies, and the country became a prey to licence and anarchy; but Oorchha was not taken, and the retiring army was harassed almost to annihilation by the Boondelas. Chumput Rae afterwards joined Aurungzeb against his brother Dara; and his son, Chutursaul, then thirteen years of age, was placed with the van of the successful rebel army. To these princes' knowledge of the passes through the country, and over the Jumna, has been ascribed Aurungzeb's success. These services, however, were forgotten by that Emperor, who, after the death of Chumput Rae, subdued Boondelcund, and attempted to convert the Boondelas to the Mahomedan faith. Chutursaul entered the imperial army as an inferior officer, and with it accompanied Raja Jeysingh of Jeypoor to the Deccan war. During its prosecution, he formed an acquaintance with the illustrious warrior opposed to them. Sivajee reminded him of his duty to his religion and country; and, after girding a sword on his loins, and commending him to the goddess Bhowanee, bade him return to his country, and achieve its independence. The advice was not lost, for Chutursaul contended with the imperial armies until the death of Aurungzeb, at which time the revenue of his possessions were rated at two millions sterling. Such is the legendary history of the Boondela Chiefs. The sixty-ninth Raja was Owdhoot Singh, adopted from the family of the Raja of Hurdwar; and the present Raja, who succeeded his father about 1817, is the seventy-second. The Raja of Oorchha is considered as the head of the Boondela tribes, and all the other Rajas receive their investiture from him.

chief; and they appear to have formed part of those bequeathed by him at his death to the Peshwa Bajeerow. These alienated lands contributed to the formation of the Soobehdarry of Jhansi, about 1742.

The remaining lands of Duteeuh continued in the hands of the Raja's descendants, of whom there is nothing remarkable recorded, until the British army entered Boondelcund, with a view to the occupation of the ceded portion of it, when the Raja Pareech-hut, requested to be received among the number of British dependents, and co-operated with his troops. A treaty was in consequence concluded with him, dated 15th March, 1804, by which he was confirmed in his hereditary possessions, on the usual terms of protection and fidelity.

During the Pindarry war, the British army was chiefly encamped in the territory of the Raja of Duteeuh, when his conduct, in affording assistance as far as his means permitted, gave much satisfaction; and on the settlement of the country, as a mark of the sense entertained of his services, all the lands formerly held by the Veechoorkur, east of the Sinde river, and known by the name of the Chowrassee, were conferred upon him, burdened only with a pension of 10,000 rupees annually, to the late agent of the Veechoorkur. The revenue of Duteeuh, as now formed, is about seven or eight lacs of rupees.

THE RAJA OF TEHREE.

This prince traces his descent from the same stock as the Raja of Duteeuh, and his family being the most ancient of the Boondela Rajas, they receive investiture from him. Great part of his possessions were wrested from him by the famous Chutursaul, by whom they were transferred to the Peshwa Bajeerow in 1735, and now form part of the lands of Jhansi. In 1809, this chief solicited to be admitted among the number of British dependents, on terms similar to those which had been concluded with the other Boondela Rajas who had come under the British authority, by the operation of the treaty of Bassein. But no connection was established until 1812, when the irruption of the Pindarries into Mirzapoor, led to a treaty with the

Raja Bickramajeet on the 23d December of that year, in order to engage him in the defence of the passes through his country. On the advance of the army, under the Marquis of Hastings, in 1817, he presented his Nuzur in token of fealty, affirming it was the first time he had ever acknowledged the supremacy of another power, though he confessed that he had been liable to have contributions extorted from him like other weak states. His revenue is about four lacs of rupees.

THE RAJA OF SUMPTER.

In 1805, this chief sought to be taken under the protection of the British Government; and, on the 22d February, a draft of an engagement of six articles was prepared, as a preliminary arrangement, which, through the non-interference policy just then adopted by Government, did not terminate in a treaty. He has made repeated applications, since that period, to be taken under British protection; but it was not deemed proper to accede to his entreaties, until the advance of the army, in the middle of 1817, when he was comprehended in the federal arrangements, and a treaty was concluded with him on the 12th November of that year. The Raja had been hitherto independent, and paid tribute to no one. The stipulations of the Company's engagement guarantee his possessions, and protection against enemies, on condition of his furnishing a contingent of horse, and attaching himself to their interests. A body of his horse joined the centre division. His dominions extend over a fertile tract of country, yielding about six lacs of rupees a-year.

RAJA OF REWAH.

After the annexation of a portion of Boondelcund to the British possessions, the intercourse with Rewah became more frequent, and was improved by reciprocal acts of friendship.

The Raja, Juesingh Deo, had expressed a desire to be taken under the protection of the British Government, which, in 1812, led to a treaty with him of defensive alliance. The

Raja's troops were to co-operate with the British, under the officer commanding the latter, in defending the passes through his country, by which the Pindarries might be expected to advance or retreat. The Rewah Government did not prove so friendly as its professions gave reason to expect, and a party of British Sepoys being attacked passing through the country, an additional force was detached to Rewah, to enforce the stipulations of the treaty, and to obtain security for the due fulfilment of them in future. The Raja having submitted unconditionally, was restored to his territories on agreeing to pay the extra expenses incurred in the operations against him, amounting to 45,000 rupees. A new treaty was concluded, dated June 2, 1813, the chief stipulations of which provide for his reception of a resident envoy, his allowing a Dawk to be established through his territory, and his acknowledging the right of the British Government to punish his refractory Jagheerdars.

Having thus acquired the power to punish the subjects of the Raja, the Jagheerdar of Suttemee was dispossessed, and his lands transferred to another. The Jagheerdar of Chourut having voluntarily surrendered himself, was reinstated in his lands, and the Jagheerdar of Semeereah was exempted from any portion of the penalty of 45,000 rupees, levied upon the Rewah Government. As the price of protection, the Raja yielded a tract of territory to the British Government, rated at 40,000 rupees per annum.

PETTY SEIK STATES.

The petty Seik principalities, south of the Sutledge, were, by the treaty with Sindhia, in 1803, taken under the protection of the British Government. When, therefore, Runjeeth Singh, of Lahore, approached, for the avowed purpose of assuming a control over these chiefs, part of whom were his tributaries for lands held by them on the north bank of that river, the British Government declared them under its protection. The declaration was supported by the advance of an adequate force, when Runjeeth relinquished his assumed right of interference with them, and recognized that claimed by the British Government, by treaty, dated 25th April, 1809. Engagements were at this time concluded with the chiefs, by which they were exempted from the payment of tribute; and they became bound to assist in repelling an invader. Interference with them is, however, limited to adjusting differences with each other, or with foreign states, and deciding cases of disputed succession. A British force is stationed, in a strong position, at Loodeeanah, on the frontier, to watch Runjeeth Singh, cover the protected Seiks, and controul their own feuds and habits of rapine and plunder. In 1814, when the late Sir David Ochterlony visited them, they exhibited a striking contrast to their former state of anarchy and turbulence.

The Raja of Patiala is the most powerful of these petty chiefs. His dominions extend over a wide tract of country between the Jumna and Sutledge rivers. His cavalry are fine martial looking troops; but his infantry, which are clothed and accoutred like the native infantry of the British army, are a miserable looking rabble. In 1815, on the conclusion of the Nepaul war, the greater portion of the lands of two of the hill chiefs, together with the fort of Juguthgurh, were transferred to this Raja. His revenue is estimated at twenty-five lacs of rupees. The British political agent with the petty Seik states, resides chiefly at the court of Patiala, where his chief employment is that of mediator between the chiefains, who are constantly quarreling; and, during these feuds, it is not uncommon for one party to storm another's village fortress, and dictate terms.

The Raja of Khytul is descended from an elder branch of the family of Patiala, and is, by inheritance, a Gooroo, or spiritual guide; and his relative, though greater in temporal power, cannot sit in his presence. His revenue is about five lacs of rupees. He is now seventeen years of age.

The Raja of Jheend is probably the next in resources. His amusements are divided between the Zunana and the stable. He was a great favourite of Runjeeth Singh, of Lahore, but he violated the hospitality of that chief, by eloping with a female favourite.

There are many other petty Seik Chiefs in the plains, and Hill Chiefs in the mountain regions, towards Deyra and Pinjore, under British protection, whom it is unnecessary to notice, except in a general way.

Hill Chiefs.—The mountain territory between the Sutledge and Tonse rivers, was wrested from the Goorkhas in 1815, but as the original princes of the country, who had been either expelled, or who had been still suffered to hold their lands, contributed in no way towards the expulsion of their oppressors, the British Government acquired a right by the conquest to the disposal of the territory. Those chiefs, however, who had taken no part in the war, either for or against the British, were restored under engagements by which they are bound to afford, when required of them, military co-operation to the extent of their means, and a stipulated number of hill porters. They are, moreover, bound to submit their disputes to the arbitration of the British Government, and to perform, in short, all the duties of allegiance. The revenues of the whole of these petty lordships, which are twelve in number, amount to four and a half lacs of rupees, of which the territories of the chiefs of Sirmore and Bussaher are estimated at eighty thousand rupees each. The former of these chiefs was required to cede a portion of his territory as the price of protection, and the latter agreed to pay a tribute of fifteen thousand rupees annually. The chiefs next in consideration were those of Keonthul and Bughat, but their lands having been forfeited, they were transferred to the Seik Raja of Patiala.

RAJAS OF DHAR AND DEWASS.

These Princes trace their origin from Subajee Puar, a Patel of the village of Multan, thirty miles north-east of

Poona, where the descendants of the elder branch of the family still retain their hereditary office of Patel. The son of Subajee, by name Krustnajee, as also his three sons, Babajee, Ryajee, and Keroojee, were at the same time Silahdars and cultivators. Babajee had two sons, Kaloojee and Sumbhajee, who were military leaders, during the contests for Hindoo emancipation. Their sons fought in the same cause, and having served under the Raja Sahoo, they claim precedence over the houses of Sindhia and Holkur, who owed their elevation to the Peshwas. The annexed genealogical tree, which is given as a specimen of those kept in Mahratta families, will shew the connection of the Rajas of Dhar and Dewass, with the Patels of Multan and others. It will also shew that a father having an only son, will allow that son to be adopted into a family of higher rank, while his place in his own family can be supplied by adoption from another in an humbler sphere.

The Patel of Multan holds lands principally in Khandes, producing 9637 rupees, and he keeps up about 25 horse.

The Raja of Dhar has the Pergunnas of Dhar, Budnawur, and Nalcha, the revenues of which may be rated at 4,00,000 rupees. He receives also 1,10,000 rupees annually from the British Government, for the district of Bairseeah, and tribute of Allee-Mohun, both of which were ceded by treaty, dated 18th December, 1821, in perpetuity to the Honourable Company: to which he has also given up in lieu of the expense of protecting his country, all his tributary rights on the principalities of Banswara and Doongurpoor. Bairseeah has since been transferred at a fixed rent to the Nuwab of Bhopâl, and the tribute of Allee-Mohun has been relinquished to its Chief. His troops amount to about 1100 horse and foot.

The two Rajas of Dewass have equal rank, but one minister officiates for both. The revenue is about 3,00,000 rupees, derived from the districts of Dewass, Sarungpoor, Allote, 200 foot, Ringnod, &c. The military establishment is 140 horse, including the British contingent of 50 horse, and 50 infantry.

GENEALOGY OF THE FAMILY OF PUAR.

Where the line is extinct, the name is given in Italics; but where adopted into another line, a number is affixed, to facilitate reference: for instance, Manajee, the son of Khundee Rao, has been adopted by Ranoojee, the son of Boobajee. Adoption is distinguished by dotted lines.

- Kalojee, a military chief under the celebrated Sivajee.
  - Krustnajee.
    - Boobajee.
      - *Krustnajee*, (5) *Mahadoo Rao* Ranoojee.
        - … *Tookoojee*, (6.) Manajee, (1) renamed Boobajee of Soopa, has a pension from the British Government of Rs. 5000 per ann.
  - Tookoojee of Gunigaom, Per. Khurda.
    - … Krustnajee, (5.)
      - … Tookajee, (6) one of the Rajas of Dewass.
  - Jewajee, Patel of Hingnee, on Goor R. one of the first Rajas of Dewass.
    - Sudaseo.
      - *Rukma.*
    - Anund Rao.
      - Hybut Rao.
        - … (2) Neelkunt Rao, renamed Anund Rao. Family estate at Deoor, but he is one of the Rajas of Dewass.
  - Manajee.
    - Yadhoorao.
      - Chundur Rao. Pension 5000 Rs.
        - Muheeput Rao, Patel of Soopa.
      - Amrut Rao. *Neelkunt Rao*, (2)
        - *Gopal Rao*, (3) Moorar Rao. Martund Rao.
    - Khundee Rao.
      - *Manajee*, (1.) Yadhoorao, Patel of Pathree. *Krustnajee*, (4.)
- Sumbhajee, a military leader under Sivajee.
  - Oudajee, Patel of Multan, near Seroor; one of the most distinguished leaders in Gujerat and Khandes.
    - *Chunder Rao.* Darkoojee.
      - Mulhar Rao.
        - … Gopal Rao, (3) renamed Eshwunt Rao, of Multan: has Jagheers, rated at Rs. 9,637.
  - Anund Rao, Patel of Kowta, near Seroor, is the first of this line, who established himself at Dhar. Died 1749.
    - Eshwunt Rao was the first confirmed as Raja of Dhar. He was alike remarkable for his valour and generosity. He fell at Paniput.
      - Khundee Rao succeeded; but, during his minority, the state appears to have declined. Died in 1780.
        - Anund Rao, the late Raja of Dhar, left a child, who died in infancy; but his widow adopted his sister's son, now called Ramchunder Puar. He has since been married to the daughter of Dhabary, by his wife, the daughter of the late Dowlut Rao Sindhia.
    - Ryajee, possessor formerly of Gungrar, and Dug, in Malwa.
      - Mulhar Rao.
        - Bulwunt Rao, and Ryajee, have a Jagheer, rated at Rs. 7,500, at Ahmedabad, near Seroor.
      - Wittul Rao.
        - Mahadoo Rao, of Soondursee.
  - Jugdeo, of Chittigaom, Perg. Nassik.
    - Darkoojee Rao.
      - Owdhoot Rao, now in Poona, has Jagheers rated at Rs 5400.
        - Darkoojee.
- Mulojee, son of Ryajee.
  - Jug Jewan Rao.
    - Mulojee. *Anund Rao. Bulwunt Rao.*
      - Abajee, Patel of Wagula, resides mostly at Nassik.
- Deerojee, son of Keerojee
  - *Sewrao. Kerojeerao.* Ramchunder Rao.
    - Sewrao. *Kerojee. Derojee. Purtab Rao.*
      - … Krustnajee, (4) Puar of Nugur Deeola, is the richest Jagheerdar in Khandes.

RAJPOOT CHIEFS IN MALWA.

The Rawul of Banswara, Bhowanee Singh, is of the same stock as the Oodipoor family. His revenue may be estimated at 3,00,000 rupees, and he pays three-eighths of it in tribute to the British Government, to which he is also obliged to furnish troops, agreeably to his means. His military establishment consists of about 1000 men, horse and foot, including the contingents of his Jagheerdars, who all belong to the same tribe.

The Raja of Purtabgurh, Sawunt Singh, has a country, the revenue of which may be assumed at 4,00,000 rupees, of which he pays 45,000 rupees in tribute to the British Government, to which he transferred his tributary obligations from the Holkur Government, in 1804. His military establishment comprises about 950 horse and foot, all Rajpoots, besides his armed Bheel subjects.

The Raja of Allee, commonly called Allee-Mohun, has a revenue rated at 45,000 rupees, including the Sayer, rated at 20,000 rupees, which belongs to the British Government, but which relinquished it to the Raja, to enable him to maintain fifty men for the security of the road between Allee and Dhar.

The Amjherra Chief, Ajeet Singh, a Rhattore Rajpoot, has a territory which should realize 1,00,000 rupees: he pays a fixed tribute of 35,000 rupees yearly to Sindhia, guaranteed by the British Government.

The Raja of Rutlam, Bulwunt Singh, is son of the late Purbut Singh. His revenue is assumed at 5,50,000 rupees, of which 84,000 are paid in tribute to Sindhia. He has no military establishment, but on occasions of emergency, the dependent chiefs of his family, who hold their Jagheers of him on feudal tenure, arm their adherents, and form his military force.

The Raja of Seeta-Mhow, has a revenue rated at 1,20,000 rupees, of which he pays 60,000 in tribute to Sindhia, and has a military establishment of 900 men.

THE RANA OF SOONTH claims descent from the ancient Rajas of Malwa. He has a revenue of about 70,000, and pays 7000 rupees in tribute to Sindhia: his Zumeendars, principally Bheels, furnish troops when required.

THE RAJA OF LOONAWARA. This chief is of an ancient family. In 1739, an ancestor, then styled only Zumeendar, it appears paid a tribute of 3000 rupees, together with the customary presents, to the royal authorities in Gujerat. In 1758, Deep Singh, his successor, was besieged by the Peshwa's troops, and after an honourable defence of his fort, he was obliged to pay down 51,000 rupees, and give hostages for good behaviour. This petty state was formerly tributary to Sindhia, and paid a fixed tribute of 12,000 rupees; but his allegiance being transferred to the British Government, the tribute has been remitted, on the condition of employing his troops to guard the passes through his country into Gujerat. The revenue is rated at 80,000 rupees.

THE RAJA OF SEYLANA, pays 42,000 rupees in fixed tribute to Sindhia. His revenue is rated at 1,20,000 rupees. He has no regular military force, but the Chiefs of his family, who hold their lands of him on feudal tenure, arm when required.

THE RAJA OF JUBOOA, Bheem Singh, a Rhattore Rajpoot, is tributary to Holkur, to whom he pays 35,000 rupees. His son, Purtab Singh, has now the chief management, and the revenue rated at 80,000 rupees, is shared equally between him and his father. He has no military force, but his subjects are Bheels, and his country is strong.

THE CHIEFS OF OOMUTWARRA. This province takes its name from two chiefs of the Oomut class of Rajpoots. They established their dominion over great part of Malwa during the decline of the Moghul empire, but were confined to their present limits by the Mahrattas. Newul Singh, styled Rawut, or Chief, resides at Rajghur, and Hunmunt Singh, styled Dewan, or Minister, at Nursing-ghur. They are of the same family, and deduce their genealogies from brothers, between whom the territory was equally divided, not into distinct tracts of country, but by each taking the alternate village. The country contains about 800 villages, and at present produces from four to five lacs of rupees. The Rawut is tributary to Sindhia, and the Dewan to Holkur. The amount of tribute from each is 85,000 rupees; that of the Rawut, however, has been commuted in 1819, for territory ceded. The Rawut besides pays 1,050 rupees to the Raja of Kota. They continue to receive a Tanka, rent or fee, from some of the districts formerly in their possession.

THE RAJA OF RAGOOGURH holds a territory realizing two lacs of rupees, and is a feudatory of Sindhia. The late Chief, Juesingh, who died about 1820, opposed himself successfully to Sindhia, who never wholly subdued him. The chiefs of his family, the principal of whom was Dhokul Singh, continued the war, and in an action with the contingent were defeated.

THE CHIEF OF MUXOODNUGUR, Bhyree Saul, styled Raja Buhadoor. Muxoodnugur is all that remains of the conquests made by the late Doorjun Saul, whom the present chief succeeded. He is descended from an elder branch of the family of the present Raja of Ragooghur. He belongs to the Khychee class of Rajpoots, from whom the tract called Khycheewara takes its name. The district under Muxoodnugur contains about sixty villages, but produces a revenue of only 5000 or 6000 rupees, the districts having been nearly destroyed during the protracted contests between the Khychees and Sindhia's government.

THE RAJA OF KILCHEEPOOR Sher Singh, styled Dewan, is of the Khychee tribe of Rajpoots. The state of Kilcheepoor has existed from one hundred and fifty to one hundred and seventy years. The family came originally from Gagrone, where their ancestors held large possessions. The districts contain about 200 villages, and the revenue, exclusive of numerous small Jagheers, amounts to 35,000 or 40,000 rupees. It is tributary to Sindhia, and pays the yearly sum of 13,500 rupees. It also pays a tribute of 1050 rupees to the Raja of Kota. Kilcheepoor lies west of Oomutwarra, and south of Harowtee.

THE CHIEF OF GAGOORNEY, Rugonath Singh, is the descendant of a family who are said to have once ruled over the two districts of Zeerapoor and Machilpoor. The present possession of the family comprises only twenty villages. It is a dependency of the Holkur state, to which it pays a yearly tribute of 1500 rupees.

THE RAJA OF MUKRAEE, Devi Sah. This chief is a Gond, whose ancestors in former days are said to have held the Punj-Muhals of Hurda and Hindia, till they were taken possession of, first by the Moghul, and latterly by the Mahratta. A tract containing forty-five villages, is all that is now left to the family. This state was a dependency of the late Peshwa, and, consequently, is now of the British Government.

BRITISH FEUDATORY CHIEFS.

Introduction.

THE difference between protected and feudatory chiefs is, that treaties were concluded with the former as independent princes, who spontaneously sought the protection of the British Government, whereas, the allegiance of the latter was either transferred by their feudal superiors, or by the events of war. The British Government, with its accustomed liberality, has, in most cases, confirmed to these feudatories in perpetuity, the lands which they had held on a life tenure, and permitted them to enjoy the same privileges they had held under their former superior, which included a supreme control on their own lands.

THE PUTWURDHUN FAMILY.

THE founder of this family was Hurry Bhut, a Konkanee Bramin, originally in the service of the Peshwa, Bajeerow Wiswanath. Of his six sons, Gowind Hurry, Trimbuck Hurry, and Ramchunder Hurry, and two of his grandsons, Gopal Rao and Purusram Bhow, rose to distinction as military leaders. Purusram Bhow is well known to the English as the leader of the Mahratta division which co-operated in the reduction of Mysore, in 1792. He died in battle in 1800, fighting against the Raja of Kolapoor, in whose vicinity the family Jagheers are situated. Of the ten chiefs composing the family, nine of them hold their Jagheers on the tenure of military service, but are only required by their engagements with the British Government to keep up one-fourth of their original contingents. Chintamun Rao, of Sanglee, however, preferred a cession of territory to serving the English; one-fourth, therefore, of his original Jagheer, equal in revenue to 1,25,000 rupees, has been resumed, and the rest, which is rated at 3,75,000 rupees, has been confirmed to him. This veteran and intelligent, but refractory and litigious, chief, is the heir of the elder branch of the family, but his claims were set aside by the Peshwa. Since the settlement of the country, he has maintained a greater number of military followers than any other of the southern Jagheerdars, Appah Dessaye Neepaunker excepted.

The nine chiefs of the Putwurdhun family, with the value of their Jagheers, and amount of their contingents of horse, one third of which serves with the Poona auxiliary horse, and two thirds remain with their chiefs, ready when called upon.

Chiefs.	Jagheers.	Horse.
Descendants of Gowind Hurry.		
Gunput Rao, styled Tattia Sahib, is now in charge of the Fort of Meerich, as heir to this branch	Rupees 1,85,336	90
Madhoo Rao Baba, styled Baba Saheb . . .	1,18,413	70
Gopal Raojee	1,01,348	70
Wamon Rao, styled Sahoneekur, from the name of his chief village	92,270	70
Descendants of Trimbuck Hurry.		
Rugoonath Rao of Shedbaul	1,22,925	70
Krushna Rao of Koorundwar	1,53,358	70
The grandchildren of Purusram Bhow.		
Gopel Rao of Jumkhundee	2,64,144	150
Gowind Rao Nana of Chinchnee	2,26,125	150
Purusram Bhow of Tazgaom, the adopted son of the late chief, now a minor, under guardianship of his reputed uncle of Jumkhundee	2,56,880	150
Total amount of the Putwurdhun contingent of Horse .		890

SOOBEHDAR OF JHANSI.

The territories of Jhansi were part of the bequest made by Raja Chutursaul to the Peshwa Bajeerow, but they appear not to have been formed into a separate government until after the Peshwa's visit to Hindoostan in 1735. The lands under Jhansi at that time were rated at 24,42,979 rupees, and were distributed as follows:—

Sindhia, Jagheer lands, .	Rupees, 14,61,361
Holkur, Enam lands, . . .	98,956
Raja Bahadoor, Pergunna of Mote, now held by the Jhansi Government in mortgage,	2,35,192
Assigned to the Deo (God) of Chinchoor,	10,688
The remaining lands are rated at .	6,36,782

The first Soobehdar of Jhansi on record, was Naroo Shunkur,* styled Raja Bahadoor, one of the most distinguished of the military leaders under the Peshwas, and grandfather to the present chiefs of Maligaom. He seems to have been appointed to Jhansi about 1764, and held the office until 1778, when, not having contributed one rupee to government, he was recalled to Poona. Naroo Shunkur was succeeded by Hurry Damodhur, who, with his brother, had each command of a party of horse in the Nizam's service, which they quitted

* The great grandsons of Naroo Shunkur hold Jagheers under the British Government in the Deccan, but as neither of them have any prospect of heirs, they have been allowed to adopt children from other families. Gopal Rao Trimbuk, the elder, has the small town of Nimbayet, in Khandes, with fourteen adjacent villages, the whole producing a revenue of 21,195 rupees: he has also an assignment of 7000 rupees upon the customs of Maligaom. His adopted son is named Shew Rao, and is now about eleven years of age. Mahdoo Rao Trimbuk, the younger brother, also styled Raja Bahadoor, has Jagheer villages in the Ahmednugur district, rated at 34,772 rupees. His adopted son is named Trimbuk Rao. The strong fort of Maligaom, in Khandes, known in the annals of Indian warfare for its protracted siege in 1817-18, was built by Naroo Shunkur, after his return from Jhansi.

for that of the Peshwa, who conferred upon them Parola and other villages in Khandes, and afterwards appointed the elder to Jhansi. His son, Siva Rao Hurry, taking advantage of the troubles of the times, rendered himself in some measure independent after the decease of the Peshwa Mahdoo Rao, in 1797. When, however, the British troops proceeded to occupy Boondelcund, agreeably to the stipulations of the treaty of Bassein, Siva Rao acknowledged himself a feudatory of the Poona Government, and entered into a treaty, by which the tribute due to his feudal superior was thenceforth to be paid through the British Government. In 1812, he applied to the British Government to have the treaty modified, so that its conditions might have an hereditary effect.

The Peshwa's remaining rights, (rated as above at 6,36,782 rupees) in the estate of Jhansi, which were held by its chief on the usual tenure of tribute and service, were transferred to the direct authority of the British Government by the treaty of Poona, in June, 1817; when the uniform attachment of the Soobehdar to the British interests induced government to relinquish the tribute, and to confirm his family in the Jagheer on a perpetual tenure, with the concession on his side of the services of a body of horse, and the usual engagements of fidelity and dependence. In deference, therefore, to the request, or wish, expressed by Siva Rao Hurry before his death, in 1817, his possessions were confirmed in perpetuity to his grandson, Rao Ramchunder Hurry. Siva Rao left three sons, but the eldest, who was father to the present chief, died during his father's lifetime.

THE CHIEF OF JULAOON AND CALPEE.

The chiefs of Julaoon and Sâgur having the same ancestor, their early history will be found in the account of the latter chief, among the Stipendiary Princes.

By the treaty of Poona, in June, 1817, the lands held by the Rana of Julaoon, in Boondelcund, on military tenure, from the Peshwa, were ceded to the British Government, which confirmed them to him in perpetuity, on his acceding to an arrangement for the cession of Mahoba, a district on the banks of the Jumna, in lieu of the tribute and military service due by him to the Peshwa, and now transferred to the British Government. The surplus revenues of Sâgur, to which he advanced a claim, as heir to the elder branch of the family of the first Soobehdar of Sâgur, were also secured to him, rated at 1,18,000 rupees. He possesses a fertile tract of country celebrated for its cotton; and his revenue is supposed to amount to about ten lacs of rupees.

THE FAMILY OF ANGRIA.

RANOJEE ANGRIA was the son of a distinguished Mahratta officer in Sivajee's fleet, and commenced life himself as second in command to the officer who held the command of the fleet, with charge of such part of the country, along the coast, from Goa to Surat, as belonged to the Mahrattas. He first distinguished himself at the capture of the strong fort of Raighur, from the Abyssinian chief of Jinjeera, in the year 1698; and, subsequently, in the reduction of that portion of the Koncan still held by the Mahomedans. In these conquests, he attempted to establish an independent sovereignty; but, having been often defeated, he at length consented to acknowledge the supremacy of the Raja of Satara, and was confirmed in possession of the whole of the territory and seaports from Viziadroog to Kolaba. In 1722, the Bombay government, incensed at his piracies, joined the Portuguese in an expedition against him,—the land forces being furnished by the latter, and three ships of the line, under Commodore Mathews, being furnished by the former; but the object of it failed, through cowardice in the Portuguese. His possessions, on his death in 1728, reverted, first, to his eldest son, Suckojee, and, in two years after, to his second son, Sumbajee, whose great-grandson now holds the estate. The indiscriminate piracies of this family on all nations approaching the western coast of India, are matter of history, and do not admit of illustration in this place. As the British power preponderated, they gradually subsided; and, after the treaty of Bassein, in 1803, they ceased altogether; while the once powerful Angria, encroached on by the Peshwas from time to time, dwindled into insignificance. At the breaking out of the war, in 1817-18, the territory in possession of the family yielded three lacs of rupees, of which about half is applied to religious purposes. The future relations between Rughoojee Angria, the present chief, and the British Government, were fixed by treaty in July, 1822.

TRIBUTARIES IN KATTEEWAR.

Introduction.

Of chiefs in the Gujerat peninsula, one hundred and thirty-seven were tributary to the Peshwa, and one hundred and eleven to the Gaekwar. The tributes, as settled with each chief individually, by General Walker, in 1809, amounted, on account of the former, to 8,54,700 rupees; and on account of the latter, to 9,79,882 rupees. Since that period, famine and other causes have combined to injure the prosperity of the province, and the falling off in the tributes may be assumed at twenty or twenty-five per cent. The Peshwa's share of the tributes was ceded to the British Government in June, 1818, at four lacs of rupees, being its value, free of the expense of collection. These turbulent chiefs are now secured against external aggression themselves, and prevented from encroaching on their neighbours; but they are free to exercise sovereign authority on their own lands, and are exempted from the British courts of law. The following are a few of the principal chiefs, as drawn up from a report written in 1827:—

The Chiefs of Bauntwa. This Talooka (which comprises eighty villages, of which thirty-six are now deserted) was given by Sulabut Khan, the second Nuwab of Joonagurh, in 1740, to his younger sons, Duleel Khan, and Sher Jumma

Khan, to be held in equal divisions by them and their descendants. The principal possessor at present is Kumal Deen, who has twenty-two villages. The other twenty-two villages are held by six proprietors, the principal of whom are Mahomed Khan, and Nuttoo Khan. Bauntwa yields a revenue of about 1,00,000 rupees, and pays a tribute of 32,000 rupees; but the villages are in a wretched state, and the six proprietors, descended from Sher Jumma Khan, are in very penurious circumstances. The Talooka is still subject to the Gadee of Joonagurh, and pays a share of the tribute, besides its own. They maintain 180 horse and 320 foot.

The Rawul, styled also Raja, and Thakoor, of Bhownugur, Vujjee Singh. The revenues of this chief are estimated at 10,00,000 rupees. The Bhownugur district itself, including the sea and land customs, is estimated at 2,00,000 rupees; and the Talooks of Gogeh, Burra-Sehore, and Omralla, under the Ahmedabad collectorate, are rated at 1,00,000 rupees. The British Government tribute is 75,400 rupees annually, and on account of the Joonagurh Zoortulubee, 23,400 rupees more. He pays also 1,36,400 rupees in tribute to the Gaekwar. Vujjee Singh is probably the richest chief in the Peninsula, and the greater part of his country is in a flourishing condition. His force is 2500 horse, and 6000 foot.

The Chief of Bujana, Dhureea Khan, is a Jhut, a tribe of Mahomedans, supposed to be the earliest converts from Hindooism, and from whom the province of Jhutwar derives its name. The revenue of Bujana is rated at 20,000 rupees, of which 5000 is paid in tribute to the British Government.

The Chiefs of Cheetul and Jaitpoor are Kattees of the Khoomaun tribe. The principal of them are Vikumsee and Mooloo-Wala. The tribute paid by Jaitpoor and Cheetul together, to the British Government, is 54,264 rupees, and the Joonagurh Zoortulabee amounts to a farther sum of 3530 rupees annually. The whole revenue is estimated at 1,50,000 rupees. The lands of both Cheetul and Jaitpoor were lately under attachment, for the debts of the Khoomaun chiefs, for whom the Jaitpoor Kattees were security. Jaitpoor is situated on the Bhâdur river, has a good strong and high wall, and contains about 12,000 inhabitants. It was in this place that the refractory Kattee chiefs usually left their families when they went out upon pillaging excursions. Military force, 200 horse and 450 foot.

The Raja of Durangdra, Oomur Singh, is head of Jhalla Rajpoots. Being entirely given up to devotion, his resources have been left in bad hands, and the estate, which comprised in 1809 about two hundred villages, has now not more than one hundred inhabited. The population is scarcely one-third of what it was, from the effects of the famine of 1813, mismanagement, and the incursions of Meyannas, and other freebooters, conjoined. The town of Durangdra, which is in good preservation, and the walls newly built, is situated on a clear stream which falls into the Runn. The revenue is rated at 1,67,900 rupees, and the tribute to the British Government is 48,909 rupees; but latterly, on account of the impoverished state of the Talooka, 40,000 rupees only have been exacted.

The Zumeendars of Dussara are Mahomedans. The estate, comprising twenty-five villages, (many of which are deserted,) bordering the Runn, on the north of Jhalawar, was, it is said, conferred upon their ancestor by the Emperor, in the eighth century of the Hejira. It is divided into two large Putties, or shares. The tribute of this Talooka, in 1809, was fixed at 14,001 rupees; but owing to the poverty of the chiefs, there are considerable arrears, and the Talooka is now under attachment. Of late years there has been scarcely half the produce, and Government made a new settlement, remitting 2000 rupees of the tribute, and 12,001 rupees are now settled for the five years from 1826.

The Chief of Goondul, Chunder Singh, has a large district in the division of Hallar: his chief towns are Goondul and Dhorajee, both large and thriving, and the district comprises one hundred and seventy-nine villages. The chief himself, however, pays little attention to the affairs of his government. His whole revenue may be rated at 4,00,000 rupees, of which he pays in tribute to the British Government 53,005 rupees, and to the Gaekwar 1,15,000 rupees. Dhorajee and Ooplaita are at present under farm to Runchoorjee Dewan, on account of the debts of the Goondul chief. Military establishment, 200 horse and 1100 foot.

THE NUWAB OF JOONAGURH, Buhadoor Khan, was placed on the Musnud in 1811, at which time he was about sixteen years of age. From the mal-administration of those who have had the management of his affairs, his country has been rapidly going to ruin, and for the purpose of freeing him from his embarrassments, Government were necessitated to place the administration in the hands of a farmer, Govindjee Jhalla, in 1823. The land revenues are farmed to this person for ten lacs and a half of kories, (including his own salary 75,000,) out of which the Nuwab receives 2,40,000 kories for his maintenance, and the remainder is set apart for the payment of his Sebundy and creditors. Besides this amount, his Highness has another source of revenue in the Zoortulabee * which is collected from most of the chiefs in Katteewar, and is now farmed to Nanjee Veerjee, a merchant of Poorbunder, at 2,23,000 kories. The Mooluck-geery collections, which were ceded to the British Government in 1811, realized last year 82,384 rupees.

The Joonagurh dynasty originated with Sher Khan Babi, who, during the confusion occasioned by the struggles between the Mahratta and Moghul for superiority in the province, about 1730, established himself in the government of Soreth, of which Joonagurh was the capital. The other chief towns are Buntlee, Kesor, Choorwaur, Soodra-Para, Oona-Dilwara, Kootianna, and Vairawul-Puttun. Joonagurh is surrounded by a well-built wall and rampart thirty feet high, with a ditch at its base excavated out of the rock, and twenty feet deep,—making the height from bottom of the ditch fifty

* The Zoortulabee and Mooluck-geery, seem to be a similar species of revenue, being a forced settlement upon every village in Katteewar, or a tribute levied to forbear plundering; the former was established by the Nuwab,—the latter at an earlier period, by the Mahrattas. Similar to this is the revenue extorted under the head of Ghas-Danu, which seems to have commenced with the Peshwa's farm of the Gaekwar's Mahals in Gujerat. Ghas-Danu, however, seems to have been exacted for the benefit of Sirdars of the Mooluck-geery army, while the Mooluck-geery exactions were for the benefit of the Prince.

feet. The inhabitants are estimated at 30,000 souls. Military establishment, 500 horse and 1000 foot.

THE CHIEF OF LIMREE is a Rajpoot. The revenues of the Limree Talook are estimated at 1,57,075 rupees: this does not include either what is derived from the Bhyad villages, or those under Ahmedabad. The tribute payable to the British Government is 51,931 rupees annually. The town of Limree is situated on the banks of the Bogwara river, but is now a place of no strength, and the walls are fast going to decay; it is, however, extensive and celebrated for the number of its moneyed inhabitants. The Talook is divided as follows:—Thirty-two Durbar villages; thirty-nine under the Bhyad (brotherhood) *i. e.* under the management of, and for the support of, cadets of the family; thirty-four under the Ahmedabad collectorate, including Dundooka, Burwala and Wuddara. Troops, 140 horse and 400 foot.

THE THAKOOR OF MALLIA, Suttajee, a Jahrejah Rajpoot. Having lost his faculties from the immoderate use of opium, his affairs are managed by his mother, a woman of talent and ability. She exhibits one of the few instances of a Rajpoot lady sitting in Durbar in the presence of Europeans. The revenue is estimated at about 70,000 kories, or 17,138 rupees, and the tribute to the Gaekwar government is 1200 rupees. Mallia has seven villages under it, and three Bhyad villages; the latter pay a share of the tribute.

THE NUWAB OF MANGROL seems formerly to have been dependent upon Joonagurh. The first who assumed the title of Nuwab was a Kusbatty, but his descendants have retained it. The principality remained independent until Omarjee, the Dewan of Joonagurh, wrested from it the villages of Seâl, Buggusra, Meyaree and Dewassa, and fixed the Mangrol share of the tribute at 11,000 rupees yearly, which the Joonagurh officers collect: and farther, to cede the half produce of the remaining forty villages of the Talooka. The Nuwab of Joonagurh has authority to decide in all cases of disputed succession, but no authority in the town of Mangrol itself, nor any share of the customs. The land revenue is estimated at about 1,25,000 kories, and the customs and town revenues amount to about a lac more of kories. The town of Mangrol is very populous, and the port much frequented by small craft.

THE THAKOOR OF MOREWEE. Jehajee, a Jahrejah Rajpoot, is the principal chief of Muchoo Kaunta. His estate comprises ninety-seven villages. His revenue is rated at 1,68,641 rupees, and his tribute is 40,001 rupees. His chief towns are Morewee and Tankaria: the latter is at present in the hands of Meiral Bhow, a Baroda shroff, for debt: it has nine villages under it, not included in the Morewee Talook: the estimate of the Tankaria revenues may be about 20,000 rupees annually. Jehajee has also several villages in Cutch under him. The Morewee villages are now in rather improving circumstances.

The legend says that the ancestor of the present Chief of Morewee, by name Rewajee, who was the eldest son of Raidhunjee, Rao of Cutch, and should have succeeded to the Gadee of that country, was murdered about 1685, by his younger brother, Pragjee; and his offspring were obliged to fly to Morewee, then a possession in Katteewar belonging to the Cutch state, which, at a subsequent period, confirmed the Talook to an ancestor of the present Chief of Morewee.

THE JAM OF NOANUGUR, Runmuljee, is the head of the Jahrejah Rajpoots. He was adopted by the widow of Jam Suttajee, the last chief, who died about 1814. The widow continued in the administration of affairs during his minority, aided by Jug-Jeewan, a Nagur Bramin, of some talent, as her minister. His government extends over the greater part of the province of Hallar, and his revenue is rated at 15,00,000 rupees, whereof 95,000 rupees are paid in tribute to the British, and a like sum to the Gaekwar government. Noanugur, the chief town, is the most populous in Katteewar, and nearly four miles in circumference. It is greatly celebrated for the beauty and texture of its cloth manufactures. The other principal towns in the Jam's dominions are, Jooria, Kumbalia, and Sutchana, which are the chief sea-ports in Katteewar, in the Gulf of Cutch, and Balumba, a well built town, containing about one thousand houses, surrounded by a double wall and ditch. The Noanugur country is at present farmed, on account of the debts of the Jam to the late Soonderjee Sewajee, for 17,25,000 kories annually; out of which the Jam receives three lacs for his maintenance, and the rest goes to pay his tribute and creditors. There are upwards of three hundred villages in his Talooka included in Soonderjee's Farm, which is now held by his son Soonderjee Dewjee. His military force is rated at 700 horse, and 3000 foot.

The Raja of Paulitana is a relation of the Raja of Bhownugur; he is, however, much in debt, and his country is at present mortgaged to a Banyan. Paulitâna is the chief place of pilgrimage in Gujerat. The principal place of worship is on the summit of the Shaitrojee hill, the bottom of which is about a mile from the town. The top is covered with temples of various kinds, but the finest is that dedicated to Parisnath; the image is of black marble, and is always adorned with a great variety of rich clothes and jewels. The sculpture in the other temples is well executed, and the gods are of white marble.

The Dessaye of Patree's estate lies on the northern extremity of Katteewar. The town was formerly reckoned a place of considerable strength; but is now much in decay. It is surrounded by three separate walls, at the inner of which is a ditch. The revenue is rated at 18,000 rupees, and the fixed tribute to the British Government is 5652 rupees. The military establishment is 20 horse and 75 foot.

The Rana of Poorbunder, Halajee, styled Pritheraj, is a Rajpoot, of the Jaitwar tribe. He is head of a petty maritime state, called Burruda, or Jaitwar, which is under the immediate protection of the British Government. The estate comprises about one hundred villages, including the forts of Chya, Ranawau, and Kundoorna, and the seaports of Nuvee-Bunder, Meannee, and Poorbunder; and realizes a revenue of four lacs of rupees. Half the port duties of the latter place, rated at 37,500 rupees, were ceded, in 1808, to the British Government, to defray the expense of one hundred sepoys, and an officer, to be stationed at Poorbunder. These port duties realized 31,230 rupees in 1826. A tribute of 30,000 rupees is also paid to the Gaekwar. The Rana is a man of little capacity. Being joined by a number of profligate associates, he raised a rebellion against his father, about 1810, and established himself in the adjacent fort of Chya, where he was besieged in the following year, by Colonel East's force, which, after sustaining some loss, succeeded in taking him prisoner, when he was delivered over to his father. Military establishment, 100 horse and 600 foot.

THE THAKOOR OF RAJKOT, Sorajee, is a minor. He has a revenue rated at 34,500 rupees. His tribute to the British Government was fixed at 20,500 rupees; but only 17,000 rupees are now exacted. The principal town is Sirdhar, which was formerly the residence of the chief.

THE THAKOOR OF SAEELA, Alluda Singh. The revenues of his district may be estimated at 35,000 rupees, of which 12,000 are paid in tribute to the British Government. In 1809, the Talooka comprised thirty-eight villages; but of these, seventeen were depopulated by the famine, in 1813. The revenue, at the first period, was estimated at 50,000 rupees; and Colonel Walker settled the tribute at 18,782 rupees. Saeela is a large walled town, situated in an open country, and upon a large tank. Serraw, a well-built walled town, west of it, is the next principal place under this Talook.

THE THAKOOR OF WANKANEER, Dosajee, has a small district in Mutchoo-Kaunta. His revenue, in 1809, was assumed at 40,000 rupees, and his tribute fixed at 18,000 rupees. The former is now reckoned 26,000 rupees, and the tribute taken is 12,000 rupees.

THE RAJA OF WUDWAUN is a minor, and the government is conducted by the mother of the late Raja, Jhallum Singh, who died in 1826. The Bhyad villages of this Talooka settle separately for their tribute. There are twenty-eight Durbar villages in this Talooka, all in a high state of cultivation. The finest cotton in Katteewar is grown in it. The tribute settled by Colonel Walker for Wudwaun, was 27,831 rupees, and the revenue may be estimated at 1,00,000 rupees.

TRIBUTARIES IN GUJERAT.

THE NUWAB, OR DEWAN, OF PAHLUNPOOR, Futtih Khan. He derives his descent from a tribe of Afghans, who, according to the Akbar Namu, occupied Bahar in the reign of Humayoon, Emperor of Delhi. Buhadoor Khan, an ancestor of this chief, was Foujdar in 1759, when Pahlunpoor was besieged by the Mahrattas, under Sudasheo Ramchunder; and after a month's fighting, during which the whole of his country was plundered and laid waste by them, he was obliged to buy them off by a payment of 35,000 rupees. Some Bramins of Jalore still do homage yearly to the Dewan, for villages received from his ancestors, who held the Foujdaree of that district till dispossessed by Aurungzeb. The present Dewan is son of Feroze Khan, who was murdered by a faction of Sindee Jemadars, in 1813. The revenue is rated at two and a half lacs of rupees, of which fifty thousand are paid, as tribute, to the Gaekwar.

THE NUWAB OF RADHUNPOOR AND SUMMEE, Zoorawur Khan Babi. An ancestor, Sher Khan Babi, was Thanadar of the district of Chowaul, in 1659; and, in 1713, Juwan Murd Khan, a grandson, was appointed Foujdar of Radhunpoor: he had several sons, the elder of whom, bearing the same name, is conspicuous, in the annals of the period, in Gujerat. He was appointed Foujdar of Summee and Moonjpoor in 1726, by the Soobehdar of the province, Moobaruz-ool-Moolk; and Mahomed Anwur, his brother, was at the same time appointed Foujdar of Radhunpoor. Juwan Murd Khan was in charge of the province of Gujerat from 1743 till 1755, when the city was besieged by the Mahrattas, and obliged to capitulate. Juwan Murd Khan retired to Puttun; but four years after, he assisted in the second siege of Ahmedabad, when it was defended by Momin Khan, Nuwab of Cambay. Some years afterwards, the heirs of Juwan Murd Khan were deprived of Puttun and other places, by Dumajee Gaekwar, who was desirous of weakening the power and influence of this family. The present Nuwab succeeded his father, Sher Khan, in 1824: he is the fourth in descent from the second Juwan Murd Khan. His revenue is about 1,50,000 rupees a-year, and he sends a horse and clothes yearly to the Gaekwar, in token of vassalage. He keeps up a military establishment of about 60 horse, and 550 infantry.

THE NUWAB OF CAMBAY, Bundeh Ali Khan, succeeded to his brother, Futtih Ali Khan, in 1822. These were sons of Momin Ali Khan, who was related to, and succeeded, Muftakhur Khan, as Mootusuddee of the Chowreeassee, (or district of eighty-four villages,) of Cambay. Cambay, formerly the principal seaport of Gujerat, is now the capital of a small compact territory, comprehended between the Muhee and Saburmuttee rivers, on the east and west, and by the British and Gaekwar possessions on the north. The revenue is rated at about 2,50,000 rupees. The Chouth was ceded by the Peshwa to the Company by the treaty of Bassein, and is rated, in the schedule, at 60,000 rupees. The Company also possess half the customs, which, in 1827, realized 34,096 rupees.

THE RAJA OF EEDUR, Gumbheer Singh, is great grandson of Anund Singh, who was a brother of Abhee Singh, the Raja of Joudpoor, and viceroy of Gujerat, between 1731 and 1736. Anund Singh, together with his enterprising brother, Rae Singh, obtained possession of Eedur about this time. Anund Singh was killed in action with the Mahrattas, in 1742, near his own fort. Eedurwara, of which this is the capital, is a mountainous and jungly country, inhabited principally by Bheels. The revenue is rated at four lacs, of which three are allotted to eight dependent chiefs. The tribute to the Gaekwar is twenty-four thousand rupees, of which six thousand are paid by the Raja, and the residue by the dependent chiefs.

THE RAJA OF AHMEDNUGUR is a son of Sungram Singh, and grandson of Anund Singh, the first Raja of Eedur. Raja Raee Singh, the brother of the latter, joined the Mahrattas in 1740, but went over to the Soobehdar, during the following year, when he had Ahmednugur, Amliara, &c. conferred upon him, in Jagheer.

THE RAWUL OF CHOTA OODIPOOR, styled Pirtheeraja,

succeeded his father Raee Singh, about five years ago. His revenues are about 1,00,000 rupees, principally road duties, or customs; the honourable Company pay about 16,000 rupees annually to him, in transit duties upon opium. He maintains about 400 or 500 Sebundies, and he can command the services of a few thousand Bheel bowmen. His Bheel subjects, however, are principally employed in cultivation, are very peaceably disposed, and comparatively civilized. The management of affairs is in the hands of the Raja's mother, a very sensible woman, aided by Gokal Bukshee, a Banian. The Raja himself, however, is not deficient in intelligence, and is old enough (twenty-six years of age) to take the conduct of affairs into his own hands.

JOINT TRIBUTARIES OF THE NIZAM AND COMPANY.

The Raja of Shorapoor, Pid Naik, commonly called the Ramoosy Raja; himself and the greater part of his subjects being of the Ramoosy tribe. The ancestor of this chief, having aided Aurungzeb in the subjugation of the Beejapoor State, of which he was a subject, was then made a Raja, and a Royal Munsubdar of 5000. The district of Shorapoor is situated between the Kistna and the Bheema, immediately above their junction, and is about forty-five miles from east to west, its greatest length. The Raja purchased a nominal independence, by paying an annual tribute to both the Nizam and Peshwa in 1816, the first received 1,45,000 rupees, the latter claimed 85,000, and each levies a fine on the accession of a new Raja. His revenues formerly amounted to eight lacs of rupees, but they do not now exceed six. In 1802, the troops which the Raja had collected to resist the Nizam's army, were estimated at 4000 cavalry, 8000 infantry, and 4000 Behdurs, or Ramoosies, who form a militia, but are employed only when urgently required. He probably has not now above 2000 men in regular pay. His principal forts are Shorapoor, Wakunkhera, Windroog, and Gurgetah.

The Raja of Gudwaul, Seetaram Bopaul, is of the

Koonbee, or cultivating, class. The district of Gudwaul is situated between the Kistna and Toongbudra, just above their junction, and extends about thirty miles from north to south. The accession of his ancestor to rank, and his own relative situation towards the Nizam and Peshwa, appear to be similar to that of the Raja of Shorapoor. The revenues may be about four lacs of rupees a-year. The tribute which the Nizam claims is 1,20,000 rupees; the Peshwa, in 1816, claimed only 17,500. The Raja has 500 troops in constant pay, and about 1000 Behdurs. His principal forts are Gudwaul, Dawur, Borpilly, and Nizamkoonda.

ABYSSINIANS.

The Seedee of Jinjeera. Seedee, or Hubshee, Mahomed Khan, the present chief, is the eldest son of the late Ibrahim Khan, who, after a reign of about twenty-four years, died towards the end of 1826. His territories are not fifty miles from Bombay, and lie along the sea coast, between the Rewdunda and Bankoot rivers, and produce a revenue of about 1,75,000 rupees. The legend sets forth, that, about the year 1489, a party of Abyssinians, in the service of one of the Nizam-Shahi Kings of Ahmednugur, disguised as merchants, obtained permission from the chiefs of the island, to land three hundred boxes, each of which contained a soldier; by which means they possessed themselves of Dhunda-Rajpoor. It afterwards formed part of the dominions of the King of Bejapoor, under whom, in the time of Sivajee, the government of the southern Konkan was held by the admiral of the Beejapoor fleet, who was an Abyssinian, and whose officers and crews were his own countrymen. Being hard pressed by the Mahrattas, the captains of the fleet appear to have formed themselves into a republic, and to have offered their services to Aurungzeb, then at war, equally with Beejapoor and the Mahrattas. Their services were accepted, and their chief was appointed admiral of the imperial fleet; for the support of which an assignment was granted on the revenues of Surat, the trade of which port, together with the ship which annually conveyed the pilgrims to Mecca, he was specially bound to protect. Since that time, till within the last fifteen or twenty years, they have been engaged in constant wars by sea and land; but this little principality maintains its independence to this day. The Seedees were terrible as pirates, and more dreaded than all others on the pirate coast. The town and district of Jafferabad, on the south coast of Katteewar, is a colony belonging to this petty state. The Seedee's personal appearance and manners are much in his favour, and his complexion is very fair for an Asiatic. His subjects talk of the mildness of his government, and recently, during a famine, Ibrahim Khan directed that all strangers should be hospitably received by his subjects wherever they entered the country.

THE GOVERNOR OF JAFFERABAD, Eyib Khan, bin Yakoob Khan, is a Seedee, or Abyssinian. He was appointed, in succession to his father, about 1808, from Jinjeera, otherwise Dunda-Rajpoor, of which government Jafferabad is a colony. It is a walled town of considerable strength, and has five villages subject to it; the revenues of each, however, do not exceed 500 rupees, and the whole of the revenues of this petty colony, including land and sea customs, may not exceed 15,000 rupees.

THE NUWAB OF SUCHEEN, Seedee Ibrahim Khan Buhadoor, is an Abyssinian by descent. His father, Abdool Khureem Khan, commonly called Balloo Meah, was the elder brother of the late Chief of Jinjeera. The latter having succeeded to the Jinjeera principality, agreeably to the will of their father, and Abdool Khureem Khan, being unable to obtain foreign aid to recover it, was induced to relinquish to the Peshwa his right of succession, and received in return a grant of the estate of Sucheen, in Altumgha grant, in June, 1791, then rated at 75,000 rupees. The Peshwa, however, never obtained possession of the island of Jinjeera. The estate of Sucheen comprises seventeen villages, and the land revenue is at present 84,000 rupees, besides which, the Nuwab receives about 10,000 rupees from other sources. His independence is acknowledged, and he has steadily refused to admit the criminal and civil jurisdiction of the British Government on his lands, though his boundary reaches within two miles of Surat.

THE DESSAYE, OR DESHMOOKH, OF SAWUNT-WAREE, is an independent Prince, ruling over a small territory situated between Goa and Malwan, and yielding from two to three lacs of rupees. Khem Sawunt, to whom this family trace their origin, was an officer under the Beejapoor kings, and held great part of the Waree country in Jagheer during the declining period of that monarchy. When the celebrated Sivajee was in the zenith of his glory, Khem Sawunt transferred his allegiance to him from Beejapoor, and was confirmed as Sur-Dessaye over all that part of the Konkan, half the revenue of which was to be made available to Sivajee, and the other half was assigned for the maintenance of a body of three thousand infantry for foreign service, besides the requisite number for garrisons. The Sawunts, however, resumed their allegiance to Beejapoor on Sivajee meeting with reverses, and on the eventual dissolution of that monarchy, Sawunt-Waree appears to have been left independent. The long wars of this petty state with the neighbouring state of Kolapoor, and occasionally with the Portuguese and British Governments, will be found detailed in larger works. Their piracies obliged the government of Bombay to send an expedition against Sawunt-Waree in 1765, and the fort of Rairee was taken, but restored on receiving security for the future, and indemnification for the past. Vingorla was also ceded, and a factory established by the British, but the Sawunts retook the place in 1780, and their piracies were renewed, and continued until 1812, when they were finally suppressed. An expedition was at this time sent against Sawunt-Waree, and after the reduction of the country, a treaty, dated 3d October, 1812, was concluded, by which Vingorla was again ceded to the British; and, for the more effectual suppression of piracy, he was obliged to agree to a detachment of troops being stationed at the seaports of Rairee and Newty, for the purpose of searching all vessels proceeding from, or arriving at, any of them.

This, however, did not prove effectual against this turbulent state, and new expeditions and new treaties became necessary in 1819 and 1820.

A GENERAL ABSTRACT of the Gross Revenues of the Presidencies of Calcutta, Madras, and Bombay, for the year ending 30th April, 1829.

	Calcutta	Madras	Bombay.	Total
Land Revenues in the ancient possessions,	£3,574,237	£846,365	£205,067	£ 13,845,113
Ditto in conquered territories,	3,144,327*	842,089†	1,448,851‡	
Ditto in territories ceded in lieu of subsidy,	1,610,538§	1,831,297‖	342,347¶	
Subsidy and tributes,	69,049**	392,355††		461,404
Monopoly of salt,	2,388,277	346,192	19,936	2,748,405
Monopoly of opium,	2,057,621			2,057,621
Monopoly of tobacco,		85,482		85,482
Customs,	831,734	126,859	394,681	2,178,566
Variable imposts and taxes,	485,422	485,422		
Post-office collections,	91,833	32,043	12,584	136,460
Marine receipts, pilotage, &c.	38,486	7,801	18,383	64,670
Farms and licences of exclusive privilege,		313,886	71,978	384,864
Mint duties at the Presidencies,	32,176	4,332	5,440	41,948
Judicial fees, &c. ditto.	85,442	13,845	17,890‡‡	117,1[illegible]7
Stamps,	327,705	56,225	5,161	389,091
Ava indemnification,	186,010			186,010
	£14,924,969	£5,338,632	£2,543,123	£ 22,695,811
The whole of these revenues for the year ending 30th April, 1829, realized,				22,691,721

* This includes the Benares territory, as well as the lands acquired on the Nerbudda, and in Burmah.
† Tippoo's late dominions.
‡ The conquered and formerly ceded Mahratta territory.
§ The Oude Cessions.
‖ From the Nuwab of the Carnatic, Raja of Tanjore, and the Nizam.
¶ From the Gaekwar.
** Tribute from Jeypoor, Bhopaul, &c.
†† Subsidies from Mysore, Travancore, and Cochin.
‡‡ This includes the provinces.

CHARGES upon the REVENUES OF INDIA, Civil, Military, and Miscellaneous, for the year ending 30th April, 1828.

	Calcutta.	Madras.	Bombay.	Total
Civil and Political.				
Charges of government,	£932,824*	£287,331*	£290,783*†	
Ditto collecting the land revenues,	993,494	626,174	260,702	
Ditto on the salt monopoly,	808,322	74,419		
Ditto — opium monopoly,	658,254			
Ditto — tobacco monopoly,		31,843		£5,488,799
Ditto — customs,	126,808	52,132	44,504	
Ditto — post-office,	89,075	29,339	18,848	
Ditto — mint,	48,773	20,406	3,637	
Ditto — stamps,	81,690	9,437		
Judicial.				
Provincial and city courts of justice,	970,616	321,266	247,799	1,698,992
Supreme court at the Presidencies,	51,179	50,485	57,647	
Miscellaneous.				
Military charges,	4,574,299	3,897,520	1,311,485‡	9,783,304
Stipends and charitable allowances, payable by treaties,	754,818	506,685	636,207	1,897,710
Provincial, Auxiliary, and Sebundy corps,	412,800		754,854	1,167,654
Indian Navy and Pilot service,	117,745	18,781	212,862	349,388
Buildings and repairs,	548,492	81,876	163,990	794,358
Surveys,			28,126	28,126
Deccan booty distributed,	600,905			600,905
Interest on public debt,	1,712,253	179,074	27,230	1,918,557
	£13,482,347	£6,186,768	£4,058,674	£23,727,795

* This includes ecclesiastical, and a variety of other charges.
† This includes £66,774, the political charges of the residencies of Baroda, Bussorah, Bagdad, Busheer, Bhooj, Bittoor, Mocha, Muscat, and Satara.
‡ This includes £99,521, the expense of Madras troops employed in the Bombay territories.